The Definitive Dream Dictionary

Diane Bellchambers

NEW
HOLLAND

To my dreams for their inspiration and to my father
for giving me the opportunity to follow my dreams.

First published in Australia in 2004 by
New Holland Publishers (Australia) Pty Ltd
Sydney • Auckland • London • Cape Town

14 Aquatic Drive Frenchs Forest NSW 2086 Australia
218 Lake Road Northcote Auckland New Zealand
86 Edgware Road London W2 2EA United Kingdom
80 McKenzie Street Cape Town 8001 South Africa

National Library of Australia Cataloguing-in-Publication Data:

Bellchambers, Diane.
The Definitive Dream Dictionary.

Includes index.
ISBN 1 74110 093 3.

1. Dreams—Dictionaries. 2. Dream interpretation—
Dictionaries. I. Title.

154.6303

Managing Editor: Monica Ban
Project Editor: Liz Hardy
Designer: Karl Roper
Production Controller: Kellie Matterson
Typeset by Midlands Typesetters
Printed in Australia by Griffin Press, Adelaide

10 9 8 7 6 5 4 3 2

TABLE OF CONTENTS

Acknowledgments

I wish to thank my family—my husband Ron, daughter Beth and
Audrey Forbes for their encouragement and support.

I would also like to thank Lucy Murray, Amanda Boyle, Gerardine Creek,
Judith Lemka, Angelika Eigenwillig and Janine Young
for their practical skills and assistance.

Part One

Analysing Your Dreams

How To Use This Dictionary

Who looks outside dreams;
who looks inside wakes.
Carl Jung

The doorway to your inner wisdom opens every night—everybody dreams

Being open to your dreams could be the best thing you ever do. I know it was for me. Every night while you're asleep you are receiving guidance from your inner self. At night you are free from the distractions of waking life ready to receive practical and spiritual guidance about life and the situations you are dealing with. These insights are offered to you with a view to moving you closer to being who you really are and what you can become.

Having a greater sense of self and our life's purpose can add meaning and direction to our journey. Imagine how different your life could be if:

- you could know the thrill of being able to forecast future events and use timing to your best advantage
- you could plot a wise course, knowing ahead of time what your soul's purpose was and where your hidden talents and best options lie
- you could be very discerning, knowing the hidden strengths and weaknesses of your associates
- you could move quickly towards your goals, knowing what subconscious beliefs were holding you back
- you could enjoy inner peace, knowing that you were able to communicate with absent loved ones beyond the bounds of time and space
- you could feel empowered by tuning into your body's wisdom and being forewarned of any developing problems (and their solutions) before physical symptoms have time to present
- you could make good career moves, receiving inspiration on demand and being able to solve complex problems creatively
- you could add meaning to your life by being able to look back on it and know what's brought you to this point
- you could see the power in the present moment pregnant with all its possibilities and be able to look at your life with contentment.

These gifts can be yours. You already own them. Your dreams come to you every night. You just need to tune into your dreams and understand them. When you follow your dreams you can live your dreams and move closer to living the life you choose to live.

Dreams tell a story about you—they make sense

Your dreams are very meaningful. We often mistakenly discount and underestimate them on the grounds that they seem like bizarre and disconnected imaginings. They are a story created by you and about your current life in pictorial form. Like a novel they have structure—a setting against which the story is played out and symbols that are like characters, each with their own unique quality and features. There is also a plot and movement in the story-line which builds to a climax and contains a con-clusion, resolution, comment or revealing insight in which you can learn something about yourself. And like the author of a novel, you have carefully and deliberately placed every character and sequence of the dream in order to create feeling, meaning and impact.

Some dreams mean exactly what they say

Some dreams are very clear and easy to understand. These dreams can come from the super-conscious mind or that part of yourself that knows all things and transcends the personality and time and space boundaries. These can be very vivid and dramatic and sometimes wake you in the middle of the night. Such dreams can shape your life in powerful ways. They can forecast the future, warn you of danger and unproductive choices, provide you with spiritual progress reports, help you communicate with others and provide you with ingenious solutions.

Denise had a nightmare about her sister Annie which illustrates this type of dream very well. In the dream Annie had fallen into a cave and was calling out for help. When Denise awoke she was prompted to call Annie interstate with no response. She found out later from her boyfriend, that Annie had not turned up at home or work for the past two days. In due course Annie was formally lodged as a missing person. She was found, but not before a member of the family picked up a letter post-marked the day after the dream. In it, Annie said not to worry that she had left her boyfriend and would contact the family when she had an alternative address. Annie later confirmed that on the night of the dream 'something was very, very wrong'.

This nightmare was literally a psychic call for help which short-circuited the slower postal system. It was picked up by someone who loved her (hence the rapport) and who also watched and had the courage to act on her dream.

Most of our dreams are symbolic—how to tell the difference

Many of our dreams are symbolic because they use associated meanings and often exaggerate to make a point. Understanding these symbols takes more skill. Dreams use symbols to portray feelings and concepts because your mind thinks naturally using pictures. We acknowledge this in our language when we say, 'I get the picture'. For example, if I told you that I looked in the mirror when I was getting ready to go to work this morning and was surprised to see another face smiling back at me, you pictured that scene in your mind's eye. You didn't mentally read a page of text.

Symbols are a very economical language because one picture speaks a thousand words; symbols are also loaded with feeling and personal relevance for dramatic effect.

They are intriguing because they stand for something other than their obvious meaning. By their nature they draw you in. A sign, on the other hand, means exactly what it says. A sign bearing the words 'Mary Street' identifies the street as Mary Street. As a symbol, a street could represent your path in life, the direction you are taking, the option you are considering or your career path.

Sometimes the boundaries blur between when a dream can be taken literally and when it requires a symbolic interpretation. For example, could it be possible that Annie's cry for help represented some aspect of Denise that needed rescuing? It's a good question to ask yourself.

First, do a reality check by asking yourself:

Could the dream be saying exactly what it seems to say?

If the answer is yes, then consider the possibility that the dream could be taken on face value. Keep it as a working hypothesis to use as another dimension in your thinking. It will be confirmed only with the value of hindsight. A further check would be of value here. Apply a symbolic interpretation to your dream and if it doesn't ring true with your current life circumstances this would add weight to the probability that it could be a literal dream, in which case, it may give you the perception and foresight to make better choices.

All your dream symbols have meaning

You may have noticed that dreams draw many of their symbols from the day's events. This is not done randomly. Dipping into your pool of experiences and recent exposures is an economical process and one that dreams use wherever possible. All dream symbols are meaningful. Your dreaming mind may target an image from a television show that you watched last night or something you saw in a magazine recently or may conjure up an image of a person who just stepped into your life. This works because symbols can have more than one meaning. Despite its other possible meanings the dreaming mind chose that symbol (it could have chosen others) because it has a personal relevance loaded with emotion and significance that is unique to you. Your dreams go to great lengths to try to make you understand.

Symbols may have many possible meanings

In order to work with symbols fully it is important to be open-ended with them rather than to constrict their meaning in the first instance. Symbols can have more than one meaning. A baby as a symbol could represent different things to different people. It could represent dependence and joy or responsibilities to a mother. It could symbolise a project or someone's 'brain child' to a businessperson or it could represent jealousy and competition to a sibling. All of these meanings can be correct and there may be others.

When we apply context the associated options will narrow down. If we consider the street symbol again in a variety of different circumstances you will see how the most probable meaning becomes clearer. If you were:

- looking for a street you could be searching for something and trying to find your way
- stumbling along a street you could be floundering through life feeling lost or struggling to find direction
- heading up a one-way street you may be feeling like you can't make your own choices, you're stuck in rut or you haven't many options open to you at the present time.

How you relate to the symbol will be the best indicator of its meaning

As you can see, symbols are very versatile and malleable. They often represent some part of yourself. Because you created them, your relationship to them holds the key to their meaning. This would take precedence over any other definition offered by well-meaning friends or a dream dictionary. You will know when your interpretation is correct. It will fit with the rest of the dream story and be relevant to your life. It will also be met with a 'yes, of course' realisation or an 'ah-ha' feeling. Your dream interpretation would also be consistent with a series of dream messages on the same issue.

Understanding personal and universal symbols

Sometimes dreams can use symbols that are beyond your experience. These are universal symbols and have meaning to our race. Because they appeared in your dream they also have significance for you at this time. These types of symbols tend to relate to major human themes we all face and they come to us at important transition times in our lives. They are often out of the ordinary in character.

They can feature mythological figures and concepts like the unicorn, the winged horse Pegasus, angels, sages, wizards and even royalty. They help us through phases like marriage, birth, illness, divorce and death, bringing us wisdom. Through universal images of the hero, the nurturer, the trickster, the victim and the saboteur they can show how we are influenced by the roles we subconsciously act out and whether these serve or hinder our growth and ambitions.

Personal symbols, on the other hand, are more common everyday things and events. If you don't own them you would likely know of them or have experienced them or could relate to them. Everyday animals like cats, dogs and horses or things like houses and vehicles or even the act of swimming, sitting for an exam, being naked in public and teeth falling out fit into this category. These are personal symbols because with some investigation you can relate to them. Dwelling on the feeling behind the image and focusing on what is happening in your life will often reveal its meaning. Their significance is unique to you.

Even here types of symbols can blur. What may be a universal symbol to one person may not be to another. The queen may symbolise a sense of destiny and devotion to duty to someone who has never met her or is never likely to meet her but she may represent herself (or some quality within the dreamer) to someone who works in her court and knows her personally.

Meditating with your dream symbols

Some dream symbols can be obscure and you may not be able to relate to them. Perhaps it's too obscure for this dictionary or maybe the leads you have don't seem to be taking you anywhere. You can mentally converse with a dream image in meditation and often something profound will reveal itself.

Just find a quiet spot where you won't be disturbed, close your eyes and go back into your dream. You'll need to be prepared to play a dual role: that of yourself and of the symbol you wish to investigate. Visualise yourself stepping into the symbol and now become the symbol (even if it's an inanimate object, make it come to life). No-one is watching so you can let yourself go. Allow yourself to run with whatever springs to mind. Don't think about the process or what you say. Just let it happen. The idea is to simply experience whatever happens and uncover the unconscious associations that gave birth to the image. It's a safe process.

Start by describing yourself, what you look like and what your function is. Then assume the role of yourself and have a mental dialogue back and forth for however long it takes, allowing the conversation to be completely free flowing until the meaning of the symbol reveals itself.

Some interesting insights usually present themselves. Here are some examples:

- One woman dreamt of seeing fish hooks in the ocean and they turned out to be barbs—family gossip directed at her the previous day.
- Another woman dreamt of a dog with permed fur! It turned out to be a self-image issue. The dog was beautiful; it didn't need curly fur to be more beautiful. This dreamer was recovering from bulimia and working with low self-esteem.
- Someone else dreamt of an old aboriginal woman hiding behind a rock. It turned out to be her shadow (a part of herself in need of recognition)—she was old, wise and repressed.

Use this fantasy technique to complement your other skills if and when you get stuck. It usually bears fruit and you will grow into it with practice.

Look at the action—context is important

Symbols are only part of the story and an important part at that. But you wouldn't read a novel and focus on just one or two characters or even read one chapter to the exclusion of the rest and expect to understand the story and how the conclusion unfolded. How the characters and symbols behave and what happens to them is vitally important in the dream story when considering its meaning. Let's look at how the meaning of our street symbol varies significantly when we consider context.

- If you were walking down a street to be met by an oncoming car that impeded your progress it may indicate that you are heading in the wrong direction
- If you were walking along a street with fast-flowing traffic the dream could be indicating that you are going with the flow or living life in the fast lane.

Context allows you to hone in on the various alternative meanings a symbol may have so you can then pick the best fit. This is the most appropriate meaning according to the dream story and to what is happening in your life at the time of the dream.

Dealing with conflicting meanings

Some symbols have meanings that can seem contradictory to each other. If we consider two street signs as a symbol, they could mean opposing things. They could represent:

- considering your options
- feeling confused
- or a left and right path—a wise versus an unwise direction or decision.

Looking at context and seeing what else is happening in the dream and your life will provide the key to the most appropriate interpretation.

Combining different symbols

Sometimes more than one image can make up a symbol and then you put the meanings together. If you are looking at two street signs and one of them has the street name 'Easy' on it, put the images together. In this case, it's a play on the words 'easy street'. Like a popular television game show dreams often use puns and figures of speech to great effect. The dream may be suggesting that you should take or are considering taking 'easy street', the easy path or option.

If you are a passenger in a sports car travelling along easy street, the dream may be referring to your need or your desire. It may also be advising you to adopt this approach. Because you are a passenger in the car and not the driver you don't have it or own it yet. It could be symbolising:

- a more playful or competitive approach to something (depending on how you view sportiness, whether you enjoy it, are competitive by nature, how you felt in the dream or if you were enjoying being driven or not)
- a way to make your path easier for you (easy street).

You could be confident that the dream may be advising you to adopt this approach if this scene was the climax of the dream and made up the dream message in the form of a result, outcome, conclusion, insight or resolution from the action preceding it. This is usually (however, not always) at the end of the dream. You could then consider adopting this approach knowing that it would be to your advantage.

However, you may feel that you already knew this about yourself and the dream is simply restating something obvious. If this scene is not the climax of the dream but an early action sequence in the drama then you could assume that the dream is using this episode to illustrate to you the issue you are currently facing. The first two-thirds of a dream usually describes your situation and how you feel. The dream will then go on to make some comment about it and how you can best handle it in the climax as the drama unfolds. Over several nights your dreams will tend to give further insights into this issue, much like piecing together a jigsaw puzzle, until another more important issue takes precedence.

Making connections, finding solutions and empowering your life

Your dreams are powerful tools that are more powerful than most people realise. Many of us are like the captain of a ship bobbing aimlessly in the ocean, having to set sail somewhere to get provisions and avoid the inevitable strong weather conditions that will surely come. With your dreams to guide you, you have the key you need to open the safe in your cabin and look at the map placed there by the shipping company. It outlines your journey, the nature of your cargo, the specifications of your ship and the reefs and tides of the ocean you need to navigate.

With this partnership your growth is potentially unlimited. You hold your destiny in your hands. The power to be who you want to be is yours. How will you choose to use it?

Your dreams can make a difference to your life as shown in the following examples.

- Carol learned what was holding her back from achieving fulfilling relationships with this dream. She was travelling along in her car when she stopped to investigate some rubbish beside the road. When she got back into her car, it wouldn't start. The dream was suggesting that she stop paying attention to feelings and attitudes that would be better disposed of. In this case, her feelings were impacting negatively on her present relationships, which had the potential to break down on her.
- Judith's dream was enlightening in another way. Interestingly, she met herself in her dream and looked somewhat enviously upon herself. She was then discussing with other people that she wasn't prepared to pay the high price of something. In waking life, Judith had argued with her partner a couple of days before the dream. She had taken a stand on principle, which she intended to adhere to. The dream shows her deeper feelings. Under her intellectual rationalisations Judith felt as if she had lost a part of herself—a part that she valued and admired. She aspired to being like that again. She had paid a high price to be right. It came at the expense of her happy relationship, which, in her case, was the strong foundation from which she went out into the world and the source of her confidence and inner

contentment. The dream had told a different story. With this realisation she made amends, changed her approach and let the issue go.

- Susan was a budding writer who wanted to know if she had the talent to be an author. She recalled the following three dreams which confirmed, encouraged and celebrated her aspirations. In the first dream, a friend insisted on giving her a string of expensive pearls for her to mind. Her friend made it clear that these were only on loan. In discussing the dream Susan felt that these were pearls of wisdom entrusted into her care and were the source of her inspiration.
- In the second dream, Susan walked passed a maternal figure from her past. The woman called out to Susan to wait; there was urgency in her voice. Susan had her own plans but sensed the importance of this opportunity and returned only to be greatly encouraged and empowered by her words. In this dream, Susan felt that she should keep her connection with her source ahead of making her own plans. This is a nurturing influence and would be the source of her empowerment.
- In the third dream, a writer had won an award and she was about to put on a dance spectacle to show Susan how she had won it. In waking life, Susan had made a commitment to writing and the dream was acknowledging and celebrating her achievement. What wonderful confirmation of her ambitions. The door was open to her and she should abandon her fear.

These dreams show how practical our inner wisdom can be and how our lives can be enriched by learning to understand them.

Putting it all together

Let's look at how to analyse a dream. I named this dream, Case Squashed.

Frank and I are in a small one-tonne truck travelling along Cross Road toward South Road. As we approach the railway crossing that intersects Cross Road at Unley Park the crossing signals start up and we pull to a hurried halt.

A suitcase that is on the back of the truck shoots off the tray and bounces across the road, coming to rest on the railway line. An express train comes at considerable speed along the line and runs over the case and crushes it.

With considerable dismay we run over to collect the case. It's damaged beyond repair, but it is full of money. We carry it back to the truck. I notice that the tray is full of olives—the large green variety.

In order to analyse a dream, ask yourself the following questions and follow these steps in sequence. This will make the process a lot easier.

- **Ask yourself how you felt during the dream. Was there a feeling you woke up with?**
  This is the first clue to understanding the dream issue. In this case, the feeling was one of impending shock. You can then ask yourself how or where in your life do you feel horrified or have been taken by surprise recently.
- **Ask yourself if the dream provides any clues to the place or setting of the dream drama much like a prop in a play?**

It could be work, health or relationships. In this case, Frank is the dreamer's work colleague and he may be symbolic or he may represent himself. We keep our minds open to both possibilities at this stage. However, he may anchor the dream at a work-related issue.

- **What are the major action sequences in the plot?**

  I'll rephrase the three main themes in broad general terms using my own words in order to move from appearance to meaning. This will reveal the plot and make the dream easier to work with.

  (a) The first dream theme seems to be that something comes to an enforced stop.

  (b) The second dream theme shows something getting damaged in the process.

  (c) The third theme illustrates that whatever is damaged has some reward or compensation.

- **In order to relate one or two of these main themes to your current life, ask yourself how or where in your life at the moment has something come to a halt?**

  Alternatively, you could ask where your plans have been stifled in some way. In this case, the dreamer, William, who's a company director, was responsible for thousands of individual shareholders and many millions of dollars. He had this dream after giving evidence in a two-day trial. The company was fighting for its survival in court, trying to overturn a compulsory acquisition by a government department. The trial had just finished and the judge would deliver his ruling in about two month's time. So the dream issue deals with litigation and the forced overturning of company plans.

- **Ask yourself what the meanings of the symbols are in order to obtain more detail from the dream.**

  This is much easier to do now that we know the dream topic. Cross Road and intersection could stand for being at a crossroad and having to make some decisions about where you go from here. In light of the dream issue, the suitcase would likely represent the legal case. The express train travelling at high speed could symbolise the government—powerful and unstoppable with predetermined plans (like a train travelling on set tracks). Money could represent compensation or damages in this issue. The large green olives are distasteful, the type you can't eat and could represent something unpalatable which leaves a bitter aftertaste.

- **What does the dream mean now if you were to restate it and insert the most appropriate meaning in place of each symbol?**

  When you read the dream back in order the dream message will unravel and reveal itself. In this case, it is a prophetic dream which predicts the outcome of the current court case. William's company will be defeated but there will compensation. However, this will be unpalatable. And, yes, the dream was correct. This was exactly the outcome several months later.

- **What recommended action would you take based on this knowledge?**

  This dream could help you to accept the inevitable. Time could be saved by making early plans in your own mind (while you wait for the decision to be confirmed) about your future and where you go from here.

- **Write a few words to honour the dream.**

  I am always grateful for the insights that my dreams give me. They are messages from the soul and can be the best counsel you'll ever have or need. I close my dream record with a simple word of gratitude on the page, which acknowledges its source. Gratitude opens you to receive. Honouring the dream reaffirms your commitment to the dreaming process, which in turn, encourages more constructive and spiritual dreams.

This book presents open options—use it as a guide

Understanding your dreams is an art that explores feelings, resemblances and similarities within the context of the dream and links these to issues confronting you or experiences you are having in your daily life. Dream symbols can be interpreted in more than one way and you can meditate on and mentally converse with obscure symbols and reveal their identity. This dictionary can be a great resource and guide you to your own inner wisdom. It can give you a starting point in which to think about your own associations and possible issues in your life. It helps you ask the right question—and you have the answers. It is not intended to be a book of answers. See if you relate to any of the key words associated with each symbol in the following chapters, or come up with your own. Explore their meanings within the unfolding dream drama and apply it in a manner similar to the Symbol in Action examples, which serve to illustrate the process. As the dreamer, you are the best interpreter of your dreams. Trusting and being open to your dream wisdom could be the first step you take to a new life. You can live your dreams. You can do it!

Getting Started

A single moment of understanding
can flood a whole life with meaning.
Anonymous

Dream gems—working with wisdom to live by

Imagine how empowered you would feel and the different choices you could make if you had received gems of wisdom at just the right moment when you needed them in your life. What would you do with these personal insights if they had been given to you? Reducing your dream messages to their essence (by rephrasing them succinctly) reveals their wisdom in a way that is clear and easy to see. Then create an affirmation (a positive statement of belief) with which to work. This will help anchor the attitude or quality your dream is recommending into your waking life.

Here are some sample dream messages like the ones you could get. It is interesting to note their power and authority. Remember, your messages will be even more meaningful because they will be designed for you about your life. They will be your words of wisdom guiding you into greater self-fulfilment.

Here are some dream messages and the corresponding affirmations you could use.

* Go forward with confidence. Don't let your fears hold you back.
  I go forward with trust and confidence. I can do it. I enjoy doing well.
* Show more love and understanding. Love is the most powerful force in the universe.
  My love flows freely through me and I pass it on to all beings. I love life and who I am.
* Be careful. Danger ahead. There's something you haven't seen.
  I proceed carefully and cautiously. I make wise decisions.
* All is well. Your motivation passes the test. Many people are benefiting from your actions.
  I feel connected with my source. I enjoy helping others.
* You will be offered a contract but you will need to shake off some restricted thinking first.
  I am flexible. I embrace all opportunities offered to me.
* Give Linda this message. Tell her I love her always and in all ways. Tell her!
  I am open to higher communication. I listen with my inner ear.
* Put aside your projected attitudes in order to be able to think about the issue clearly.
  I have the courage to see things as they are.
* Be careful. Watch your diet.
  I honour my body. I guard my health.
* Be confident. Project yourself. People will respond.

I am confident. I like people. People like me.

- Be patient. Wait for a turn of events.
  I walk my path with humility and grace. I watch events unfold with perfect timing.
- Slow down. Things are starting to get away from you.
  I am patient. I take things in my stride.
- The best is yet to come.
  My destiny unfolds before me. I gratefully accept the opportunities presented to me.
- You're not prepared. Build up your expertise first.
  I am thoroughly prepared. I enjoy feeling confident.
- Take comfort. The results don't concern you.
  I enjoy doing my best. I know the result will be the highest good for all concerned.
- Ignore the passing parade. You will need self-discipline.
  I keep focused. I enjoy having more time to achieve my goals.
- Keep on keeping on.
  I walk my path with persistence and determination. I enjoy the journey.
- Take your career to the next level. Move on.
  I see the bigger picture. I seize the moment. The future is in my hands.
- Nurture your ambitions. Start small. Grow tall.
  My ambitions take me to where I want to go. I proceed step by step.
- You haven't reached your destiny yet. There's much work to be done. Don't worry you're not alone. Help comes from beyond the grave.
  I am preparing my way. I am supported by those who love me. I feel strong.
- The work you do will define you as you will define the work you do.
  I make my work what it is. It makes me who I am.
- You prefer to stay where you are but you can't see clearly because of strong attachments.
  I let go of past thinking. I see things anew.
- You will receive unexpected help.
  I gratefully receive any help that's offered.
- A soul wants to be born to you.
  The soul that wants to be our baby is very welcome and deeply loved.
- Your father will pass over to the other side. You will meet again.
  I accept the inevitable with poise and grace.

How to recall your dreams

Remembering your dreams and gaining some skills is the key to receiving their wisdom. You can increase your dream recall by following these steps.

- Be aware of your day issues before going to bed, particularly your emotional ups and downs.
- Try to go to sleep when you are not too tired.
- Repeat the affirmation: 'I will remember my dreams tonight', and make this the last thought on your mind before drifting off to sleep.
- Have a drink of water before you go to bed. This will prompt you to go to the

bathroom during the night and give you another opportunity to recall your dreams.

- Keep a dream journal next to your bed. This will send a message to the sub-conscious mind that you are serious about remembering your dreams.
- Build an interest in dreams by reading and talking about them. Dreams come in response to what's in your heart and mind during the day.
- Wake slowly before the alarm. Waking suddenly to an alarm can blast the dream away.
- When you wake, recollect your impressions before opening your eyes. Keep tracing back any dream memories without thinking about the dream and this will bring the dream into the conscious mind where you may have about an hour to write your dream down. You can then analyse it at your leisure during the day. Eighty per cent of the dream is otherwise lost in the first two minutes.
- Record your dream segments if you feel there was more to the dream than you remember. These fragments are the most memorable parts of the dream and recording them will help to build recall.
- Taking your dreams seriously and then acting on them will help close the circle and reinforce more rich and rewarding dreams.

Keeping a dream journal

My dream journals are a spiritual record of my journey and they make interesting reading to look back on and will still have relevance in the years to come. Yours will also be a valuable record of your spiritual guidance whose wisdom you can share with loved ones and make it part of your family history. Honouring it will give you great satis-faction and keeping it clear and easy to read will make it a more useful reference to review and enjoy.

Use the dream diary pages in the back of this book to record your dreams. They are a helpful resource, which you can photocopy to compile your own dream journal. There is plenty of space to record even long dreams and the prompts in the Dream Insights section have been designed to guide you through the process and help you explore your dream so as not to overlook any steps. You will have more success, however, if you have fun with a creative exploratory spirit within the framework provided.

- There is a Contents page so you can look up your dream by dream title for quick reference.
- The Dream Review page will help you see your 'dream gems' at a glance and make compelling reading.
- The Recurring Dream page will help highlight those dreams that are calling out for special attention. Dreams repeat themselves in different ways if it's an important issue and we haven't understood their message. If they continue to be ignored and the issue is an ongoing one, they can build into nightmares in order to wake us to what they want to us to know.
- The Recurring Dream Symbol page will help you to compile your personal glossary of dream symbols which may recur and save you time.

Here are some hints to help you.

- Use the left-hand page to record your dream.
- Give your dream a title—one that embodies its most dramatic image or feeling.
- Record the dream in the present tense to highlight the emotion. For example, use 'I run away' rather than 'I ran away'.
- Use the dream sheets provided. They give you plenty of space with prompts that you can use to analyse your dream.
- Work on at least one dream a week. This can overcome information overload and dreams will repeat themselves in other ways if the issue is important.
- Watch a series of dreams, particularly if you're going to make a big decision or you are dealing with a difficult issue.
- Review your dreams monthly or from time to time. They will be very enlightening and the rewards will help to reinforce your commitment to watching your dreams.
- Allow up to six months to develop your skills to such a point that you can rely upon them to serve you on demand as a life skill whenever you need. You can then use it at crisis or critical points or as you wish in your life. It will be a personal skill that you'll treasure forever.

Part Two
Dream Symbols

Chapter 1
Animals

*In the glance of the speechless animal there is a discourse that
only the soul of the wise can really understand.*
Indian poet (anonymous)

Animals can represent particular qualities within you, such as your natural impulses, strong emotional needs or thoughts and sensations that you perceive and nurture. Consider these possible meanings with any others specifically listed.

How to get the best value from this chapter

- See if you relate to any of the key words or questions and explore your own meanings which may override those given here.
- Look at all possibilities and apply the most appropriate for your situation.
- Rephrase the Life Issue questions to broaden their personal relevance to you, if necessary, by using other words with similar meanings.
- You can also turn any question around (including those you formulate) to see if you relate to them better, by asking them in a slightly different way. For example, rephrase it as a need rather than a desire or belief or vice versa.
- The Symbol in Action examples show how to apply context or link meaning with action.

Desires and needs as opposed to outcomes and results

If a symbol represents an issue you are currently facing, then it may be indicative of your feelings, desires, beliefs or needs. This would usually occur in the first two-thirds of a dream, which often illustrates the issue you are dealing with and how you feel about it.

If a symbol comes in the form of a resolution, outcome, insight, solution or conclusion in the climax, usually at the end of the dream, then it may indicate a consequence, result or your dream advice to you.

Symbol	Symbol In Action *Look for feelings, desires, needs, beliefs or situations, explore literal meanings, apply any puns and idioms*	Possible Life Issues *Look for where, what and who this reminds you of, apply key words to thoughts, feelings or situations, explore literal meanings, apply word plays and figures of speech*
Animal	See the Introduction and Common Dream Theme at the beginning and end of this chapter, respectively.	
Anteater (spiny)	**Anteater with its nose in a burrow:** Sticking your nose into something **Tucking head in:** Refusing to face something **Curling into a ball:** Insulating yourself; needing to trust.	Curious; prying; gentle; innocent; harmless; prickly sensitivities (spiny); unapproachable Are you protecting yourself or being self-defensive? What do you need to uncover?
Antelope	**Stampeding antelopes:** Going along with the crowd; needing to reveal yourself **Herd of antelopes grazing:** Lost in a crowd; group protection **Butting antelopes:** Being headstrong.	Thick-skinned; versatile; leaping from one thing to another; speed; elope Where are you leaping ahead? What are you running away from?
Ape	**Apes playing around:** Imitating others; being silly **Apes grooming:** Combining strength and compassion **Group of apes feeding:** Valuing past connections.	Ancestral connections; mimicking others; copying others' ideas; origins; going ape What are you dealing with that's being influenced by, or linked with, the past? Where are you showing or needing inner strength?
Armadillo	**Burrowing:** Getting to the bottom of something; being undermined or undermining others **Rolling into a ball:** Feeling defenceless; being defensive **Upturned armadillo:** Feeling vulnerable; reversal of circumstances.	Self-protection; defensive attitudes; personal boundaries Where have you put barriers between yourself and others? What's holding you back from being open with yourself and others?

Symbol	Symbol In Action	Possible Life Issues
Baboon	**Baboons playing:** Being mischievous; interacting with others **Baboons eating:** Feeling supported by group or family ties **Trying to capture a baboon:** Needing to be more socially orientated.	Social convictions; gregarious; group-minded Are you reaching out to others? Where are you sharing common objectives?
Badger	**Dead badger:** Being passive or timid **Badger chasing a person:** Feeling annoyed or annoying others **Badger at work:** Domineering employer; bossy tendencies; needing to be assertive.	Aggressive tendencies (vicious); quick to anger Are you feeling badgered? Where do you need to push ahead?
Bandicoot	**Catching a bandicoot:** Seeking independence **Bandicoot on alert:** Feeling on edge **Bandicoot running:** Feeling threatened or dominated.	Swift; quick thinking; nervousness; doesn't infringe on others; independent What are you keeping to yourself? Where do you need to act quickly?
Bat	**Cave full of bats:** Social ties or connections **Hanging in trees:** Seeing things upside down; turning an issue around **Bat blinking:** Showing no emotion: wouldn't bat an eyelid.	Hidden fears; suspended judgments; rebirth; reversal; renewal; intuition (sound vibrations); sense of timing (hibernates); blind as a bat; batty What can't or don't you want to see? What are you fearful of?
Bear	**Bear about to attack:** Feeling intimidated or intimidating others **Lifting a bear up:** Having endurance: bearing up **Bear at a market:** Falling stocks: bear market.	Strength; forceful opinions; sense of timing (hibernates); lovable; cute; bringing to bear; bear hug; bear in mind; bear down upon Where are you using your power and influence? Are you being overbearing?
Beaver	**Beaver building:** Being energetic and dependable	Intelligent; achieving; striving; cooperative; skilful; tenacious; adaptable; well-suited

Symbol	Symbol In Action	Possible Life Issues
	Beaver dam: Blocking your emotions **Beaver wrestling with something:** Being intrusive; meddling in others' affairs; confronting your work ethic.	(amphibious); eager beaver Are you being conscientious and industrious? What are you enthusiastic about?
Bilby	**Bilby feeding:** Finding inner peace and contentment **Bilby burrowing:** Digging yourself into a hole; having tunnel vision **Bilby looking around nervously**: Looking over your shoulder; scaring yourself; being distrustful.	Nocturnal lifestyle; burying your feelings (burrowing); loner (solitary); alert; frightened Are you undermining yourself or others? Where are you being perceptive?
Boar	**Boar attacking you:** Feeling vulnerable or threatened **Hunting a boar:** Showing courage; confronting difficulties **You having a boar's head:** Boring others: they're such a bore.	Aggressive tendencies; dangerous; fearless; impulsive; courage; irrational; impulse to suicide Are you acting against your own self-interest? Are you feeling bored?
Buffalo	**Large herd of grazing buffalo:** Affluence; manifesting ideas **Captured buffalo:** Restricting supply; harnessing spiritual energy **Stampeding buffalo:** Plans taking off quickly; dispersed energy.	Stored energy; spiritual force; sacred ideals; good provider; prayer; gratitude; big head Are you receiving abundance? Where are you connecting with your source?
Bull	**Being chased by a bull**: Feeling bullied or intimidated **Bull standing next to a gate***: Being reckless: bull at a gate **Bull in a market place:** Large rise in stock prices: bull market.	Uncompromising views; caught in a rut; dishonesty; Taurus; no bull; bull in a china shop; bullying; bullseye; take the bull by the horns Are you being impulsive and charging forward? Where are you using your power?
Camel	**Camel drinking:** Need staying power	Weighed down; whingeing (moans); treading carefully

Symbol	Symbol In Action	Possible Life Issues
	Camel train: Group persevering through difficult times **Camel being cut up:** Strength, endurance or tolerance being undermined.	(cushion-footed); endurance Where have you taken on too much? Are you feeling resentful or complaining?
Cat	**Buying a cat:** Developing intuition **Cat walking:** Showing off; making your mark: catwalk **Cat coming out of a bag**: Revealing a secret: letting the cat out of the bag.	Independent; intuitive; disconnected; indifferent; inquisitive; cat call; catty; cat nap; cat-o'-nine-tails Are you being uncaring? Where have you cut yourself off from others?
Cattle	**Cattle grazing**: Nurturing domestic circumstances **Cattle being herded:** Being led by others **Being slaughtered:** Sacrificing yourself or your principles.	Crowd behaviour; domestic issues; group influences Where can't you think for yourself? Are you being linked with others?
Chameleon	**Chameleon changing colours:** Being fickle; accommodating others; adjusting or reinventing yourself **Looking for food**: Serving your self-interest **Chameleon running away:** Fear of change.	Variable; versatile; conflicting; changeable; unpredictable; persevering Are you being adaptable? Where do you need to change or be flexible?
Cow	**Herd of cows:** Going along with the crowd **Hard to handle cow:** Making a stand **Boy with a cow:** Wild and unreliable behaviour: cowboy.	Good provider; docile; passive and compliant; sacred; green pastures; great mother; old cow Where are you serving others? Are you feeling used and neglected?
Coyote	**Coyote attacking you:** Self-deception; self-sabotage; needing to laugh at yourself **Coyote hunting:** Feeling misled or conned; misleading others **Pack of coyotes:** Group deception or illusion.	Wisdom; intelligence; deception; illusion; trickster; balances risk and safety; foolish Are you weighing up risk? Do you sense that things are not as they seem?

Symbol	Symbol In Action	Possible Life Issues
Deer	**Stroking deer:** Showing compassion **Stalking deer:** Harmful motives; lacking innocence **Two deer:** High cost or consequences: too dear.	Beauty; inner beauty; gentleness; love; grace; agility; mental acumen; innocence; listening; compassion; vulnerability Where are you showing charm and grace? What is precious and dear to you?
Dingo	**Dingo attacking you:** Feeling victimised, threatened or cheated **Dingo attacking prey:** Scheming; being ruthless **Holding a dingo cub:** Evolving deception; growing suspicions.	Elusive; calculating; deceptive; vanishing What needs to be exposed and brought out into the open? Where are you dealing with dishonourable intentions?
Dog	**Leading a dog to work:** Bringing loyalty into the workplace **Dog at dawn:** Changing luck; every dog has its day **Dog in the house:** Being in trouble: in the dog house.	Devotion; protection; self-defence; courage; loyalty; best friend; service; fear; aggression; threatening; dog box; dog tired; dog's life; dog's body Where do you need to show or receive unconditional love? Are you are in a dependent relationship?
Donkey	**Donkey carrying a heavy load:** Feeling overburdened **Picture of donkey on a calendar:** Very long time: donkey's years **Donkey working:** Feeling undervalued; dreary work: donkey work.	Persistence; servile; stubborn; simple-minded; being a donkey; donkey vote Are you feeling used? Where are you standing your ground?
Dunnart	**Dunnart hiding:** Not revealing your feelings **Dunnart watching:** Needing to be more alert **Dead dunnart:** Unable to accommodate others.	Shy; mental alertness; not obvious; adaptable (camouflaged) Are you being reticent, reserved or overlooked? Are you feeling well suited to your job or fitting into your environment?
Echidna	See Anteater in this chapter.	
Elephant	**Friend riding an elephant towards you:** Other people's	Good memory; big issues and responsibilities; weighty

Symbol	Symbol In Action	Possible Life Issues
	responsibilities; needing to remember someone **Struggling to lift an elephant:** Feeling weighed down or overburdened **Elephants stampeding towards you:** Powerful force behind you or to contend with.	problems; exaggeration; powerful; gentle; social; being overweight Are you dealing with hefty issues? Where are you relying on your memory?
Elk	**Elk feeding:** Enjoying passionate emotions **Elk charging you:** Uncontrolled feelings and desires **Elk running away:** Denying your feelings; lack of cohesion.	Magical; wild; untamed emotions; staying with the familiar; keeping to your own gender Are you being emotional? Do you need to be more spontaneous?
Ferret	**Ferret in a burrow:** Bringing feelings or issues to the surface **Ferret hunting:** Forcing your attitudes or opinions onto others **Breeding ferrets:** Being more proactive.	Curious; unearthing beliefs or solutions; disclosure; savage; unpredictable; ferret out What are you searching for? What are you uncovering?
Fox	**Fox with prey:** Feeling or being manipulated; being clever **Fox in a hole:** Needing to take cover: fox hole **Woman wearing a fox fur:** Classy and trendy: foxy lady.	Cunning; untrustworthy; intelligent; blending in with others; adaptable (camouflaged); unpredictable; foxtrot Are you out-manoeuvring or outwitting others? Where are you serving your own ends?
Frog	**Little frog in a big pond:** Feeling insignificant or lost **Person coughing while holding a frog:** Unable to speak freely: frog in the throat **Frogs hopping in sequence:** Pushing an idea or project forward: frogmarch.	Hidden beauty; transformation; cleansing attitudes or emotions; progressing in leaps and bounds; rain Have you overlooked the deeper significance of something? What has potential or could be developed?
Giraffe	**Giraffe eating leaves at the top of a tree:** Feeling stretched; striving to achieve **Giraffe alone:** Standing out; being noticed	Rising above the crowd; higher perspective; standing tall; stretching; far-seeing Where have you got a higher vision?

Symbol	Symbol In Action	Possible Life Issues
	Giraffe unable to eat something on the ground: Inability to relate to others; stiff neck.	Are you holding your head up high?
Goat	**Rams locking horns:** Opposing something head-on **Goats playing:** Fooling around: acting the goat **Goat at night:** Zodiac sign of Capricorn.	Knowing where you're going (sure-footed); headstrong; undiscriminating; sexuality; scapegoat; ramming a point home; getting on your goat Where are you being forceful or arrogant? What's annoying you?
Gopher	**Gopher trying to get attention:** Feeling used or undervalued **Gopher burrowing:** Undermining yourself or others; needing more information **Gopher eating:** Setting goals.	Cowardly; hidden beliefs or inclinations; go-for; go for it; go-getter Where could you be more motivated? What have you underestimated?
Hare	**Hare running:** Being impulsive **Hare urging you on:** Arrogance or overconfidence **Hare pulling something:** Trickery or deception: pulling a fast one.	Bold; fast; urgency; recklessness; boastful; conceited; splitting hairs Are you acting without thinking? Where do you need to be more cautious or modest?
Hippopotamus	**Leading a hippopotamus:** Being in control **Hippopotamus sitting on you:** Feeling weighed down **Hippopotamus swimming:** Receiving support.	Massive problems; significant issues; feeling awkward; being overweight Where are you dealing with big issues or huge responsibilities? What are you overemphasising?
Hog	See Pig in this chapter.	
Horse	**Horses running free:** Freedom of movement **Horse tied up:** Feeling restricted or disempowered **Riding a black stallion:** Harnessing strength; gaining assistance.	Stamina; strength; movement; progressing through a situation; assistance; power; horse sense; horsing around Where are you feeling powerful and strong? Do you need to harness your drive and energy?

Symbol	Symbol In Action	Possible Life Issues
Hyena	**Hyena eating:** Feeding on others; being victimised **Hyena attacking you:** Being taken advantage of; being sacrificed **Pack of hyenas:** Group underhandedness or deceit.	Predatory; perseverance; aggressive tendencies; untrustworthy; following the crowd (pack behaviour) Where are you exercising your power or following your self-interest? Are you being relentless or intrusive?
Jackal	**Jackal-headed god:** Need to move on; rite of passage **Jackal attacking you:** Feeling undervalued; time to go **Jackal hunting:** Being victimised or victimising others.	Unwelcome influence; drudgery; underworld; underhanded; death; Anubis (Egyptian god of the dead) What are you going along with that you don't approve of? Are you going through a period of transition?
Jackass	**Jackass eating:** Enjoying playing the fool **Riding a jackass:** Playing the fool to your advantage **Being kicked by a jackass:** Feeling unappreciated.	Masculine energies; irresponsible attitudes or actions; servitude; ass Are you feeling used and neglected? Do you feel foolish or have you been misguided?
Kangaroo	**Riding a kangaroo:** Making rapid progress **Sleeping kangaroo:** Inertia **Kangaroo with joey:** Nurturing new plans; family support.	Bounding; stamina; adaptable; speed and mobility; manoeuvrability Where are you progressing in leaps and bounds? Are you moving forward despite hostile circumstances?
Koala	**Koala eating:** Digesting ideas **Koala looking at several trees:** Choosing between options **Several koalas in many trees:** Holding on; many alternatives to consider.	Being choosy; selective attitudes or feelings; considering options; slow progress What are you holding on to or can't let go of? Are you being laid-back?
Ladybird	**Ladybird on your wallet:** Financial prosperity or good fortune **Several ladybirds:** Group of insignificant or irrelevant matters	Good luck; insignificant issues; small; beautiful; blemished reputation (black spots) Where are things working out for you?

Symbol	Symbol In Action	Possible Life Issues
	Dead ladybird: Loss of good fortune or fortuitous circumstances.	Are your motives tainted?
Lamb	**Lambs being herded:** Being sacrificed or manipulated; feeling vulnerable: lamb to the slaughter **Pet lamb:** Nurturing innocence **Flock of sheep:** Being led; following the crowd.	Helpless; gentle; innocent; persecution; self-victimisation Where are you following others? Are you being a good provider?
Leeches	**Leeches on you:** Sapping your strength; feeling drained **Leech in your kitchen:** Domestic free loader **Leech on your office door:** Taking advantage of others at work.	Taking from others; free-loader (parasite); permeating attitudes or beliefs (percolates); blood sucker Where are you taking advantage of others or where are they doing it to you? What information or intuitions are filtering through to you?
Leopard	**Being cornered by a leopard:** Finding yourself in a tight situation: put on the spot **Leading a leopard to work:** Showing mental acumen at work **Leopard with no spots:** Acting out of character: changing your spots.	Adept; shrewdness; secrecy; fearlessness; cunning; strength; hot spots; changing your spots Are you showing exceptional skill and ability? Could you be more discerning?
Lion	**Being a lion-tamer:** Showing mastery and daring **Lion with mouth open:** Dangerous position; feeling vulnerable or powerless **Lion on loan to you:** Having the best or largest part: lion's share.	Authority; leadership; daring; fearlessness; pride; power; zodiac sign of Leo; lion-hearted; lionise Where are you acting on your convictions? Are you showing courage and strength?
Lynx	**Lynx feeding:** Feeling whole and in tune **Lynx chasing you:** Scared to face yourself or look deeper **Sick lynx:** Talking too much; gossiping; breaking a confidence; needing to speak up.	Silent; afraid to speak up; lost secrets; ancient knowledge Where do you need to express yourself? What have you missed or lost?

Symbol	Symbol In Action	Possible Life Issues
Mole	**Mole with mound of dirt:** Exaggerating: making a mountain out of a molehill **Being attacked by a mole:** Destructive unseen influences **Mole digging:** Searching for answers; looking inwards.	Destructive attitudes or actions; uncovering beliefs or solutions (burrowing); unseen; small; blind Are you being undermined or undermining others? What can't you see or have overlooked?
Monkey	**Monkey at work:** Being dishonest: monkey business **Monkey on your back:** Feeling dependent **Moulding a monkey out of clay:** Being made to look foolish: make a monkey of.	Mischievous; imitating others; mimic; monkey's uncle Are you adopting others' values and expectations? Where is your attitude or dedication less than serious?
Moose	See Elk in this chapter.	
Mouse	**Mouse caught in a trap:** Feeling inadequate; feeling stuck **Mouse plague:** Overwhelming irritations **Mouse running across the floor:** Needing to face your fears.	Meekness; quiet; timid; scrutiny; fearful; mousy What is gnawing away at you? Where could you be more assertive?
Mule	**Mule carrying a heavy load:** Feeling oppressed **Mule not moving:** Being obstinate; taking a firm stand **Mule in your front yard:** Domestic endurances.	Stubborn attitudes; beast of burden; weighed down Are you feeling used and neglected? Where do you feel burdened?
Opossum	See Possum in this chapter.	
Otter	**Otter in your kitchen:** Being inconsistent at home **Otter at work:** Being good-natured at work **Several otters:** Group of inconsistent people or feelings; blocked attitudes or emotions.	Inconsistency; blocked feelings (builds dams) Have you been unpredictable? Do you need to be more fun-loving?
Ox	See Bull in this chapter.	

Symbol	Symbol In Action	Possible Life Issues
Panda	**Patting a pander:** Indulging yourself or others: pandering **Freeing a pander:** Valuing inner beauty and peace **Panda in a car:** Feeling guilty; needing to measure up; panda car.	Black and white; cute; lovable; tranquil feelings Are you seeing things in black-and-white terms? What do you find attractive in yourself or others?
Panther	See Leopard in this chapter.	
Pig	**Pig eating:** Getting more than your due **Pig being slaughtered:** Overcoming selfish or greedy tendencies **Pig with wings:** Seeing the impossible or improbable: pigs will fly.	Treating oneself; mercenary; bad manners; being tempted; selfish police; informer; hogging something; pig-headed; snout Where are you lacking self-discipline? Are you indulging yourself?
Porcupine	See Anteater in this chapter.	
Possum	**Possum squealing:** Enjoying the sound of your own voice; making a fuss **Possum pretending to be dead:** Being flexible or adaptable; pretence **Possum eating:** Taking what you need; self-interest.	Cute; nocturnal lifestyle; perceptive; grasping motives; making yourself heard (loud squeal); strategic; clever; playing possum Where aren't you considering others? Are you showing pretence?
Potoroo	**Potoroo behind a bush:** Hiding from life; lack of curiosity **Potoroo exploring:** Discovering new ideas and feelings **Captured potoroo on your colleague's desk:** Needing to mind your own business.	Nosy; inquisitive; curious feelings or ideas What are you sticking your nose into? What are you curious about?
Rabbit	**Rabbit burrowing:** Digging a hole for yourself; digging yourself in **Rabbit hopping:** Hopping from one task or person to	Fertility; fertile ideas; prosperity; sexual accomplishment; gregarious; gentle; fear; uncovering solutions or beliefs (burrowing)

Symbol	Symbol In Action	Possible Life Issues
	another; can't settle **Rabbit plague:** Resources being eaten away.	What's increasing rapidly? Where are you undermining yourself or others?
Raccoon	**Feeding a raccoon:** Expressing basic instincts and urges **Raccoon biting you:** Being deceived **Many raccoons:** Group under-handedness.	Nocturnal lifestyle; thief; seeing what others can't; racketeer Are you taking without giving? Where are you being perceptive?
Ram	**Ram climbing a steep hill:** Strong desire to achieve **Ram butting a wall:** Forcing matters and getting nowhere: butting one's head against a wall **Rams butting each other:** Opposing or confronting others.	Pioneering spirit; leadership; male power; energy; hostilities; conflicting feelings; lack of diplomacy; zodiac sign of Aries Are you ramming your point home? Where are you dealing with new beginnings?
Rat	**Smelling a rat:** Aroused suspicions **Rat chewing:** Letting things gnaw away at you **Rats playing:** Betraying yourself or others: play the rat.	Poverty; disease; unhealthy attitudes or habits; filth; squalor; hoarding; ratbag Are you feeling betrayed? What don't you like about yourself or others?
Rhinoceros	**Rhinoceros charging:** Unstoppable events **Rhinoceros attacking you:** Feeling vulnerable or threatened by big responsibilities **Rhinoceros eating:** Being overweight.	Unpredictable outcomes or behaviour; huge problems; aggressive tendencies; uncontrolled temper; little intelligence; self-protection What's taken a surprise turn?
Salamander	**Slippery salamander:** Can't get a hold of something **Eating a salamander:** Listening to hearsay; being spirited; having vision **Dead salamander:** Short-sighted thinking.	Heat; spirit; energy; fire (fire elemental); invent (cooking implement); prolonged and drawn out; fabrication (mythical reptilian creature); adaptable (amphibian) Are you being passionate? Where do you need to be flexible?

Symbol	Symbol In Action	Possible Life Issues
Sheep	**Sheep following the leader:** Being too trusting or easily led **Killing a sheep:** Sacrificing yourself or being a martyr **Sheep with wolf's head:** Cunning pretence: wolf in sheep's clothing.	Passive; submissive; silly imitation; peaceful; trust issues; following without thinking; sheepish Where aren't you thinking for yourself or lacking originality? Have you fleeced someone?
Skunk	**Having a skunk with you:** Being defensive **Breeding skunks:** Developing undesirable qualities within you **Skunk at the office:** Unpleasant colleague; under-handed work practices.	Thinking in black-and-white terms; foul-smelling; self-protecting behaviour; defensive attitudes; repulsive; respect; reputation Are you being offensive? What doesn't smell right?
Sloth	**Sloth eating:** Feeding inefficient thoughts and practices **Leading a sloth:** Taking control or directing lazy tendencies **Sloth sitting down:** Lack of progress.	Slow-moving; passive; immobile; unable to move forward; deliberate; reticent; gentle; slothful Where can't you get motivated? What are you feeling indifferent towards?
Snail	**Eating snails:** Enjoying taking your time; indulging yourself **Many snails eating:** Strong destructive feelings, thoughts, forces or habits **Killing a snail:** Impatience; wanting things to move faster.	Creeping; attitudes that creep up on you; destructive habits or beliefs; slow; snail's pace Where are you making slow progress? What is getting at you?
Squirrel	**Squirrel eating:** Being conscientious **Squirrel collecting food:** Conserving your resources **Squirrel burying nuts:** Needing patience; holding onto your feelings; being prepared.	Hard-working; thrifty; quick; hoarder; gathering your energies Are you being economical? Do you need to save your energy?
Tiger	**Tiger eating prey:** Being victimised or victimising others **Patting a tiger:** Facing your fears **Tiger chasing you:** Feeling	Strength; dominance; domineering opinions; powerful opponent; fear; female energies; paper tiger Where are you showing power,

Symbol	Symbol In Action	Possible Life Issues
	threatened; denying your own power.	strength or skill? Are you feeling intimidated or being coerced?
Weasel	**Weasel talking:** Misleading remarks: weasel words **Weasel walking away:** Evading your responsibilities **Capturing a weasel:** Revealing deceit.	Slender bodied; treachery; betrayal; disloyalty; sly; stealth; slinking away; covert tactics What are you trying to weasel your way out of? Are you betraying yourself or others?
Wild animals	See Common Dream Theme at the end of this chapter.	
Wolf	**Wolf on your verandah:** Feeling threatened; seeking wisdom; confronting difficulties: wolf at your door **Sheep with wolf's head:** Being a hypocrite: wolf in sheep's clothing **Pack of wolves:** Group cunning.	Sneaky; crafty; greedy; fear; threatening situations; moon; intuition; admiration; wolf whistle; cry wolf Are you having a problem with trust? Where are you deceiving your-self or dealing with deception?
Wombat	**Wombat burrowing:** Being undermined or undermining others; digging in **Wombat sleeping:** Showing a lack of determination **Wombat eating:** Maintaining your resolve and persistence.	Solid thinking; heavy concepts; uncovering solutions or beliefs (burrowing); placid; tenacity; nocturnal lifestyle; seeing things others can't; perceptive Where are you showing strength and resolve? What are you searching for?
Worm	**Worm crawling:** Worming your way into something; responsibili-ties creeping up on you **Worms on your head:** Feeling remorseful: worms of conscience **Worm's eye:** Needing humility: worm's eye view.	Unworthy; creepy; taking from others (parasitic); downtrodden; no backbone Where are you feeling undervalued or insignificant? What is giving you the creeps?

Common Dream Theme: Being chased by wild animals

To dream of being chased by wild animals can symbolise running away from, or repressing, your spontaneous self, being fearful or feeling emotionally threatened by your natural urges and impulses.

Chapter 2
Birds

No bird soars too high if he soars with his own wings.
William Blake

Birds soar above the earth and can represent your spiritual connections, high ideals, expansion, love, joy, hopes and flights of fancy. Consider these possible meanings with any others specifically listed.

How to get the best value from this chapter

- See if you relate to any of the key words or questions and explore your own meanings which may override those given here.
- Look at all possibilities and apply the most appropriate for your situation.
- Rephrase the Life Issue questions to broaden their personal relevance to you, if necessary, by using other words with similar meanings.
- You can also turn any question around (including those you formulate) to see if you relate to them better, by asking them in a slightly different way. For example, rephrase it as a need rather than a desire or belief or vice versa.
- The Symbol in Action examples show how to apply context or link meaning with action.

Desires and needs as opposed to outcomes and results

If a symbol represents an issue you are currently facing, then it may be indicative of your feelings, desires, beliefs or needs. This would usually occur in the first two-thirds of a dream, which often illustrates the issue you are dealing with and how you feel about it.

If a symbol comes in the form of a resolution, outcome, insight, solution or conclusion in the climax, usually at the end of the dream, then it may indicate a consequence, result or your dream advice to you.

Symbol	Symbol In Action *Look for feelings, desires, needs, beliefs or situations, explore literal meanings, apply any puns and idioms*	Possible Life Issues *Look for where, what and who this reminds you of, apply key words to thoughts, feelings or situations, explore literal meanings, apply word plays and figures of speech*
Albatross	**Albatross nesting:** Taking time out **Albatross flying:** Needing resilience **Albatross in a storm:** Ability to weather and endure.	Endurance; extended journey; patience; fierce; effortless (glides) Where are you showing endurance or perseverance? What are you taking in your stride?
Bird	See Introduction and Common Dream Theme at the beginning and end of this chapter, respectively.	
Bluebird	**Bluebird singing:** Receiving good news; feeling joyous **Bluebird in your garden:** Happy domestic circumstances **Many bluebirds:** Group or family joy.	Happiness; joy; song; singing your praises; colour blue; spiritual values Are you feeling happy and content? Are you feeling inspired?
Bowerbird	**Bowerbird collecting shiny items:** Being dazzled **Bowerbird in courtship dance:** Seeking attention **Bowerbird with lots of things:** Needing to clear your clutter.	Curiosity; curious notions; attraction; hoarder; colouring your life (likes colour) Are you accepting people or events on face value? Are you holding onto ideals or ideas that no longer serve you?
Brolga	**Brolga calling others:** Needing to be heard **Brolga unable to move:** Blocking the flow **Brolga dancing:** Being creative; celebrating who you are.	Graceful; rhythm; uninhibited feelings; dance; expressing yourself (trumpeting) Are you celebrating your achievements? Do you need to go with the flow?
Buzzard	**Buzzard feeding:** Being consumed by your feelings; feeding your appetites **Hunting with prey in its mouth:** Dissatisfaction; unfulfilled	Exploit; devour; greedy; insatiable appetites Are you disadvantaging yourself or others? What can't you get enough of?

Symbol	Symbol In Action	Possible Life Issues
	Buzzard attacking: Being picked on; victimising yourself or others.	
Canary	**Canary let out of cage:** New beginnings; letting go; danger **Sick canary:** Being sensitive; detrimental conditions **Cat eating canary:** Feeling guilty: looking like the cat that swallowed the canary.	Delicate; harmony; song; restricted; unexpressed emotions (caged); lightness; yellow Where are you feeling confined? What do you want to sing about?
Cassowary	**Cassowary eggs:** Developing respect **Cassowary attracting others:** Standing up for your rights; gaining recognition **Being attacked:** Feeling vulnerable; being defensive; loss of reputation.	Respect; reputation; independence; self-protection; self-defensive attitudes; daunting opponent Where are you being defensive? Do you feel isolated or disconnected from others?
Chicken	**Chickens escaping:** Fears running wild **Capturing chickens and locking them up:** Plucking up courage; containing your fears **Old chicken:** Aging or maturing: no spring chicken.	Faint-hearted; shirking responsibilities; retiring; weakness; failure to act; being chicken; chicken feed; chicken-hearted Are you questioning whether you measure up? Where are you feeling you could do better?
Cock	**Cock's eye:** Revealing yourself: cock one's eye **Cock standing above others:** Feeling superior: cock one's nose **Cock that won't fight:** Doubting your argument.	New dawn; male energies; penis; new beginnings; half-cocked; cock shot; cock-up cock-and-bull story; Where have you got energy and drive? Are you making a new start?
Cockatoo	**Cockatoo talking in a cage:** Speaking without thinking **Cockatoo in the bush:** Farmer: a cocky **Cockatoo laughing at you:** Being cheeky or cocky.	Loud; flamboyant; group ties; social; friendship Where are you showing off? Are you speaking your mind?

Symbol	Symbol In Action	Possible Life Issues
Condor	**Condor flying:** High-flyer **Condor nesting:** Developing spiritual aspirations **Condor searching for prey:** Being visionary.	High-flying; high ideals; clarity; perceptive; large; endangered Are you gaining perspective? Are your opportunities taking you places?
Crane	**Crane migrating:** Changing your position; moving on **Crane carrying something in its mouth:** Bearing responsibility; the machine: crane **Crane on your desk:** Working on a long-term project.	Clumsiness; stupidity; feeling awkward; sense of timing (migratory); longevity; carrying a heavy load or responsibilities Where have you vision or a higher perspective? Do you need flexibility?
Crow	**Crow flying:** Moving decisively: as the crow flies **Tree full of crows:** Group goals and determination **Eating a crow:** Feeling humiliated: eating crow.	Clarity; focused thought; decisiveness; law; higher order; shape-shifter (expanded con- sciousness); shamanism; South Australian: Croweater What are you crowing or boasting about? Do you need to be more single- minded?
Cuckoo	**Cuckoo looking for a nest:** Feeling inadequate **Cuckoo nest:** Feeling violated; intrusion **Cuckoo's eggs:** Growing laziness.	Laziness; taking from others (lays eggs in other's nests); cuckoo clock Are you infringing on others? Where are you adopting others' views or values?
Dove	**Doves on your shoulder:** Seeking inner peace **Letting doves fly:** Promoting harmony **Dead dove:** Lack of agreement or understanding.	Freedom; gentleness; innocence; scope; independence; peace; rapport; feeling connected; infor- mation; Holy Spirit Are you making peace with yourself or others? Who are you communicating with?
Duck	**Duck in water:** Being in your element: like a duck to water **Pair of ducks:** Being in love; bonding with others	Fair game; unseen and emerging; ducky; dead duck What are you ducking or avoiding?

Symbol	Symbol In Action	Possible Life Issues
	Duck in shotgun sights: Being set up: sitting duck.	Are you feeling vulnerable?
Eagle	**Eagle flying overhead:** Feeling vulnerable; being ruthless **Seeing eagle's eyes:** Being perceptive; needing vision or perspective: eagle eyed **Eagle feeding young:** Supporting others' ideals.	Swift; targeting; far-reaching outlook; higher ground; air; high ideals; America; legal eagle Do you need to act quickly or decisively? Are you being focused and perceptive?
Emu	**Young emu:** Acquiring or needing speed **Emu running away:** Avoiding responsibility; needing fast reactions **Sick emu:** Being slow and inattentive.	Fast; issues that are difficult to grasp; attentive; taking action; avoidance (buries head in the sand) Are you shirking your responsibilities? Where do you need to spring into action?
Falcon	**Falcon nesting:** Developing intuition **Falcon tethered:** Feeling restricted **Falcon with prey:** Success; being quick to act.	Visionary; victory; aspirations; quick-witted (agile); mental acumen; receptive (tilts its head to listen); strength; beauty; fertility; Horus; Eye of Horus (falcon-like) Where do you need to act quickly? Are you enjoying a sense of freedom?
Flamingo	**Flamingo preening:** Seeking attention; promoting yourself **Flamingo eating:** Valuing or needing flexibility; acclimatising yourself **Many flamingos:** Group conformity.	Adaptable; flexible (inhabits brackish lakes); pink; red; tall; elegance (long-limbed); descent (bill bent downward) Where are you standing out? Have you fitted in to suit your circumstances?
Flying	See Introduction and Common Dream Theme at the beginning and end of this chapter, respectively (also see Human Actions in Chapter 10).	
Frogmouth	See Nightjar in this chapter.	

Symbol	Symbol In Action	Possible Life Issues
Goose	**Following a goose:** Following your intuition **Cooking a goose:** Feeling exposed: your goose is cooked **Killing a goose:** Sacrificing the future: kill the goose that lays the golden egg.	Mother Earth; grounded; nurturing; conformity; folk wisdom; foolish; leading or following others; goose flesh; goose step; silly goose; Mother Goose Who or what are you nurturing? Where are you in step with others?
Grouse	**Young grouse:** Developing a rhythm **Grouses fighting:** Finding fault; having grievances **Dead grouse:** Loss of passion and energy.	Dance; movement; moving through an issue or crisis; complaining; excellent; well done: grouse Where are you blindly following others? What are you strongly attracted to?
Hawk	See Falcon in this chapter.	
Hen	**Hen laying eggs:** Providing for others **Hen nesting:** Getting your house in order **Hens fighting:** Conflicting feelings; issues of service and servitude.	Nesting urges; family interests; productive; nurturing feelings Where are you putting family interests first? Do you need to be more productive?
Heron	**Young herons:** Growing self-confidence **Heron looking around:** Needing to be alert **Heron flying overhead:** Freedom; rising dignity.	Self-esteem; multiple skills; dignity; readiness; vigilance What are you wading into? Where are you balancing several tasks?
Honeyeater	**Honeyeater nesting:** Growing joy and happiness **Sick honeyeater:** Unable to see the pleasure in life **Many honeyeaters being joyous:** Group happiness or pleasure.	Small; song; singing your praises; happiness; descent (bill curving downward); extracts sweetness What is going well? Where are you taking the best offer?
Hummingbird	**Hummingbird flying:** Making yourself heard	Small; colourful; joy; great energy; exceptional responsiveness; manoeuvrability (can fly in

Symbol	Symbol In Action	Possible Life Issues
	Hummingbird on a flower: Enjoying the sweetness of life **Trying to catch a humming-bird:** Needing to move faster.	any direction) Where are you proceeding with speed? Do you need to manoeuvre yourself or manipulate a situation?
Ibis	**Trying to catch an ibis:** Needing to be better informed **Ibis at work:** Intelligent pathway to career or business **Dead ibis:** Lacking foresight.	Hermes (Greek messenger god); soul; wisdom; discernment; enlightenment Where are you gaining insights? Are you seeking greater awareness?
Kingfisher	**Kingfisher diving:** Going after your desires **Two kingfishers:** Feeling devoted **Dead kingfisher:** Being unfaithful.	Togetherness (flies in pairs); faithfulness; happy marriage; peace; joy; descent (captures by diving) What are you plunging into? Are you in love or have a sense of attachment?
Kite	**Kite flying:** Needing to test something first: fly a kite **Kite with prey:** Hurting others with gossip; feeling hurt by what others say **Kite at work:** Speaking up at work.	Loud; chattering; gossip; high-flying; high ideals Where have you got a high profile? Are you being too talkative?
Kookaburra	**Pair of kookaburras:** Enjoying your relationship **Kookaburra behind you:** Feeling as if others are laughing at you **Dead kookaburra:** Inability to laugh at yourself.	Laughter; joyful feelings; happiness; having a laugh Do you need to enjoy life more? What aren't you taking seriously?
Lark	**Lark at dawn:** Showing enthusiasm; needing to make a start: rise with the lark **Lark singing:** Feeling happy: happy as a lark **Larks playing:** Being fun-loving or light-hearted: it's a lark.	Happiness; evolution; highs and lows (rises and falls quickly) Are you larking around? Where are things evolving or moving forward?

Symbol	Symbol In Action	Possible Life Issues
Lyrebird	**Lyrebird behind bushes:** Feeling overlooked; lack of confidence **Captured lyrebird:** Exposing pretence **Dead lyrebird:** Needing to be yourself.	Limitation; timid; self-conscious; hidden; pretence; mimic; copying others; liar Are you imitating others or living by their expectations? Where do you need to express yourself openly?
Macaw	**Macaw nesting:** New potentials **Capturing a macaw:** Taking ownership; being revealed **Many macaws:** Group passion.	Colour red; fiery energy; new beginnings; elusive beliefs (nests on high cliffs) What are you feeling passionate about? What's out of reach?
Magpie	**Magpie collecting items:** Thieving tendencies **Magpie defending territory:** Being self-defensive; needing to protect yourself; taking ownership **Dead magpie:** Indecisiveness; lost opportunity.	Protection; song; swift; thief; quick to attack Where are you seeing things in black and white? Do you need to be more decisive?
Mockingbird	See Lyrebird in this chapter.	
Nightingale	**Nightingale singing:** Bringing happiness to others **Nightingale migrating:** Being in a state of transition **Sick nightingale:** Feeling out of harmony.	Melodious; moving on (migrates); night; song of love (often heard at night) Where are you in harmony with others? Are you in love or being loved?
Nightjar	**Nightjar calling:** Forging ahead; creating new opportunities **Capturing a nightjar:** Needing to pound away at something **Sick nightjar:** Inability to hammer out a solution.	Iron-working industry; blacksmith (call is similar to striking an iron); tough Are you hammering a point home? Where have you nerves of steel?
Oriole	**Oriole feeding:** Feeling satisfied; nurturing a relationship **Oriole at work:** Enjoying a sense of achievement **Dead oriole:** Lack of enjoyment.	Colour yellow; black; spring; new beginnings; new growth; announcement; marriage; joy What are you affirming? Where are you enjoying a rewarding alliance?

Symbol	Symbol In Action	Possible Life Issues
Osprey	**Osprey flying:** Being tolerant and objective **Osprey nesting:** Developing ideas; expanding your vision **Sick osprey:** Being narrow-minded.	Broad-thinking (broad-winged); scope; potential; attractive; appealing (feathers used in hats) Where have you got bright ideas? Are you being open-minded?
Ostrich	See Emu in this chapter.	
Owl	**Owl in the dark:** Gaining clarity; having foresight **Trying to catch an owl:** Seeking intuitive awareness **Owl on your telephone:** Power of silence.	Solemn; wisdom; transformation; observation; intuition; nocturnal lifestyle; see what others can't; silence; introspective; night owl Are you being perceptive and discerning? Where are you seeking guidance?
Parakeet	**Breeding parakeets:** Spreading love; supporting others **Caged parakeets:** Unable to express love; restricted by or holding onto love **Selling parakeets:** Looking for rewards; conditional love; undervaluing love.	Love; leaving your mark (long-tailed) Where are you feeling loved? Are you being affectionate or light-hearted?
Parrot	**Parrot in a cage:** Being limited by others' views and beliefs **Parrot at work:** Inability to express yourself freely at work **Killing a parrot:** Needing to be true to yourself.	Imitating others; insincere motives Are you adopting others' values and expectations? Where are you speaking without thinking?
Partridge	**Partridge feeding:** Enjoying love **Partridge on your shoulder:** Loving yourself; inner conflict **Dead partridge:** End of hostilities.	Inharmonious (discordant cry); love call; communication Where aren't you in accord with others? Are you speaking of love?
Pelican	**Pelican feeding its young:** Supporting others **Pelican flying overhead:** Spiritual freedom **Pelican crossing a road:** Reaching a crossroad; guidance and control issues.	Christ; parental love; guardian; protection; nurturing; pelican crossing Are you sacrificing yourself? Where are you being protective?

Symbol	Symbol In Action	Possible Life Issues
Penguin	**Penguin swimming:** Being adept in your field **Penguin hiding in a burrow:** Feeling self-conscious; needing to lighten up **Dead penguin:** Lack of humour; serious situation.	Agile (flightless); mental acumen; comical; community; accomplished; fierce What hasn't got off the ground? What looks the part but lacks substance?
Pheasant	See Lyrebird in this chapter.	
Pigeon	**Holding a pigeon:** Being pigeonholed or categorised **Pair of pigeons:** Feeling complete; dual issues; two sides to an issue **Pigeon target for shooting:** Feeling victimised.	Love; shy; good communicator; messenger; paternal influence (male protects eggs); pigeon pair; clay pigeon; pigeon-toed; stool pigeon; carrier pigeon Are you being targeted? Where are you being a good communicator?
Quail	**Quail hiding:** Fear of freedom; feeling unable, or being unwilling to face your fears **Quail feeding:** Being nurtured by love; fuelling your fears **Dead quail:** Overcoming your fears; lack of passion.	Summer; love; heat; red; cower Are you shrinking from your responsibilities? Where are you feeling fearful?
Raven	**Raven on your shoulder:** Sensing more to an issue **Raven at work:** Being consumed by your work **Dead raven:** Lack of self-interest; needing to think of yourself.	Mysterious; devouring; flexibility; communication; intellect; adaptability; plunders; taking from others; fear; ravenous What's sapping your energy or enthusiasm? Where are you dealing with dishonesty?
Robin	**Robin building a nest:** Building a relationship **Robin singing:** Sensing new possibilities; happiness and joy **Caged robin:** Unable to take new opportunities.	Spring; new beginnings; new growth; messenger; new love; colour red; passage of time Are you facing new beginnings? Where have you got new hope?
Rooster	**Rooster crowing at you:** Seizing opportunities; making a start; enthusiasm	Noisy; show off; domestic issues; self-glorification; little regard for others; dawn; recurring ideas;

Symbol	Symbol In Action	Possible Life Issues
	Two roosters: Twin opportunities; double benefit **Sick rooster:** Needing to promote yourself; being reticent.	messenger Are you drawing attention to yourself? What are you initiating?
Seagull	**Seagulls feeding:** Being easily satisfied; needing to be more selective **Seagulls squawking:** Making a fuss; being upfront **Seagulls fighting:** Competing needs; conflicting with others.	Scavenger; loud; making yourself heard; crowd; ocean; unconscious Are you taking whatever you can get? Where are you competing with others?
Sparrowhawk	**Sparrowhawk eating:** Emerging female energies or strength **Sparrowhawk on your shoulder:** New openings or beginnings **Sick sparrowhawk:** Losing your identity.	New beginnings; female-dominance; (male is smaller and clumsier than the female); bird of Horus Are you facing new opportunities? Where is there a strong female influence?
Stork	**Stork eating:** Domestic satisfaction **Stork delivering a baby:** Launching a new project; pregnancy **Stork dropping a baby:** Aborted plans; fruitless endeavour.	New beginnings; fertility; fertile ideas; birth; domestic happiness; abundance Are you developing a new idea or project? Where have you got great expectations?
Swallow	**Swallow eating:** Swallowing your words **Swallow not eating:** Unable to accept **Solitary swallow in the heat of day:** Don't jump to conclusions: one swallow doesn't make a summer.	Swift; quick-witted; summer; spring; messenger; new ideas or growth; fertility; metamorphous What can't you swallow? Are you facing new beginnings?
Swan	**Swan eating:** Spiritual aspirations **Swan flying:** Freedom; gaining poise **Group of swans:** Group dignity.	Spirit; grace; beauty; strength; serenity; intuition; poise; goddess; light; swanning; swan song Where are you demonstrating grace and humility? Are you trying to find your spiritual purpose?

Symbol	Symbol In Action	Possible Life Issues
Turkey	**Holding onto a turkey:** Possessiveness **Red turkey:** Being angry: red as a turkey cock **Woman with a turkey's head:** Lacking discernment: she's a turkey.	Provider; spirit of giving; Christmas; gratitude; Thanksgiving; Turkey: the country Where are you giving of yourself or to others? Are you seeking gratitude?
Vulture	**Vulture eating corpse:** Being picked on **Dead vulture:** Ending of a threat **Many vultures:** Predatory group.	Predatory motives; force; forceful opinions; devouring; taking from others; transforming; regeneration Are you serving your self-interests? What's outlived its usefulness?
Wagtail	**Wagtail flying:** Feeling joyful; keeping yourself busy **Two wagtails together:** Being in love **Dead wagtail:** Loss of energy or motivation; falling out of love.	Constant motion; can't settle; love; delight; leaving something behind (long tail); magic potions (in myth) Where do you need to slow down? What's constantly changing?
Wren	**Wren eating:** Feeding your curiosity **Wren singing:** Feeling joyous; in harmony with others **Wren nesting:** Growing shyness.	Busybody; gossip; curious; timid; sounds good (warbling song); aggressive; WRENS (Women's Royal Naval Service) What have you got to sing about? What's aroused your curiosity?

Common Dream Theme: Flying

This exhilarating experience can symbolise a new-found freedom to achieve your goals; an ability to move on or let go of old limitations; gaining a wider new perspective; being or seeing yourself as a rising high-flyer.

Did you know?

You can wake up in a dream and will yourself to fly?
This would be a lucid dream experience with no unconscious symbolism;
it would be an exhilarating experience!

Chapter 3
The Body and Its Components

Your body doesn't lie. If you listen to it carefully,
it will tell you everything you need to know to keep you healthy.
Sara Henderson

The body can represent itself, forewarn of possible health problems and present its own solutions. It may also symbolise the state of your thoughts and emotions. Consider these possible meanings with any others specifically listed.

How to get the best value from this chapter

- See if you relate to any of the key words or questions and explore your own meanings which may override those given here.
- Look at all possibilities and apply the most appropriate for your situation.
- Rephrase the Life Issue questions to broaden their personal relevance to you, if necessary, by using other words with similar meanings.
- You can also turn any question around (including those you formulate) to see if you relate to them better, by asking them in a slightly different way. For example, rephrase it as a need rather than a desire or belief or vice versa.
- The Symbol in Action examples show how to apply context or link meaning with action.

Desires and needs as opposed to outcomes and results

If a symbol represents an issue you are currently facing, then it may be indicative of your feelings, desires, beliefs or needs. This would usually occur in the first two-thirds of a dream, which often illustrates the issue you are dealing with and how you feel about it.

If a symbol comes in the form of a resolution, outcome, insight, solution or conclusion in the climax, usually at the end of the dream, then it may indicate a consequence, result or your dream advice to you.

Symbol	Symbol In Action *Look for feelings, desires, needs, beliefs or situations, explore literal meanings, apply any puns and idioms*	Possible Life Issues *Look for where, what and who this reminds you of, apply key words to thoughts, feelings or situations, explore literal meanings, apply word plays and figures of speech*
Abdomen	**Bloated abdomen:** Having too much; excess; abundance or prosperity **Holding the abdomen in pain:** Health warning; unable to accept **Vomiting:** Unpalatable: turns one's stomach.	Health warning; absorbing food or ideas; assimilate; complain; take in; bellyful; greedy guts; bellyache What are you trying to digest? Where are you trusting your gut feelings?
Ankles	**Broken ankle:** Warning; being too rigid **Doing ankle exercises:** Loosening up; adapting **Massaging your ankles:** Needing to be more flexible.	Flexibility; inflexibility; feeling guilty Do you need to bend? What's given you mobility?
Anus	**Being constipated:** Health warning; holding onto undesir-able feelings or attitudes **Experiencing diarrhoea:** Disposing before you can evaluate; needing quick release or immediate attention **Toilet blocked with your faeces:** Blocked feelings; unable to discard or let go.	Release; eliminate; superfluous; feeling relieved; unwanted ideas or desires; sexuality What are you discarding or rejecting? What's undesirable or no longer useful?
Appendix	**Being in pain:** Health warning; emotional pain **Having your appendix out:** Health warning; needing remedial action; doing without **Living without an appendix:** Making adjustments; being adaptable.	Health warning; inner pain; emotional imbalance; secondary addition What have you overlooked that could have serious implications? Have you blocked your emotions?
Arch of foot	**Looking at an arch:** Being impudent; appearing smart; saucy look: an arch look	Cover; facade; protection; weak point; reinforce; upholding values or your position; an arch rival

47

Symbol	Symbol In Action	Possible Life Issues
	Standing under an archway: Taking cover; shielding or defending yourself **Standing on top of an arch:** Needing support.	Where are you being a strong support? Are you feeling vulnerable?
Arms	**Arms tied behind your back:** Inability to act; lacking commitment **Picking up a gun:** Standing your ground; opposing others; confronting difficulties; feeling angry: up in arms; defending yourself: arming yourself **Putting up your elbow:** Making room: elbow room; being pushy or forceful.	Protection; justice; power to act; strength; retain; equipping yourself; aggressive; hostilities; weapons; embrace; armful; arm in arm Are you being defensive? What are you holding onto?
Back	**Arching your back:** Being provoked: got your back up **Lying down on your back:** Backing out of commitment; backing down **Carrying a heavy backpack:** Feeling burdened: have on one's back.	Courage; resolve; strength; support; dependability; willpower; feeling behind; needing to catch up; concealment; backing out; backup; backchat; backblocks; taking a back seat Where are you showing backbone? What are you turning your back on?
Bladder	**Full bladder:** Holding onto undesirable feelings or attitudes; not letting go **Bladder infection:** Health warning; emotional pain or undesirable feelings **Wearing a catheter:** Health warning; needing help to release emotional issues.	Water; being wordy; feeling relieved What are you releasing? What are you inflating?
Blood	**Heart pumping blood:** Health warning; circulation of ideas; feeling connected with others **Looking at blood cells:** Health warning; hereditary factors; family ties: runs in the blood	Loss; circulation; distribution of ideas; menstrual cycle; emotions; life force; essence; heart; ill-feeling; linkage; lineage; stubborn; passion; red; injury; high birth: blood ties; blue blood; bloodshed

Symbol	Symbol In Action	Possible Life Issues
	Blood pouring out of the body: Injury; unable to contain your emotions; loss of vitality; sacrificing yourself or your values.	Are you being bloody-minded? Where is there bad blood between you and another?
Body	See Introduction in this chapter.	
Brain	**Observing brainwaves:** Having a bright idea: brainwave **X-ray of a brain:** Needing to think more deeply; looking for proof; uncovering causes **Seeing an object sitting on a brain:** Being obsessed with an idea: having something on the brain.	Conscious mind; intellect; thoughts; smart or inventive thinking; brainwash; brainchild; brainy What are you brainstorming? What are you dwelling on or having to think about?
Breasts	**Admiring breasts:** Attraction to a person or idea; being passionate **Suckling a breast:** Seeking love and protection; reverting back; phase of life **Having breast cancer:** Health warning; lack of self-nurturing.	Nurturing others; affection; life's phases; sexuality; unconditional love; mother; abundance; protectiveness; breaststroke; breast cancer Do you need to nurture yourself? What's supporting you?
Brow	See Forehead in this chapter.	
Buttocks	**Loose buttocks:** Lack of stamina or motivation **Tight buttocks:** Feeling desirable; having energy and strength **Sitting down:** Not using your power; not getting anywhere; inertia or inaction.	Capability; energy to move forward; might; behind; seat of power; potency; strength; upright; mooladhara chakra (energy point in yoga) Where are you using your power? Are you standing tall?
Chest	**Lifting a weight off your chest:** Feeling or being relieved **Person sitting on your chest:** Emotional burdens; feeling weighed down **Chest X-ray:** Health warning; needing to take a deeper look; uncovering causes.	Health warning; secrets; burdens; feelings; storage Where are you playing your cards close to your chest? What do you need to get off your chest?

Symbol	Symbol In Action	Possible Life Issues
Colon	See Intestines in this chapter.	
Crown	See Head in this chapter.	
Ears	**Someone whispering in your ear:** Receiving a secret; listening to your intuition **Blocked ears:** Health warning; not listening; having a closed mind **Having donkey ears:** Listening to silly ideas.	Inner ear; attentive; discriminating; receptive; spiral shape; intuition; eavesdrop; earshot; earbash; earache; earmark Where do you need to listen to yourself or others? Are you being intuitive?
Eyes	**Having penetrating eyes:** Being perceptive; seeing through a situation; having foresight **Seeing an eye on your wallet:** Watching your finances or personal security: keeping an eye on **Eyes closed:** Being unaware; not watching; avoidance.	Inner awareness; third eye; window of the soul; discernment; awareness; perception; visualise; mind's eye; realisation; observant; flirting; leading others on; I; eyewitness; eye-opener; eyeing What do you need to look at? Have you had your eyes opened?
Face	**Putting on make-up:** Improving your self image; your public face **Seeing two faces looking at each other:** Face to face; confronting yourself or others; being two-faced **Having no face:** Being overlooked; unable or unwilling to face an issue.	Individuality; self-image; personality; expression; humiliation; putting on an appearance; facelift; facing things What issues are you facing? Have you suffered a loss of face?
Feet	**Having a foothold:** Gaining support **Sore feet:** Questioning your beliefs; lack of progress **Losing your footing:** Losing ground; instability; being footloose and fancy free.	Footing; support; foundation; founding principles; reflexology; mobility; preparation; progress; infantry; linear measure; foot; footman; foot-slogging; footprint; footloose Where are you gaining a foothold? Are you following in someone's footsteps?

Symbol	Symbol In Action	Possible Life Issues
Fingers	**Finger pointing the way:** Setting your goals; following directions **Finger pointing at someone:** Making accusations; being accused **An object slipping through your fingers:** Losing your grip.	Connection; keeping in touch; purpose; direction; penis; your grip on things; fingerprint Have you had your fingers burnt? Who are you wrapping around your little finger?
Forehead	**Smooth forehead:** Straightforward thinking **Frowning brow:** Disapproving: frowning on **Covered forehead:** Concealing your thinking; lacking intuition.	Advanced thinking; extrasensory perception; intellect; outward; third eye; brow chakra (energy point in yoga) Where are you being forward-thinking? Are you being broad-minded?
Hair	**Permed hair:** Trendy thinking **Grey hair:** Old-fashioned thinking; being out of touch **Bald head:** Lacking ideas; loss of self-image; ageing; loss of self-esteem; lacking power or influence.	Vitality; personality; self-image; thoughts; hairline; hair's break What's been hair-raising? Where do you need to keep your hair on?
Hand	**Right hand:** A wise direction or choice **Holding hands:** Having a connection; relationship **Something falling out of your hands:** Losing control; being out of control: out of hand.	Openness; begging; communication; healing; service; control; means of achievement; hand mudras (yoga); hand language; hands down; hand over; handwriting; hands off; hands up What are you holding onto? What's out of your hands?
Head	**Head in the sand:** Unwillingness to consider an idea **Being scalped:** Being taken advantage of **Admiring your head:** Being head-hunted.	Taking the lead; being influential; achievement; highest thoughts; intuition; director; pituitary gland; crown chakra (energy point in yoga); heady; headway; headwind; headstrong; heading Are you directing events or people? Where are you being headstrong?
Heart	**Having no heart:** Being heartless; lacking compassion	Health warning; flow of emotions; love; compassion;

Symbol	Symbol In Action	Possible Life Issues
	Being stabbed in the heart: Being emotionally hurt **Heart attack:** Health warning; emotional blockage; lack of circulation; being heartbroken.	circulation; soul; essence; life force; affection; heartbreaking; heartfelt What have you taken to heart? Where should you follow your heart?
Heel	**Turning on your heels:** Changing your thinking **Having cold heels:** Needing patience: cool one's heels **Sore heels:** Questioning your beliefs; lack of progress.	Foundations; belief system; adaptability; support; mobility; your leanings; change of thinking; high heels; well-heeled; Are you being brought to heel? Where are you head over heels?
Hips	**Broken hip:** Health warning; being inflexible **Having a hip replacement:** Health warning; needing greater adaptability **Sitting on a rich person's lap:** Living in the lap of luxury.	Mobility; making progress; adjustment; flexibility; movement; sexual function; 'hip, hip hurrah' Where are you mobilising support? Do you need to be flexible?
Intestines	**Irritable colon/intestines:** Health warning; refusing to let go; blocked feelings **Having an X-ray of the intestines:** Health warning; needing to look deeper; review and evaluation; uncovering causes **Having intestines operated on:** Health warning; needing to take remedial action.	Health warning; release; eliminate; ruling out options What needs to be released? What do you need to absorb and assimilate?
Jaw	See Teeth in this chapter.	
Kidneys	**Unable to urinate:** Holding on **Kidney infection:** Health warning; emotional blockage; unable to let go **Releasing kidney stones:** Health warning; releasing emotional pain.	Health warning; kidney stones; clarifying; discarding; filtering emotions What do you need to purify? Where do you need to filter out negativity?
Knees	**Kneeling:** Needing to be humble; paying homage; needing respect; subservient	Submission; reverence; flexibility; piety; ability to bend; up and down; kneecap;

Symbol	Symbol In Action	Possible Life Issues
	In water up to your knees: Meeting emotional resistance **Having a knee operation:** Health warning; lacking mobility; needing emotional flexibility; taking remedial action.	knee-deep; kneeling Where have you been brought to you knees? Are you involved in a joint exercise?
Legs	**Lifting your leg up:** Receiving or expecting support **Someone pulling your leg:** Being deceived **Falling down:** Loss of confidence; losing power; losing ground.	Power; achievement; moving forward; mobility; step by step; performance; legging it; pull the other leg Are you moving forward? Where haven't you got a leg to stand on?
Lips	**Smiling:** Feeling content; happy outcomes **Applying lipstick:** Covering up your words; being politically correct; conforming; social acceptance **Closed lips:** Unwilling to speak up; keeping secrets.	Speech; insincerity; opening; sexuality; expression; self-image; pleasure; giving lip; lip reading; lipstick Where do you need to express yourself? What are you giving lip service to?
Liver	**Infected liver:** Health warning; blocked feelings **Having an X-ray of your liver:** Health warning; looking deeper; uncovering causes **Holding a liver:** Needing a liver transplant; transforming your feelings.	Health warning; endurance; stress; anger; base emotions Where do you need purification? Do you need to be more refined?
Lungs	**Holding your breath:** Being stubborn; holding onto your feelings; keeping quiet **Using the breath in meditation:** Harmonising your energies; feeling in tune **Can't breathe:** Unable to express yourself; can't cope.	Breath of life; energy; life force; interaction; free-flowing; rhythm; inward and outward; lunge Where can you breathe easily? Are you holding your breath?
Marrow (Bone)	**Strong bones:** Enjoying inner strength **Having an X-ray of the bone marrow:** Health warning;	Health warning; subconscious mind; inner strength; deep (cavity); fatty; profound; self-protection;

Symbol	Symbol In Action	Possible Life Issues
	looking deeper; uncovering causes **Having no bone marrow:** Health warning; lacking inner strength.	shielded; interior; vegetable: marrow Do you need to look inward? What are you concealing?
Mouth	**Seeing a mouth full of food:** Receiving a mouthful of abuse **Kissing another:** Having feelings for another; being attracted to a person or idea **Open mouth:** Feeling surprised; being devouring.	Swallowing; ingesting; taking in ideas; eating; diet; kissing; entrance; opening or opportunity; pleasure; estuary; mouthed Where are you speaking out? Do you need to speak up?
Muscle	**Lean muscles:** Ability to perform; being capable **Sore muscles:** Being inflexible **Pulled muscles:** Health warning; being too flexible.	Elasticity; movement; strength; resistance; tone; interconnections Do you need to strengthen up? What's cramping your style?
Navel	**Pierced decorated navel:** Honouring past connections; valuing your relationships **Having no navel:** Feeling lost; independence **Enlarged navel:** Feeling in tune with yourself; needing to reflect.	Contemplation; relationship; dependence; independence; interdependence; connection; needs; umbilical cord Where are you providing support? Are you connecting with your source?
Neck	**Broken neck:** Health warning; suffering: getting it in the neck **Sticking your neck out:** Feeling exposed; taking a risk **Having a stiff neck:** Being rigid or inflexible.	Connection; speaking out; vulnerability; sexuality; willpower; ability to stand up for yourself; throat chakra; necklace Where are you sticking your neck out? Are you looking for balance between the mind and the body?
Nervous system	**Seeing a nervous-looking person:** Worrying too much; lacking confidence; needing composure; watch out **Having a pinched nerve:** Being too sensitive; painful point; your sore spot **Nervous breakdown:** Health warning; feeling unable to cope;	Emotional stability or instability; excitable; timid; interactive; information; anxiety; warnings; apprehensive Are you highly strung? Are you being intuitive?

Symbol	Symbol In Action	Possible Life Issues
	lacking emotional control; needing detachment.	
Nose	**Following your nose:** Being straightforward; knowing where to go **Looking at a nose on a face:** Transparent or easily seen: plain as the nose on your face **Turning your nose up:** Showing contempt.	Discernment; curiosity; prying; protrusion Are you being nosey? Where is your nose out of joint?
Pelvis	See Hips in this chapter.	
Penis	**Erect penis:** Enthusiasm; being passionate; attracted to an idea or person; working creatively; making inroads towards your goals **Limp penis:** Lack of perform-ance; apathy; low self-esteem; lacking creativity **Inability to achieve an erection:** Health warning; emotional or mental blockage.	Planting a seed; generation; pleasure; penetrating; attraction; power; creativity; lust; dominance; performance; male energies; giving What do you desire? Are you rising to a challenge?
Scalp	See Head in this chapter.	
Shoulders	**Seeing two people shoulder to shoulder:** Making a joint effort: shoulder to shoulder **Frozen shoulder:** Health warn-ing; avoiding your responsibilities **Cold shoulder:** Being unfeeling; unable to warm to an idea or person; feeling rejected.	Conscientious; strength of character; interest; attachment; responsibilities; joint of meat: shoulder; cold shoulder Where are you shouldering responsibilities? What are you carrying?
Skeleton	**Skeleton in the cupboard:** Having secrets; hiding something **Tall skeleton:** Standing tall; feeling proud **Skeleton at work:** Structuring your plans; dealing with remains; tidying up; getting back to basics.	Principles; body; remains; outline; material world; structure; plan; indispensable part; hard; framework; mobility; death (the grim reaper) Do you need to stand up for yourself? Where do you need more structure?

Symbol	Symbol In Action	Possible Life Issues
Skin	**Birthmark on your skin:** Your individuality; individual; feeling exposed; self-conscious **Jumping out of your skin:** Feeling overjoyed **Thick skin:** Not taking offence.	Responsiveness; feelings; sensitivities; vulnerability; complexion; extremity; perimeter; outer limits; flexibility; confining; covering; skin deep; thin-skinned; skin-tight; skinhead Are you being too sensitive? What have you taken as far as it can go?
Skull	**Skull and crossbones:** Death; health warning; end of a habit, attitude, relationship, conflict or stage of life **Thick skull:** Being slow to get the point **Skull on your desk:** Being headhunted.	Thoughts; intelligence; attitudes; mortality; death; impermanence; thick skull What are you thinking about? Are you in a period of transition?
Solar plexus	**Inflamed solar plexus:** Health warning; festering sensitivities **Solar plexus being X-rayed:** Health warning; needing to take a deeper look; uncovering causes **Solar plexus chakra (energy point in yoga):** Greater awareness.	Health warning; shock; stress; confronting; sensibilities; emotions; fear; intuition; nerve centre; connections; chakra; point of exit and entry Where are you following your gut instincts? What are you fearful of?
Soles of feet	**Sore feet:** Feeling uncomfortable; being sensitive **Wearing no shoes:** Freedom of thought; feeling impoverished; no basis **Wearing tight shoes:** Restricting thinking.	Sensitivity; individual thinking; grounding; mobility; earthiness; grounded; foundations; beliefs; solitary; sole Where do you need soul? Are you doing it alone?
Spine	**Straight spine:** Upholding high principles; upstanding position **Having a curved spine:** Health warning; bending your principles **Broken spine:** Health warning; lacking character.	Strength; toughness; pillar of support; passage; channel; kundalini energy (yoga); nerve centre; spines; spine-bashing; spine-chilling Where do you need to show backbone? Are you being spineless?
Spleen	**Two spleens:** Receiving immunity; strong resentments	Health warning; moroseness; hostility; resistance; immunity;

Symbol	Symbol In Action	Possible Life Issues
	Spleen being X-rayed: Needing to look deeper; uncovering causes **Ruptured spleen:** Health warning; harmful negativity.	protection; self-defences (produces antibodies); irritability Are you venting your anger? Where are you feeling bitter or resentful?
Stomach	See Abdomen in this chapter.	
Teeth	**Clenched teeth:** Being determined; holding in anger; being aggressive; desiring revenge; warning others **Long tooth:** Feeling your age; ageing attitudes **Toothache:** Health warning; speaking without thinking.	Early stages; difficulties; self-respect; public image; aggression; maturational development; speech; sweet tooth Where are you having teething problems? What are you getting your teeth into? (Also see Common Dream Theme at the end of this chapter.)
Thighs	**Powerful thighs:** Standing on principle; needing strength; staying power **Pulled thigh muscle:** Health warning; unable to make the distance **Weak thighs:** Lacking enthusiasm or support.	Ability; competence; energy; power and influence; force; might; endurance; support; stamina; womb and phallic symbol (in myth) What are you powering through? Where do you need to stand up for yourself?
Throat	See Neck in this chapter.	
Thumb	**Upward pointing thumb:** Great satisfaction; congratulations: thumbs up **Thumb pointing down:** Disapproval **Sore thumb:** Lacking support.	Power; support; consent; validation; identification; thumb print; thumbscrew Where are you feeling under the thumb? What are you thumbing your nose at?
Toes	**Broken toe:** Health warning; loss of balance; losing your grip **Six toes:** Overdoing it **Toe missing:** Needing balance or stability.	Balance; mobility; minor details; offended feelings; restless; uneasy; agitated; part of a shoe; toe-ragger Who has stepped on your toes? Where are you feeling toey?

Symbol	Symbol In Action	Possible Life Issues
Tongue	**Passionate kiss:** Getting involved; tasting the pleasures of life; sexuality **Forked tongue:** Being insincere **Twisted tongue:** Unable to speak your mind; can't be heard.	Communication; taste; swallowing your words; sexuality; expressing yourself Do you need to hold your tongue? Where are you feeling tongue-tied or embarrassed?
Uterus	See Womb in this chapter.	
Vagina	**Painful vagina:** Health warning; not giving of yourself **Weeping vagina:** Losing creativity; being too compliant **Oversized vagina:** Needing to be open; too receptive; willing to receive.	Female energies; sexual power; receptivity; passion; open-minded; amenable; creativity; responsive; generation Are you being receptive? Where are you being submissive?
Vulva	See Vagina in this chapter.	
Womb	**Expanded womb:** Developing a new concept or project; new possibilities; pregnancy **Giving birth:** Manifesting your plans **Having a miscarriage:** Health warning; idea whose time has not yet come; aborted plans.	Conception; gestation; birth; creativity; fertility; fertile ideas; Mother Earth; potential; hidden depths Where are you being original? What have you conceived or developed?

Common Dream Theme: Teeth falling out
*Dreaming of teeth falling from your mouth can symbolise a
loss of face, public image or self-esteem; speaking thoughtlessly; feeling
or being defenceless; having a maturing approach or simply ageing.*

Chapter 4
Buildings and Places

A man travels the world over in search of
what he needs and returns home to find it.
George Moore

Buildings can symbolise different states of consciousness, patterns of thinking and beliefs that you hold. Consider these possible meanings with any others specifically listed.

How to get the best value from this chapter

- See if you relate to any of the key words or questions and explore your own meanings which may override those given here.
- Look at all possibilities and apply the most appropriate for your situation.
- Rephrase the Life Issue questions to broaden their personal relevance to you, if necessary, by using other words with similar meanings.
- You can also turn any question around (including those you formulate) to see if you relate to them better, by asking them in a slightly different way. For example, rephrase it as a need rather than a desire or belief or vice versa.
- The Symbol in Action examples show how to apply context or link meaning with action.

Desires and needs as opposed to outcomes and results

If a symbol represents an issue you are currently facing, then it may be indicative of your feelings, desires, beliefs or needs. This would usually occur in the first two-thirds of a dream, which often illustrates the issue you are dealing with and how you feel about it.

If a symbol comes in the form of a resolution, outcome, insight, solution or conclusion in the climax, usually at the end of the dream, then it may indicate a consequence, result or your dream advice to you.

Symbol	Symbol In Action	Possible Life Issues
	Look for feelings, desires, needs, beliefs or situations, explore literal meanings, apply any puns and idioms	*Look for where, what and who this reminds you of, apply key words to thoughts, feelings or situations, explore literal meanings, apply word plays and figures of speech*
Abattoir	**Slaughtered animal:** Sacrificing yourself or others **Animals being slaughtered:** Feeling used; being disregarded **Closing a door on abattoir:** Confronting exploitation.	Base emotions; disembodied; disconnected; butchered; violence; torn apart Have you killed off part of yourself? Are you feeling violated?
Abyss	See Canyon in this chapter.	
Accountant's office	**Being with your accountant:** Needing to account **Paying money to your accountant:** Owning up; needing to explain; business **Being chased by your accountant:** Plagued by your conscience; feeling exposed.	Accountability; reckoning; assessing yourself; explanation; liability; feeling responsible; thinker; economy Where do you feel you don't measure up? Are you evaluating yourself?
Airport	**Busy airport:** Confusion; new possibilities; considering your options **Catching a plane:** Adopting new ideas; changing your thinking **Planes taking off:** Successful endeavours; spiritual principles; higher thinking; new perspective.	High ideas; mind; activity; coming and going; higher planes; journey into the unknown; arrivals and departures; commercial interests; terrorism Where are your plans taking off? What's coming and going?
Alley	**Alley named 'Good':** Confirming your position: making your alley good **Running down an alley:** Short-term thinking **Dark alley:** Lacking direction; feeling vulnerable.	Narrow thinking; shortcut; risky position; not seeing the whole picture; blind alley Are you taking chances? Where do you need clarity?
Antique shop	**Buying antiques:** Being traditional **Expensive antiques:** Exclusive thinking; paying a high price	Old-fashioned thinking; not moving forward; time-honoured custom; dated attitudes

Symbol	Symbol In Action	Possible Life Issues
	Cluttered antique shop: Too many outdated ideas.	Where is your thinking out of date? Are your attitudes unchanging?
Apartment	**Small apartment:** Restricted thinking **Big apartment block:** Needing soul **Friend's apartment:** Adopting others' values and expectations.	Temporary thinking or position; small; vacation; spacious; set of ideas; soulless Are you in a state of transition? Where are you accepting convenience?
Apartment building or condominium	**Empty apartment building:** Soulless; feeling isolated **Full apartment building:** Seeing connections; diversity **Derelict apartments:** Discarded ideas; no longer useful.	Interconnectedness; set of ideas; community; universal mind Where are you embracing the whole picture? Are you dealing with relationships?
Arena	**Arena with clapping crowd:** Being the centre of attention; needing to put yourself forward **Being an umpire in an arena:** Dealing with hostilities; needing discernment; striving for balance **Crowd jeering you:** Feeling exposed.	Centre of attention; spectator; scene of activity Where are you dealing with conflict? Are you judging yourself or others?
Art gallery	**Admiring artwork:** Appreciating beauty; seeking approval **Buying artwork:** Acquiring inner peace **Painting a picture:** Imitating; striving for perfection; being creative.	Beauty; inner beauty; pleasure; culture; bringing something into manifestation; design; exhibiting; peaceful attitudes and feelings Where are you seeking self-expression? Are you being creative?
Attic	**Looking out of an attic window:** Being an observer; feeling isolated **Cluttered attic:** Old memories **Friend's attic:** Needing to adopt other values; higher values you haven't owned yet.	Higher thinking; memories; spiritual self or principles Where do you need a higher perspective? What needs sorting out?
Bank	**Bank overflowing with money:** Abundance; prosperity	Prosperity; saving; value system; commerce; financial concerns;

61

Symbol	Symbol In Action	Possible Life Issues
	Bank robbed: Feeling cheated; losing your values **Bank closed:** Limited resources; lack of trust; restricted access.	emotional or financial deposits and withdrawals; safe-keeping; custody issues; trust Are you keeping stock of your resources? Where are you investing time and energy?
Bar	**Drinking at a bar:** Entertaining new ideas; drowning your sorrows; running away **Bar door shut:** Feeling excluded **Running away from a bar:** Refusing to accept: won't have a bar of.	Emotional or mental barriers; interaction; exchange of ideas; social gathering; decadence; pressure (barometric); bars; barred Where are you lacking self-discipline? Are you feeling under pressure?
Barn	**Barn full of animals:** Strong desires **Barn falling down:** Undermining emotions **Burning barn:** Consuming emotions.	Animal instincts; lower levels of consciousness; stockpile of thoughts, feelings or resources; outbuilding; metric unit Where are you being influenced by unconscious urges and impulses? Are you being easily led or manipulated?
Barracks	See Dormitory in this chapter.	
Basement	**Searching a dark basement:** Recovering information **Files in a basement:** Unconscious memories; subconscious beliefs **Crowded basement:** Unconscious group urges and behaviour.	Unconscious; founding principles; starting point; lacking awareness; lowest part; groundwork Are you going back to basics? Where have you been rocked to your foundations?
Bathroom	**Cleaning bathroom:** Self-purification **Dirty bathroom:** Offensive feelings or attitudes **Old bathroom:** Outdated beliefs.	Cleansing thoughts or feelings; purifying; sterile approach; unproductive views Are you sanitising your thoughts or actions? Where do you have an unblemished record?

Symbol	Symbol In Action	Possible Life Issues
Beach	**Walking along a beach:** Dwelling on things **Wild ocean beach:** Turbulent emotions **Safe shore:** Needing peace and regeneration; feeling secure.	Cleansing; safety; relaxation; renewal; border between states of consciousness; emotions; beach head; beached Are you reflecting on your life? Where do you need to relax?
Beauty parlour	**Being treated at a beauty parlour:** Improving your self-image; increasing your self-esteem **Admiring your skin in a beauty parlour:** Being shallow; needing to look deeper: beauty is but skin deep **Beauty parlour closed:** Unwilling to change.	Self-interest; self-consciousness; beauty; inner beauty; make-over; vanity Are you seeking transformation? Where do you need to make a good impression?
Bedroom	**Asleep in bed:** Being unaware; apathetic; dreams and dreaming; being a dreamer **Lying in bed with someone:** Having rapport; being onside; personal and familiar **Getting dressed in a bedroom:** Denying your inner self; scared of intimacy.	Sleep; affections; private secrets and aspirations; sexual connections; haven; retreat Where are you enjoying intimacy? What are your private hopes and dreams?
Bookstore	**Browsing a bookstore:** Searching for solutions **Buying a book:** Being open to new ideas **Closed bookstore:** Being closed-minded; inability to access the subconscious.	Knowledge; enlightenment; seeking solutions; new awareness; resource; your personal resources; unconscious; super-conscious; memorable Are you seeking answers? Where have you got a wealth of knowledge?
Bridge	**Swing bridge:** Swaying convictions; needing to be careful **Crowded bridge:** Change in group thinking or circumstances **Broken bridge:** Unable to change.	Decision-making; goal-setting; change; progressing; upper and bony part of the nose; bridge head; bridging finance Are you in transition? Where are you moving on?
Broadcasting station	**Being on talkback radio:** Ability to give and receive information	Transmission; public exchange; announcement; misinformation; teaching; advertising your views;

Symbol	Symbol In Action	Possible Life Issues
	Being a radio announcer: Advising or teaching; disclosure **Confronting an announcer:** Revealing a secret; misinformation.	communication; reaching out to others Where are you giving out information? Are you promoting yourself?
Building	See Introduction in this chapter.	
Cabin	**Sitting in an aircraft cabin:** Journeying into the unknown **Building a log cabin:** Seeking simplicity; retreating; down to earth **Log cabin burning down:** Rejecting simplicity.	Humility; simplicity; modest views; poverty; refuge; cramped; small considerations; cabin boy Where are you feeling humbled? Who has cramped your style?
Campus	See College in this chapter.	
Canyon	**Approaching a canyon:** Confronting obstacles; facing limits **Climbing a canyon:** Overcoming your fears; facing a challenge **Falling into a canyon:** Fear of the unknown; losing ground or status; being taken in.	Danger; obstacles; fear; barrier Are you facing difficulties? Where are you being limited by your personal boundaries?
Castle	**Building a castle:** Emotional defences; being in control; taking leadership; rising self-esteem **Trying to enter a castle:** Needing to be open; trying to get through **Castle ruins:** Outdated position; irrelevant feelings or attitudes.	Self-esteem; privileged position; protection; safe attitudes; security; make-believe world; stately residence; privacy; dominance; castles in the air; sandcastle; king of the castle Are you seeking power and influence? Where are you being defensive?
Cathedral	See Church in this chapter.	
Cave	**Exploring a cave:** Exploring your unconscious beliefs; facing your fears; questioning your values **Exiting a cave that is not on your land:** Exploring values that you don't own	Unconscious; hidden; deep; dark; fear; subsidence; sinking principles; giving in; cave in; caveman Where are you looking inwards? Are you losing ground?

Symbol	Symbol In Action	Possible Life Issues
	Cave collapsing on you: Warning; being undermined or undermining others.	
Cemetery	**Walking out of a cemetery:** Moving on; letting go of the past; discarding **Being in a cemetery after the mourners have left:** Holding on to the past; can't let go **Cemetery at night:** Fearing the unknown.	End of a feeling, attitude, relationship or habit; demise; fear; grieving; loss; transition; passing; burying the past What should you lay to rest? What are you mourning?
Chasm	See Canyon in this chapter.	
Chemist	**Being given a prescription:** Needing to change your ways; being open-minded; healing; needing to take responsibility **Can't decide in a chemist shop:** Confusing choices; too many options **Closed chemist shop:** Lack of options; being closed-minded.	Dispensing advice; rehabilitation; laws of combination; making choices; remedies; taking corrective action; collection of ideas; feeling a chemistry between yourself and others Where are you following prescribed advice? Do you need to take remedial action?
Church	**Seeing Christ in church:** Finding your spiritual self; enlightenment **Church with no spire:** High ideals that fall short of your expectations **Empty church:** Lack of spiritual direction; being bound by dogma; having no support.	Christianity; dogma; spiritual beliefs; salvation; forgiveness; protection; having faith; defensive; church-goer; church house Do you need to forgive yourself or others? Are you being restricted by your beliefs?
Circus	**Watching a circus:** Considering change; entertaining ideas; being an observer **Performing in a circus:** Being the centre of attention; putting on an act **Animals escaping from a circus:** Being undisciplined; wanting to run away.	Transient; uproar; control; disturbance; converging; disciplined; compulsive Are you being entertaining? Where are you in transition?

Symbol	Symbol In Action	Possible Life Issues
City	**Congested city:** Blocked pathways; slow progress; feeling anonymous **City at night:** Exciting opportunities **Polluted city:** Unhealthy options; feeling uncomfortable; can't breathe.	Commerce; community; other views; important concepts; hustle and bustle; excitement; career; finance; business; employment; security issues; support system Where are you seeking opportunities? Are you wheeling and dealing?
Cliff	**Looking up at a steep cliff:** Reaching an impasse; facing a challenge **Hanging over a cliff:** Being in a vulnerable position; needing help **Falling to the bottom of a cliff:** Danger; going too far; reaching your limits; losing ground or status; hitting rock bottom.	Vantage point; perspective; reflection; crisis point; boundaries; precarious position Where have you reached a standstill or stalemate? Are you being forced to make a decision?
Closet	**Closet with door open:** Feeling exposed; feeling vulnerable **Closet with no door:** Nowhere to hide **Hiding in a closet:** Can't face something; don't want to be seen; being secretive.	Narrow-thinking; suffocating; private; safe; hidden childhood memories; past; closeted; water closet Where are you feeling trapped with nowhere to go? Are you feeling smothered?
Clothing store	**Wearing evening clothes:** Feeling dignified; elegance **Wearing sports clothes:** Being competitive **Wearing business clothes:** Being responsible; needing to be business-like; respected.	Self-esteem; roles you play; image; new attitudes Where are you trying on a new outlook? Do you need a new self-image? (Also see Common Dream Theme in Chapter 17.)
College	**Being with students on campus:** Learning life's lessons; gaining understanding **Campus with no students:** Unwilling to learn; believing that no-one else understands **Holding lots of books:** Higher learning; spiritual principles.	Higher learning; advanced thinking; exchange of ideas; experiment; self-education; training; enlightenment; collegian Are you developing your thinking? What are you learning that's new?

Symbol	Symbol In Action	Possible Life Issues
Compound	**Climbing into a compound:** Locking yourself in; restricting or protecting yourself **High compound:** Highly challenging obstacle **Escaping from a compound:** Freeing yourself up; overcoming limitations.	Limitations; barriers; combining; complication; compound Are you feeling confined or restricted? Where have you reached your limits?
Concert hall	**Listening to a concert:** Being receptive; open to inspiration **Playing in a concert:** Working with others; compatibility; coordinated effort **Empty concert hall:** Lacking inspiration.	Upliftment; harmony; power; cooperation; music of the spheres Are you working harmoniously with others? Where do you feel uplifted and inspired?
Convent	See Monastery in this chapter.	
Corner house	**Buying a corner house:** Having two perspectives **Driving into a corner house:** Feeling trapped or restricted: driving yourself into a corner **Turning past a corner house:** Making a change: turning the corner.	Exposed; outer edge; being on the outer; meeting of two positions; cornerstone Are you at a crossroad? Where have you cornered the market?
Corridor	**Corridor leading to a door:** Transition; moving on to new opportunities; being or feeling led **Crawling down a corridor:** Feeling tentative about your progress **Blocked corridor:** Lacking options.	Rite of passage; your prospects; journey; crossing; change; progressing through a crisis, issue or situation Are you facing openings or opportunities? Where do you need to move forward? (Also see Hallway in this chapter.)
Courthouse	**Facing a magistrate:** Being brought to account **Receiving a sentence:** Facing the consequences of your actions; karma **Derelict courthouse:** Avoiding repercussions; delayed justice.	Justice; law; order; accountability; measuring up; standards; court martial; kangaroo court What has pricked your conscience? Where are you feeling weighed down?

Symbol	Symbol In Action	Possible Life Issues
Crater	**Falling into a crater:** Reopening old wounds **Climbing out of a crater:** Putting the past behind you **Several craters:** Outdated grievances.	Old scars; past record; cavity; gap in your thinking; unavoidable; unchanging Where are you holding onto the pain of the past? Have you been scared?
Crossroads	**Looking at two crossroads:** Choosing options; evaluating **Crossroads with no signs:** Feeling undecided; lack of guidance **Train coming through a crossroad:** Unstoppable forces or events.	Crisis; turning point; decision time Do you need to change direction? Are you facing a transition?
Department store	**Browsing a department store:** Seeing what's on offer **Making a purchase:** Making a commitment **Empty department store:** Lacking options.	Resources; personal reserves; having means; commerce; spending; choices; manipulated; transactions Where are you considering your options? Are you being tempted by something?
Desert	**Traversing a desert:** Lack of feeling for yourself or others; great achievement; endurance **Looking for water in a desert:** Feeling lost; needing support; fighting for your survival **Looking at a huge expanse of desert:** Never-ending challenges; enduring hardships.	Barren; unproductive; fruitless endeavours; inhospitable; absence of emotion or opportunities; need; insufficiency; abandon: desert; his just desserts What have you abandoned? Where are you feeling alone and unsupported?
Dining room	See Kitchen in this chapter.	
Dormitory	**Being in a full dormitory:** Adopting common values; cooperating with others **Dormitory falling down:** Being uncooperative; rejecting others **Empty dormitory:** Unwillingness to conform; feeling isolated.	Group learning; feeling alienated; enforced living; common values Where do you have to conform? Are you feeling restricted?

Symbol	Symbol In Action	Possible Life Issues
Drugstore	See Chemist in this chapter.	
Elevator	**Broken elevator:** Lack of movement; stagnation; loss of energy **Being trapped in an elevator:** Feeling helpless or vulnerable; lack of control; going nowhere; lack of progress **Elevator crashing to the ground:** Falling from grace; loss of position; losing ground; going backwards; dashed hopes; demotion.	Higher goals or purpose; hopes and aspirations; rising and falling; promotion or demotion; rise or fall in status; increasing or decreasing energy or motivation Where are you being elevated? Are things going up and down?
Factory	**Busy factory:** Being efficient; unthinking responses **Empty factory:** Being apathetic; feeling isolated; lacking support **Derelict factory:** Inefficient or outmoded work practices.	Industrious; efficient; repetitious; mechanics of the mind; stability; monotonous; business Are you being productive? What's predictable or boring?
Farmhouse	**Cooking in a farmhouse:** Going back to basics; slaving away; feeling trapped; being independent **Burning farmhouse:** Rejecting basic values; loss of innocence **Derelict farmhouse:** Old-fashioned values; values that no longer serve you.	Honest values; down to earth; independence; unpretentious; grounded; provider Are you simplifying your life? Where are you working hard?
Field	**Looking over a field:** Seeing the bigger picture: field of vision **Moving from wooded area out into a field:** Receiving clarity; becoming clearer **Walking through a field:** Being out in the field; getting involved: taking to the field.	Openness; clarity; room to move; space; fertile ideas or endeavours; exploration; expanse for growth; wider perspective; field day; field marshal Where are you seeing things clearly? What's being brought out into the open?
Fire station	**Putting out a fire:** Gaining emotional control; being a hero **Firehouse on alert:** Being	Flammable; destructive; erupting issues or feelings; passionate emotions; combustion;

Symbol	Symbol In Action	Possible Life Issues
	aware of destructive forces **Empty firehouse:** Needing to rely on your own resources; lacking support; lack of passion.	enthusiasm; raw energy; heated feelings; hot issues; excited; fiery; fireworks; fire away What needs rescuing? What could blow up and explode?
Football oval	**Playing football:** Joining forces; being disciplined; cooperating with others; being competitive; sense of fair play **Barracking for your team:** Giving approval; being one-sided; voicing your feelings **Brawl between players:** Conflicting feelings; competing needs.	Cooperation; competition; rules; training; discipline; community; opposing forces; conquest or defeat Where are you being a team-player? Are you playing by the rules?
Forest	**Surrounded by thick undergrowth:** Subconscious beliefs that are holding you back **Dense forest:** Loss of perspective; can't see your way forward; much to consider **Lost in forest:** Feeling confused: can't see the wood for the trees; needing direction: not out of the woods yet.	Narrow perspective; confusion; short-term view; subconscious mind Are you being short-sighted? What are you taking a close look at?
Fort	**Climbing into a fort:** Taking protective measures; watching your back; lack of trust **Defending a fort:** Being defensive **Burning fort:** Needing to be open; feeling defenceless or vulnerable.	Danger; self-protection; emotional barriers; self-defences; bracing yourself Where are you defending yourself? What are you guarding against?
Fountain	**Admiring a fountain:** Appreciating beauty; seeking wisdom **Putting detergent in a fountain:** Feeling agitated; corruption **Standing under a fountain of light:** Receiving spiritual wisdom.	Beginnings; rejuvenation; fountain of wisdom; fountain of youth Do you need to connect with your source? Where are you feeling composed or tranquil? (Also see Spring in Chapter 14.)

Symbol	Symbol In Action	Possible Life Issues
Funeral parlour	**Attending a funeral:** Mourning; letting go; reviewing the past **Your funeral:** Denying a part of yourself; your problem; it's your funeral **Your partner's funeral:** Warning; changed feelings; end of a relationship.	Death; closure; passing; dark; resolution; ending of a habit, attitude, idea, relationship, condition or circumstance What have you lost? What do you need to lay to rest?
Gaol	**Being in gaol:** Feeling boxed in; restricted or imprisoned; enduring limitations **Gaol cell with door open:** Being offered a way out; freedom from limitation; hope; seeing a way forward **Escaping from gaol:** Breaking free; having more time; making changes; breaking bonds; taking control.	Confined thinking; self-regulations; impediments; limitations Where are you feeling restricted? Are you feeling at others' beck and call?
Garage	**Car in garage:** Body needing repair; having the right skills **Garage with no car:** Not needing renewal; opportunity to review and overhaul **Untidy garage:** Being disorganised; needing to clear your clutter; feeling confused.	Renewal of energies or purpose; storage; reserves; regeneration; rectification; having the means; resources What needs repair? What are you maintaining?
Garden	**Flowering garden:** Fertile ideas; inner beauty **Weeding a garden:** Organising your thinking; eradicating the undesirable **Overgrown garden:** Being disorganised; neglect of self or others; lack of care; avoiding responsibilities.	Developing attitudes; sowing ideas; planning your life Are you being lead up the garden path? What are you cultivating?
Gas station	See Petrol Station in this chapter.	
Gift shop	**Buying a gift:** Giving to others; owning your own gifts or talents	Giving of yourself; giving and receiving ideas, talents, offerings or capabilities

Symbol	Symbol In Action	Possible Life Issues
	Well-stocked gift shop: Many talents to offer **Gift shop with no customers:** Unknown gifts or talents.	Where are you giving to others? What gifts do you own?
Graveyard	See Cemetery in this chapter.	
Greenhouse	**Greenhouse with thick growth:** Productive ideas; thriving in the right conditions; adapting well **Empty greenhouse:** Physical environment without love **Greenhouse with dead growth:** Fruitless endeavours; unable to adapt.	Invented concepts; ingenious plans; encouragement; artificially produced What are you cultivating? Where are you providing the right environment?
Gym	**Working out:** Being self-disciplined; pushing yourself **Being a spectator:** Assessing your performance; unwilling to commit **Unable to join in class:** Feeling that you don't measure up.	Training; transformation; competition; ambition; discipline; model thinking; make-over Where are you in training? Are you hoping for perfection?
Hallway	**Walking along a hallway:** Being directed; following opportunities; moving on; making progress; searching **Choosing a doorway:** Considering your options **Blocked hallway:** Being obstructed.	Admittance; access; rite of passage; gateway; threshold; interchange of views; transition What are you gaining access to? Where are you moving forward? (Also see Corridor in this chapter.)
Harbour	**Ship in harbour:** Adopting a safe position; taking shelter; needing time out; ship comes in **Many boats moored:** Group security **Ship unloading in harbour:** Off-loading your feelings; releasing your responsibilities.	Retreat; sanctuary; protection; stabilisation; stable ideas or views; security Where are you seeking refuge? Are you harbouring a grudge?
Hardware store	**Buying items:** Acquiring skills **Busy store:** Choosing popular options	Self-improvement; physical aspects; body; personal tools

Symbol	Symbol In Action	Possible Life Issues
	Empty shelves: Lack of choice.	Where have you got the right skills? Does your physical body need attention?
Health food store	See Health Food in Chapter 7.	
Hidden rooms	**Exploring a hidden room:** Discovering potential talents; revealing unknown parts of yourself **Being trapped in a hidden room:** Held back; feeling vulnerable; being manipulated (even unknowingly) **Finding a ghost in a hidden room:** Haunted by your fears.	Hidden talents; unconscious beliefs; obscure; unexplored areas of consciousness; cover up; repressed What haven't you considered? What are you concealing from yourself or others?
Highway	See Road in this chapter.	
Hospital	**Sick in hospital:** Needing transformation **Hospital with no staff:** Receiving no support; lack of options **Derelict hospital:** Not receiving the right kind of help; out-of-date practices.	Sickness; repair; death; resurrection; regeneration; unhealthy attitudes, habits or outcomes Where do you need repair and renewal? What needs to be healed?
Hotel	**Visiting a hotel:** Revisiting an issue; moving on **Busy hotel:** Coming and going; new ideas; diversity **Empty hotel:** Not welcoming change.	Fleeting issues; temporary circumstances; change; business; sexual liaisons Where are you in transition? Are you in a passing phase?
House	**House in disrepair:** Neglecting yourself or your responsibilities; being unfit; ill-health **New rooms:** Extending your thinking or field of influence **Upper and lower levels:** Different levels of consciousness (subconscious and super-conscious mind).	Consciousness; awareness; belief system; body; family roots; astrological term: house Where is your focus? What is the state of your body?

73

Symbol	Symbol In Action	Possible Life Issues
Industrial buildings	**Large industrial building:** Big venture; being ambitious **Refurbished factory:** Renewed enthusiasm; resurrecting your goals **Disused warehouse:** Lacking goals or drive.	Diligent; hard-working; motivated; endeavours; drive; ambition; business; organisation; finance Where are you being industrious? Are you taking on new enterprises?
Island	**Visiting an island:** Seeking refuge; feeling alone; taking time out; needing to reflect; holiday **Being marooned:** Being out of touch; unable to connect with others; needing to do it alone **Hostile island:** Emotional isolation; hurting yourself.	Isolation; individuality; detachment; seclusion; solitude Where are you feeling isolated? Are you cut off from your feelings?
Jail	See Gaol in this chapter.	
Jetty	**Walking along a jetty:** Projecting yourself; prolonged negotiations; far-reaching consequences **Erecting a jetty:** Taking a risk **Broken-down jetty:** Blocked options; short-term thinking.	Long-term thinking; projections; feeling drained; taking risks; extension; lengthen; increase; continuation Where are you extending yourself? What are you peering into?
Kitchen	**Cooking food:** Nurturing yourself or others **Cooking with books nearby:** Altering the truth: cooking the books **Serving a meal:** Dishing out ideas; teaching others.	Preparation; feeding; knowledge; presenting information Where are you serving up ideas? Are you cooking up a plan?
Lake	**Seeing your reflection in a lake:** Higher self; contemplating life; being an observer **Swimming in a lake:** Taking things in your stride **Lake whipped up by the wind:** Inner turmoil; feeling unsettled.	Emotions; tranquillity; reflections; meditating; turmoil; life experience Are you feeling calm and reflective? Where are you dipping into your pool of experience?

Symbol	Symbol In Action	Possible Life Issues
Lawn	See Garden in this chapter.	
Library	**Looking through a library:** Being open **Large library:** Reviewing past experiences; memories; searching the mind **Library with no people:** Not learning from the past; experiences to still explore; not looking within.	Knowledge; collection of experience; collective unconscious; akashic records (record of all things); karma; past Where are you looking for answers? Are you evaluating your life? (Also see Bookstore in this chapter)
Lighthouse	**Being guided by a lighthouse:** Higher knowledge; wise approach; warning **Lighthouse shining on you:** Revealing insight: bringing to light **Looking inside a lighthouse:** Going within.	Brilliance; enlightenment; knowledge; illumination; radiance; safe attitudes or position Where have you seen the light? What are you looking at in a new light?
Living room	**Empty living room:** Lacking connections **Renovated living room:** Making new contacts **Derelict living room:** Neglected relationships.	Family relations; public image; relaxation; group ideals; daily interactions Where are you cooperating with others? Are you evaluating your relationships?
Mall	**Walking along a mall:** Considering your options **Busy mall:** Making popular choices **Empty mall:** Lack of choice.	Commerce; finance; centre of things; making choices; real estate; good positioning Where are you shopping around? Are you being materialistic?
Marshland	**Sinking into quicksand:** Tenuous position; being drawn in **Trying to traverse the landscape:** Dealing with difficult circumstances **Walking around a marshland:** Avoiding problems.	Dangerous ground; uncertainty; sinking; insecurity; quagmire; emotional instability Where can't you hold your ground? Are you in an insecure position?
Meadow	See Field in this chapter.	

Symbol	Symbol In Action	Possible Life Issues
Mental institution	**Inside a mental institution:** Warning; needing time out; out of touch with reality; eccentricity **Outside a mental institution:** Questioning your sanity or emotional stability; questioning whether things make sense **Can't get into a mental institution:** Lack of support; having credibility; sound thinking.	Way off the mark; way-out ideas; unsound thinking Where do you have some strange ideas? Do you need to think differently?
Military plant	**Empty factory:** Feeling defenceless; needing to be open **Working in a military plant:** Needing to protect yourself; watching your back; feeding problems **Deciding between two opposing military plants:** Having a conflict of interest.	Self-defences; munitions; confrontation Where are you dealing with conflict? Are you being defensive?
Mine	**Probing a mine:** Making inquiries; digging deeper; digging in; searching; looking within **Extracting minerals:** Gaining subconscious insights **Collapsed mine:** Inaccessible; not facing issues; unwilling to delve deeper; unable to look within.	Inner workings; store of knowledge; excavation of information; subconscious mind; ideas or plans not manifested; yourself: mine Are you a mine of information? What are you unearthing? (Also see Cave in this chapter.)
Monastery	**Being with others in a monastery:** Sharing common values **Empty monastery:** Beliefs that no longer serve you; needing to discard your values; feeling unfulfilled **Derelict monastery:** Needing to look within; ignoring your conscience.	Religious order and values; spiritual values and aspirations; segregation; common beliefs; conscience What are you aspiring to? Are you isolating yourself from others?
Mortuary	See Funeral parlour in this chapter.	

Symbol	*Symbol In Action*	*Possible Life Issues*
Mountain	**Looking at a mountain range:** Feeling daunted; many challenges ahead **Snow-packed rugged mountain:** Very difficult circumstances; feeling overwhelmed; bracing yourself for a challenge **Climbing a mountain:** Confronting your problems.	Obstacle; hard choices; barrier; contest; difficulty; trial Where are you facing a large challenge? What has impressed you?
Museum	**Looking through a museum:** Evaluating past experiences **Can't get into a museum:** Blocking out the past **Derelict museum:** Discarded beliefs or memories.	Long-standing ideals; memorabilia; show-casing the past; traditions; museum piece Are you revisiting the past? Where is the past impacting you?
Nursery	**Nursery full of babies:** New beginnings; lots of potential; nurturing new talent **Tending a nursery:** Developing potential **Can't get into a nursery:** Unable to make a start; can't get off the ground.	Children; breeding; new beginnings; new ideas; developing attitudes, qualities or endeavours; training; education What are you nurturing? What is growing within you?
Nursing home	**Being in a nursing home:** Being patient; inability to move forward; needing support; transition **Working in a nursing home:** Needing compassion; supporting others; accepting the inevitable **Nursing home full of people:** Group acceptance.	Losing your grip; holding on; acquiescence; inescapable facts or situations; ageing Where are you biding time? What do you have to accept?
Office building	**Your office:** Business concerns; your responsibilities; living up to others' expectations **Office door closed:** Unable to fulfil your responsibilities; lack of opportunity **Many office doors open:** Many business opportunities; multiple talents or skills.	Roles you play; intentions; duty; business; study; responsibilities; planning ideas; important task Are you holding office? Where are you fulfilling responsibilities?

Symbol	*Symbol In Action*	*Possible Life Issues*
Outhouses	**Locked in an outhouse:** Can't accept the present **Trying to find an outhouse:** Seeking independence; living in the past **Decrepit outhouse:** Old-fashioned values; outmoded practices.	Discounted ideas or options; punishment; ostracised; prohibited; withdraw; withdrawal into yourself; abolished Where are you releasing the past? Are you feeling excluded?
Outer space	**Staring into outer space:** Feeling overwhelmed, insignificant or unfulfilled **Lost in outer space:** Drifting; aimless; don't belong **Travelling through outer space:** Exploring new horizons; feeling on the outer; out of touch with reality; needing to be down to earth.	Wonder; unknowable; wide scope; meaningful; unknown; final frontier; void; vacant; futile endeavours Are you exceeding your limits? Where are you dealing with infinite possibilities?
Park	See Forest in this chapter.	
Parsonage	**Being a parson:** Ministering to others; teaching; expounding wisdom; being dogmatic **Being in a parson's home:** Having spiritual aspirations; needing guidance **Barred parsonage:** Rejecting your values; feeling excluded; unqualified.	Spiritual principles; responsibilities; religious ideals; holy; Christian Where are you serving others? Are you feeling guided or inspired?
Path	See Road in this chapter.	
Petrol station	**Filling your car with fuel:** Driving yourself; being motivated; energetic **Filling your car with the wrong fuel:** Poor performance; wrong circumstances; mixed feelings **Petrol pump with no fuel:** Lacking energy; poor diet; feeling drained; being apathetic.	Diet; energy; fuel; repair; drive; stamina; motivation Where do you need to refuel your efforts? Do you need to get going?
Pier	See Jetty in this chapter.	

Symbol	Symbol In Action	Possible Life Issues
Police station	**Building a police station:** Becoming totalitarian; developing a conscience **Rioting outside a police station:** Unable to accept authority; sense of injustice; being rebellious **Burned-down police station:** Lack of discipline or self-discipline; being denied justice; absence of law and order.	Force; justice; law and order; being apprehended; conscience; protection; custody; running away; consequences and repercussions; karma Are you unable to accept authority? Do you feel guilty?
Post office	**Collecting mail:** Receiving news; being open and receptive; intuitive awareness **Looking through mail:** Searching for information; looking for answers; interest in others' opinions **Mail delivery to the wrong address:** Getting the wrong idea; not listening.	Receiving a delivery; appointed station: post Do you need to get the message? Where are you communicating with others?
Public building	**Trying to get into a public building:** Seeking public approval **Looking out of a window in a public building:** Feeling exposed; awareness of the bigger picture; sensing the greater good **Derelict public building:** Neglecting the public interest; having a poor public image.	Visibility; public appearance; public spirited; community values: public life, public interest, public relations Are you seeking publicity? Where are you concerned with public opinion?
Pyramid	**Climbing to the top of a pyramid:** Reaching the pinnacle of your career; sense of achievement; wide view or perspective **Going inside the Great Pyramid:** Being initiated; making a transition **Meditating under a pyramid frame:** Receiving spiritual insights; rejuvenation.	Mystery; initiation; higher perspective; apex; past; shift in consciousness Where are you channelling your energies? Have you made a point?

Symbol	Symbol In Action	Possible Life Issues
Railway station	**Catching a train:** Being predictable; taking others with you; moving on; expecting others to give way to you; having right of way; taking a rite of passage **Missing a train:** Lost opportunity: a train of events **Train crash:** Warning; forced halt to your plans.	Power; officialdom; predestined routes; unstoppable; transition through life's stages; travel; convoy; being with others; acquiring skills: training What's gone off the rails? Do you need to get back on track? (Also see Subway in this chapter.)
Restaurant	**Closed restaurant:** Having a closed mind; lacking options **Food you can't eat:** Can't accept; unpalatable options; rejecting ideas **Meeting others in a restaurant:** Exchanging views; diversity of opinion; being open-minded.	Food for thought; exchange of ideas; new possibilities What are you digesting or taking in? Where are you making choices?
River	**Fast-flowing river:** Having momentum; making rapid progress **Crossing a river:** Making a transition; the other side: death; Underworld king, Hades **Dammed river:** Blocked emotions; inability to go with the flow.	Flow; momentum; direction; taking your own course; out-pouring of emotion Where do you need to go with the flow? Do you need to circulate?
Road	**Road with treasure:** Achieving your goals; travelling down the road to success **Coming to a dead end:** Meeting obstacles; getting nowhere **Road with no end:** Can't see the end in sight; needing endurance.	Life course; route to objectives; choices you make; direction; pathway Where are you headed? What goals have you set yourself?
School	**Visiting a preschool:** Dealing with fundamentals **Sitting for an exam:** Evaluating yourself or your performance **Old school:** Traditional values;	Learning; evaluation; education; personal growth; training; discipline; acquiring knowledge; school tie Where are you learning from your experiences?

Symbol	Symbol In Action	Possible Life Issues
	being old fashioned; out of date; opportunities, privileges or connections.	Are you evaluating yourself and your life? (Also see Sitting for an Exam in Common Dream Theme at the end of this chapter.)
Skyscraper	**Looking up at a skyscraper:** Feeling inspired; daunted; considering the challenge ahead **Being on the top of a skyscraper:** Feeling isolated; looking down on others; seeing the bigger picture **Skyscraper crashing down:** Tumbling finances; damage to your career; reaching the pinnacle of your career; crushed hopes and plans.	High point; spiritual insight; finance; career; central business district; security; high-flyer; imagination; foresight; self-exile Are you striving for high ideals? Where are you sensing far-reaching possibilities?
Stairs	**Climbing stairs:** Taking the next step; rising to a challenge; exploring higher levels of thinking **Falling down stairs:** Falling from grace; dropping back; losing ground or position; going backwards **Blocked stairwell:** Unable to move forward; denied access; can't connect.	Connecting levels of consciousness; connections and interconnections; interdependence Are you experiencing ups and downs? Where do you need to make progress?
Subway	**Dark subway:** Confronting your fears; stepping into the unknown **Fast subway:** Having momentum; events moving too fast; feeling like you can't keep up **Dangerous subway:** Warning; feeling vulnerable.	Subconscious mind (below); loss of control; dark; underground; predestined route or direction; power; officialdom Where are you relinquishing control? Are you being predictable? (Also see Railway station in this chapter)
Supermarket	**Looking through a supermarket:** Considering alternatives **Busy supermarket:** Making popular choices	Resources; food for thought; personal reserves Where are you making choices? Are you dipping in or propping up your resources?

Symbol	Symbol In Action	Possible Life Issues
	Empty shelves: Lacking options; depleted resources; unsustainable goals.	(Also see Groceries in Chapter 7.)
Swimming pool	**Taking swimming lessons:** Gaining self-control; acquiring skills; adopting spiritual practice **Swimming in a pool:** Needing discipline; making progress; spiritual aspirations; being motivated **Unable to swim the distance:** Lacking endurance; unwilling to go the distance; lack of commitment; not ready.	Water; emotions; spiritual activity; self-discipline; technique; swimmingly What are you dipping into? Where are you directing your energies?
Temple	**Walking up to a temple:** Searching for meaning **Can't open the temple door:** Unwilling to look within; denied access; emotional blockages; feeling excluded **Overrun temple:** Neglected spiritual life.	Spiritual aspirations; worship; conscience; point in the head: temple Where do you need to treat your body as the temple of the soul? Are you aspiring to or applying spiritual principles? (Also see Monastery in this chapter.)
Tent	**Putting up a tent:** Being adaptable or flexible **Tent flapping in a storm:** Feeling unsure; weathering trying circumstances **Dismantling a tent:** Changing your circumstances; unwilling to be flexible.	Temporary; making a transition; feeling insecure; communing with nature Are things changing? Do you need to move on?
Tower	See Skyscraper in this chapter.	
Tunnel	**Looking for an entrance:** Searching for solutions; needing to be open **Crawling through a tunnel:** Exploring the unknown or the subconscious mind **Collapsed tunnel:** Shutting out the past; denied access.	Subconscious mind; dark; rite of passage; journey; making connections; accessing different levels of consciousness; transition Are you bringing up the past? Where do you need to tread carefully?

Symbol	Symbol In Action	Possible Life Issues
Twin Towers	**Being in the Twin Towers:** Feeling used; looming threat; targeted **Watching the Twin Towers fall:** Feeling shocked or helpless; historical events; being a witness **Rebuilding the Twin Towers:** Overcoming difficulties; transforming yourself; picking up the pieces; endurance and determination; building a new future.	Fears; national security; feeling undermined or threatened; heroism; being destructive What can't you trust? Where are you feeling victimised?
University	See College and/or School in this chapter.	
Volcano	**Volcano erupting:** Emotional outbursts **Running away from flowing lava:** Avoiding the consequences **Dead volcano:** Emotional stability; lacking passion.	Temperamental outbursts; fire; fiery energy; expansion; violent feelings; passionate; blowing your stack What could explode? Where are you being volatile?
Waiting room	**Busy waiting room:** Group condition; needing lots of patience **Empty waiting room:** Unwilling to take advice; rejecting assistance **Sitting in a waiting room:** Waiting your turn; seeking help; expecting outcomes.	Patience; anticipation; tolerance; suspending plans; enduring situations; restraint; pause; seeking help Is your life on hold? Where do you need patience?
Wardrobe	See Closet in this chapter.	
Waterfall	**Looking at a waterfall:** Needing emotional release or transparency **Dried-up waterfall:** Lacking emotion; feeling drained; nothing to give **Huge waterfall:** Releasing of strong emotions; being emotional.	Emotions; liberation of feelings; letting go; water Have you fallen from grace? Do you need to discharge your feelings?

Symbol	Symbol In Action	Possible Life Issues
Well	**Stumbling across a well:** Finding unexpected strength or support **Falling down a well:** Needing help; losing ground or status; being pulled down **Dried-up well:** Lacking inspiration; depleted energy or reserves; no support.	Abundance; inspiration; spirit; sacred beliefs; state of health; source of supply; dark; deep; secrecy; mystery; wellspring Where are you reaching into your reserves? Do you need to connect with your source?
Windmill	**Wind farm:** Productive alternatives; prosperity **Still windmill:** Stagnant thinking; making no progress; lack of power **Constructing a windmill:** Conserving energy; working efficiently.	Unconventional thinking; unusual possibilities; air; movement; breath; energy; flatulence: wind Where are you powering along effortlessly? Are you being alternative in your thinking?
Zoo	**Being a zoo-keeper:** Maintaining control or self-control **Letting animals out of a zoo:** Freeing yourself from limitations; being irresponsible **Closed-down zoo:** Previous limitations.	Lacking control; trapped; borders; frontiers; breaking new ground; mayhem Where are you feeling restricted? Are you on public display?

Common Dream Theme: Sitting for an exam

Finding yourself taking an exam that you haven't studied for can symbolise a lack of planning; feeling unprepared; pressured; inadequate to the task; lack of self-belief; needing to examine yourself and evaluate your priorities or being unable to fulfil your own or others' expectations.

Chapter 5
Colour

*People are like stained-glass windows. They sparkle and shine
when the sun is out, but when the darkness sets in,
their true beauty is revealed only if there is a light from within.*
Elizabeth Kubler-Ross

Colours can symbolise various emotions. The depth and clarity of colour can indicate the strength of its particular qualities within you whilst muddied variations can represent the presence of its negative aspects.

How to get the best value from this chapter

- See if you relate to any of the key words or questions and explore your own meanings which may override those given here.
- Look at all possibilities and apply the most appropriate for your situation.
- Rephrase the Life Issue questions to broaden their personal relevance to you, if necessary, by using other words with similar meanings.
- You can also turn any question around (including those you formulate) to see if you relate to them better, by asking them in a slightly different way. For example, rephrase it as a need rather than a desire or belief or vice versa.

Desires and needs as opposed to outcomes and results

If a symbol represents an issue you are currently facing, then it may be indicative of your feelings, desires, beliefs or needs. This would usually occur in the first two-thirds of a dream, which often illustrates the issue you are dealing with and how you feel about it.

If a symbol comes in the form of a resolution, outcome, insight, solution or conclusion in the climax, usually at the end of the dream, then it may indicate a consequence, result or your dream advice to you.

Symbol	Symbolism	Possible Life Issues
	Look for feelings, desires, needs, beliefs or situations, explore literal meanings, apply any puns and idioms	*Look for where, what and who this reminds you of, apply key words to thoughts, feelings or situations, explore literal meanings, apply word plays and figures of speech*
Black	**Positive:** Obscure; incomprehensible; mystifying What can't you fathom? **Negative:** Mourning; despair; animosity Where are you feeling melancholy?	Infinity; negative ideas or feelings; fashionable; darkness; contrast; denial of joy; serious; death; grounding; things look black; black and white; in the black; black mark.
Blue	**Positive:** Faithful; industrious; dependable Where are you being loyal and faithful? **Negative:** Gloomy; hopeless; argumentative What's making you feel depressed?	Spiritual attainment; aspirations and ideals; cold; neutral; conformity; respect; security; calming; masculine; responsibility; serious; winter; authority; blue skies; feeling blue; make a blue; had a blue; blue in the face; true blue; out of the blue; blue blood; blue chips.
Brown	**Positive:** Humility; commitment; material values Where are you focused on material goals? **Negative:** Stagnation; bored; negativity What has browned you off?	Stability; earthy; neutral; functional; secular interests; depression; brown out.
Coral	**Positive:** Loving; caring; friendliness Where are you being open and accepting? **Negative:** Isolated; need for love Are you being aloof?	High energy; delicate or sensitive.
Gold	**Positive:** Spiritual qualities and power Where are you showing spiritual strength and courage? **Negative:** Material affluence and talents Where are you focused on material power or wealth?	Spiritual wisdom; knowledge; prosperity; abundance; remuneration; value; status; gold-digger.

Symbol	Symbol In Action	Possible Life Issues
Green	**Positive:** Affluent; flourishing; functional Where are you thriving? **Negative:** Restless; insatiable; jealousy Are you degrading others?	Regeneration; personal or spiritual growth; health; healing; vitality; spring; anticipation; composure; serenity; greed; practical; maturity; envy: green with envy.
Grey	**Positive:** Uncertainty; clouded; vague Where are you considering shades of grey? **Negative:** Apprehension; anxiety; despair What's looking hopeless?	Institution; depression; conformity; denial of joy; old age.
Indigo	**Positive:** Dignity; respect; integrity Are you holding high aspirations? **Negative:** Self centred; deceiving; prejudiced Where are you feeling disheartened or depressed?	Intuition; psychic abilities; idealism; the blues.
Light	See Common Dream Theme at the end of this chapter.	
Magenta	**Positive:** Exciting; fun-loving; passionate Are you being energetic and dynamic? **Negative:** Serious; desire to shock; zealous Are you being intense?	Personal transformation; freedom; letting go.
Orange	**Positive:** Daring; benevolent; caring Where have you got altruistic motives? **Negative:** Deceiving; boasting; dependent Are you relying heavily on others?	Cooperation; vitality; amicable; communicative; cordial; joy; freedom; optimism.
Pink	**Positive:** Adoration; delight; clarity	Love; calmness; feminine energies; warm-hearted; caring;

Symbol	Symbol In Action	Possible Life Issues
	Where are you being kind and loving? **Negative:** Lack of self-belief and assertiveness Are you being submissive or dependent?	affectionate; devotion; achievement; intuition; self-love and acceptance.
Purple	**Positive:** Dedication; unity; healing Where are you showing unconditional love and compassion? **Negative:** Passion; anger; rage What is irritating you?	Spiritual leader; spiritual awareness; royalty; devotion; healing; faith; passion; purple heart; purple with rage.
Red	**Positive:** Bold; determined; direction Where are you showing energy and passion? **Negative:** Attacking; narrow-minded; ruthless What are you pursuing relentlessly?	New beginnings; determination; desire; anger; power; excitement; action; force; energy; aggression; blood; injury; sexuality; embarrassment; mooladhara chakra (yoga); red light district.
Turquoise	**Positive:** Revitalising energies; communication Where have you got composure and poise? **Negative:** Reserved; critical; sarcastic Are you being intolerant?	Expressing yourself; clarity; balance.
White	**Positive:** Highly attuned; spiritually inspired Where are you following your intuition? **Negative:** No negative aspects.	Intuition; light; purity; innocence; infinity; absolute; clarity; enlightenment.
Yellow	**Positive:** Quick-thinking; agile mind; alertness Where are you showing wisdom? **Negative:** Judgmental; gossiping; absent-minded Are you disapproving of others?	Intellect; wisdom; light; cowardice; mental acumen; enjoyment; being yellow.

Common Dream Theme: Seeing the light

Seeing the light in your dream can symbolise realisation, illumination, inspiration or finding a solution to your problems. If the dream was very vivid and moving it may be a recollection of a spiritual experience that you've had during the night on inner levels of consciousness.

Chapter 6
Fish and Marine Life

The stranded fish thinks only of the sea.
Mirābāi

Fish can represent spiritual thought and wisdom, Christianity, your need to flow with life or keep emotionally buoyant. They can also symbolise whether you feel in or out of your element, your suspicions ('fishy'), what's elusive and hard to catch, your unemotional or passionless side (being a 'cold fish') or abundance and fertility. Consider these possible meanings with any others specifically listed.

How to get the best value from this chapter

- See if you relate to any of the key words or questions and explore your own meanings which may override those given here.
- Look at all possibilities and apply the most appropriate for your situation.
- Rephrase the Life Issue questions to broaden their personal relevance to you, if necessary, by using other words with similar meanings.
- You can also turn any question around (including those you formulate) to see if you relate to them better, by asking them in a slightly different way. For example, rephrase it as a need rather than a desire or belief or vice versa.
- The Symbol in Action examples show how to apply context or link meaning with action.

Desires and needs as opposed to outcomes and results

If a symbol represents an issue you are currently facing, then it may be indicative of your feelings, desires, beliefs or needs. This would usually occur in the first two-thirds of a dream, which often illustrates the issue you are dealing with and how you feel about it.

If a symbol comes in the form of a resolution, outcome, insight, solution or conclusion in the climax, usually at the end of the dream, then it may indicate a consequence, result or your dream advice to you.

Symbol	Symbol In Action *Look for feelings, desires, needs,* *beliefs or situations, explore literal* *meanings, apply any puns* *and idioms*	Possible Life Issues *Look for where, what and who this* *reminds you of, apply key words to* *thoughts, feelings or situations,* *explore literal meanings, apply word* *plays and figures of speech*
Anchovy	**Eating anchovy:** Enjoying prosperity **Buying anchovy:** Accepting transparency **Dead anchovy:** Rejecting others; feeling isolated.	Abundance (packed together closely); transparency (transparent); unpalatable (salty); sociable (gregarious) What are you finding hard to accept? Where do you need to be open?
Barramundi	**Eating barramundi:** Adopting a balanced approach **Several barramundi:** Group flexibility **Dead barramundi:** Inability to adapt.	Balance of male and female energies (changes sex); large; impressive; alert; mentally agile; adaptable (lives in fresh and salt water) Do you need to adjust to your circumstances? Are you questioning your sexual preferences?
Carp	**Eating carp:** Accepting the undesirable **Many carp:** Rebellious influences; several setbacks **Dead carp:** Regaining control.	Unpalatable; unappealing; intangible; subtle; hidden; menacing; propagation; out of balance What are you finding undesirable? What's out of control?
Catfish	**Eating catfish:** Eating your words **Catching catfish:** Setting new goals **Dead catfish:** Rejecting negativity.	Extending yourself (elongated); losing interest (tapering tail); harmful; unprincipled gossip; catty (poisonous spines) What's tapering off? Are you hurting yourself or others?
Clam	**Clam opening:** Expressing yourself; opening up; revealing something **Clam being prised open:** Pressured; letting go; dealing with forces beyond your control	Hidden beauty; great value; holding on to your values; inner self; lack of communication: clam up What are you suppressing? Where are you being secretive?

Symbol	Symbol In Action	Possible Life Issues
	Closed clam: Concealing information; needing to keep things to yourself; being private.	
Coral	**Swimming over coral:** Seeing new possibilities **Being scratched by coral:** Hurting yourself or others; being uncompromising **Bright coral:** Promoting yourself; being flamboyant.	New formations; framework; structure; inflexible; supportive; showy; vivid; superficial (hollow); empty; unconscious (ocean) Are you involved in new developments? Where are you being rigid, inflexible or unforgiving?
Crab	**Crab walking around:** Sidestepping an issue **Crab in the sky:** Zodiac sign of Cancer **Crab with pincers attacking you:** Being hurt by criticism or self-criticism.	Emotional; changes with the tide; grasping; inflicting harm; crabby nature Where have you been inconsistent? Are you being bad-tempered?
Dolphin	See Swimming mammals at the end of this chapter.	
Drowning	See Common Dream Theme at the end of this chapter.	
Dugong	See Swimming mammals at the end of this chapter.	
Eel	**Eel hiding:** Hidden deceit **Seeing an eel:** Revealed deception; facing your fears; treachery **Being chased by an eel:** Feeling threatened.	Developing wisdom (spawns after 10 years); evasive; untrustworthy (slimy skin) Are you being misleading? What's maturing slowly?
Estuary perch	**Eating a perch:** Accepting your limitations **Dropping a perch:** Sliding values; falling status **Dead perch:** Inability to adapt.	Limitations (compressed body); adaptable (uses salt and fresh water); silver; high ideals; elevated position: perch Where are you limiting yourself or others? Do you need to be more flexible?

Symbol	*Symbol In Action*	*Possible Life Issues*
Fish	See Introduction in this chapter.	
Flathead	**Holding a flathead:** Being pessimistic; reflection; narrow mindedness **Flathead burrowing into the seabed:** Refusing to face something; concealing yourself; self-protection **Several flatheads:** Many setbacks.	Melancholy; meditation (upturned eyes); setbacks (depressed head); retreat; excavating (burrows into seabed); unconscious What are you uncovering? Do you need to look within?
Flounder	**Catching a flounder:** Adopting a wait-and-see approach **Gutting a flounder:** Revealing deception; looking deeper; self-analysis **Several flounder:** Changing group perceptions.	Uncomfortable position; sensitivities (prickly scales); mind shift (eye moves around the head); veiled; false appearance; adaptable; flexible (develops camouflage when needed); holding back (waits for food on the seabed); Are you floundering? What's not as it seems?
Flying fish	**School of flying fish:** Spiritual growth **Trying to catch a flying fish:** Aspiring to the top; wanting faster progress **Dead flying fish:** Feeling uninspired; lack of mobility.	High ideals; rising high; travelling swiftly; mobility; high-powered; efficient What's taking off? Where are you leaping ahead?
Garfish	**School of garfish:** Abundance **Gutting garfish:** Self-analysis; looking deeper **Eating a garfish:** Being flexible or adaptable.	Projections (spear-like snout); abundance (silver stripe); attachment (attaches eggs to plants); flexible (soft bones) What are you attached to? What are you projecting onto others?
Goldfish	**Admiring goldfish:** Seeking abundance; appreciating inner beauty **Goldfish devouring others:** Desirable image with questionable motives	Gold; subtle; spiritual notions; delicate; goldfish bowl Are you lacking privacy? What requires sensitivity?

Symbol	Symbol In Action	Possible Life Issues
	Many goldfish: Spiritual aspirations.	
Groper	**Choosing groper on the menu:** Seeking change **Gutting a groper:** Ending conflict; self-analysis **Fighting groper:** Resisting change; struggling; confronting difficulties.	Female energies; intuition (all begin as females); transformation (some change into males); conflict; resistance (powerful fighter); groping around What are you trying to find? What are you transforming?
Jellyfish	**Floating jellyfish:** Being carried along by feelings or events **Stung by jellyfish:** Warning; being stung or hurt by gossip **Looking at a jellyfish:** Seeing through a situation.	No backbone; far-reaching; stingers; jelly legs Where do you need transparency? Do you need more courage?
Jewfish	**Eating jewfish:** Taking from others **Gutting a jewfish:** Self-analysis; looking deeper **Several jewfish:** Group self-interest.	Cannibalise (eats its own kind); shallow (inhabits reefs and seabeds); having depth; important (large) Are you hurting yourself or those you love? Where do you have flexibility?
Leatherjacket	**Catching a leatherjacket:** Being defensive **Gutting a leatherjacket:** Self-analysis; looking deeper **Many leatherjackets:** Multiple opportunities.	Thick-skinned; opportunistic; defensive attitudes; self-protection (spine) Are you impervious to criticism? How are you making the best use of your opportunities?
Lungfish	**Eating a lungfish:** Being flexible **Seeking a lungfish:** Health warning (lungs); needing independence (room to breathe) **Dead lungfish:** Unable to accept.	Needing to take a breath (has lungs and gills); spiritual rhythm (inhaling and exhaling); self-protection (protected species); mind (large head); narrow vision (small eyes); great survivor; adaptable; missing link (can live on land and water) What's worth protecting? Do you need to slow down?

Symbol	Symbol In Action	Possible Life Issues
Mangrove Jack	**Eating a mangrove Jack:** Being aggressive; taking ownership; achieving a rhythm **Mangrove Jack hiding:** Concealing your motives **Several mangrove Jacks:** Conflict of interest.	Aggressive; being overbearing; taking possession; (powerful jaws); appealing (handsome); ebb and flow; mangrove Where are you feeling exposed? What are you concealing?
Marlin	**Catching marlin:** Blazing the trail; grappling with big issues **Marlin dropping off the fishing line:** Lost opportunity **Several marlin:** Big issues; group acknowledgment; abundance.	Significant (large, heavyweights of the ocean); sluggish; recognition; big prize; abundance Are you receiving big rewards? Where are you spear-heading the way?
Mullet	**Mullet eating:** Considering sound ideas **Dead mullet:** Dullness; lack of awareness; unconsciousness **Several mullet:** Group transparency.	Most valued beliefs (esteemed as food); tough; solid (thick-muscled); clarity; transparency (covering gelatinous film); stunned mullet Where are you clarifying your thinking? Are you accepting greater transparency?
Mulloway	**Eating mulloway:** Being apathetic; intuitive awareness **School of mulloway:** Group apathy **Dead mulloway:** Lack of intuition.	Large; inactive; group awareness; intuition (responds to sonar); something doesn't smell right (stench) Where are you distinctive or have unique ideas? Are you being intuitive?
Murray cod	**Fishing for Murray cod:** Being receptive; fishing for ideas **Dead Murray cod:** Stagnation **School of Murray cod:** Group realisations.	Looking inwards (concave head); colour green (mottled green); refreshing (fresh water) Do you need to look within? Where are you looking at large issues?
Octopus	**Octopus spraying ink:** Concealing your views; clouding issues	Wisdom; camouflage; formidable power; having influence; shy; retiring; health warning: blue-ringed octopus

Symbol	Symbol In Action	Possible Life Issues
	Looking for an octopus: Seeking power or inner wisdom **Wrestling with an octopus:** Getting entangled; possessiveness.	Who has you in their grasp? Where are you exerting your influence?
Oyster	**Breeding oysters:** Cultivating inner beauty **Eating oysters:** Being taken advantage of; protecting or depriving yourself **Diving for oysters:** Searching for inner strength or beauty.	Concealed thoughts; self-defences; delicacy; eaten alive; hidden beauty; oyster bar What has hidden potential? Are you feeling defenceless?
Piranha	**Attacked by piranhas:** Being victimised **Seeing a river full of piranhas:** Hopeless situation **Dead piranha:** Previous threat.	Ravenous appetite; selfish; grasping; craving (powerful jaws) What are you hungry for? What's devastated you?
Platypus	See Swimming mammals at the end of this chapter.	
Prawn (red)	**Being allergic to prawns:** Health warning; can't accept an idea; overreaction **Catching prawns:** Seeking inner wisdom; expressing your feminine side **Dead prawn:** Lack of intuition; resisting change.	Communication; intuition; feelings; female dominance; matriarch (female larger than the male); grace; slender; self-transformation Are you being intuitive? Where are you changing?
Rainbow fish	**Eating a rainbow fish:** Accepting greater transparency; gaining vision **Catching a rainbow fish:** Seeking clarity **Dead rainbow fish:** Lacking vision.	Visionary (large eyes); clarity (semi-transparent); diverging paths (forked tail) What's becoming clearer? Where do you feel divided?
Salmon	**Eating salmon:** Being determined; needing to return to your source; seeking renewal **Salmon being eaten by a bear:** Unsuccessful comeback **Dead salmon:** Unproductive endeavours.	Fertile; prolific; comeback; re-emergence; resolve; willpower (swim against the current) Where are you struggling? Are you going against current or popular thinking?

Symbol	Symbol In Action	Possible Life Issues
Saratoga	**Eating a saratoga:** Spreading ideas; teaching **Several saratogas:** Conflict of interest **Dead saratoga:** Ending conflict; not speaking out.	Ancient; refreshing (fresh water); talkative (mouth holds fertilised eggs); conflict (fighting fish) Where have you got competing needs? Are you being aggressive?
Sardine	**Opening a tin of sardines:** Feeling hemmed in; many aspects to an issue; being one of many; others to consider **Eating sardines:** Health recommendation; having a lot to think about **Sardines being processed:** Handling many things at once.	Crowding; abundance; tight squeeze; cramming ideas; being busy Are you being squeezed or put under pressure? Where are you suppressing yourself?
Seal	See Swimming mammals at the end of this chapter.	
Shark	**Shark attacking you:** Feeling threatened or intimidated; hidden danger **Shark in an aquarium:** Controlling your power; repressed feeling **Dead shark:** Previous threat.	Danger; forceful opinions; formidable opponent; swindler; unseen fear; power; shark bait Where do you feel that you could be attacked? Are you misusing your power?
Shellfish	**Eating shellfish:** Developing new ideas **Collecting shellfish:** Gathering potential **Cooking shellfish:** Preparing your thoughts; supporting others.	Embryonic; potential; hard; protected; restrictive; supporting What are you developing? Where are you reaching your boundaries?
Snapper	**Eating snapper:** Being practical; short tempered **Lifting up a snapper:** Acting quickly: snap up **Several snapper:** Group of entrepreneurs.	Abrupt change; quick; eager; superficial (lives in shallow water); expedient; pragmatic; realistic (opportunistic feeders); snap; snapshot; snap to it; snap out of it; snap one's fingers; snappy Do you need to act quickly? Where are you being aggressive?
Sole	**Eating sole:** Needing soul **Gutting sole:** Self-analysis	Restricted vision (both eyes are on one side of the head);

Symbol	*Symbol In Action*	*Possible Life Issues*
	Several sole: Group prejudice.	prejudice; narrow-mindedness; opinionated; solitary: sole; soul Are you showing bias? Where are you standing out or being alone?
Sooty grunter	**Eating a sooty grunter:** Being distracted; barging in; can't see what you're looking for **Breeding sooty grunters:** Developing depression **Dead sooty grunter:** Rejecting interference.	Intruding (barges at each other); unfocused; hidden; black; depressing; big mouth (known as blubber lips) Are you interfering? Where are you saying too much?
Squid	**Catching a squid:** Protecting yourself; being defensive **Many squid:** Group confusion **Dead squid:** Being apathetic.	Self-protection; clouding issues (sprays ink); self-propulsion; number ten (10 arms); original; beginnings; leadership Are you making things more confusing? Where are you motivated?
Starfish	**Starfish partially visible in the sand:** Holding back; being cautious; showing some of your talents; partial regeneration **Dead starfish:** Lacking influence **Several starfish:** Group influence.	Regeneration; healing; number five (radial arms); influential; brilliant; star Do you need renewal? Where are you receiving recognition?
Sturgeon	**Gutting a sturgeon:** Self-analysis **Dead sturgeon:** Lack of individuality **Several sturgeons:** Group victimisation.	Shallow (reef-dweller); distinctive (vivid colourings); victim (target for spear fishers) Are you feeling persecuted? Where are you standing out?
Sweetlip	**Catching a sweetlip:** Rare opportunity; being shallow **Slippery sweetlip:** Unable to hold on; letting things slide **Dead sweetlip:** Rejecting the superficial.	Rare; unusual; uncommon; shallow (reef-dwellers); colour red Where are you being exceptional? What's proving elusive?

Symbol	Symbol In Action	Possible Life Issues
Swordtail	**Eating a swordtail:** Needing balance or flexibility **Breeding swordtails:** Developing balance or flexibility **Dead swordtail:** Lacking balance or flexibility.	Colour orange; balance of male and female energies (female can change sex); adaptable (changes colour); sword Do you need balance? Where are you being flexible?
Tailor	**Eating a tailor:** Digesting ideas; being touchy **Gutting a tailor:** Self-analysis; looking deeper **Many tailors:** Group adaptability.	Bruises easily; large; absorbing ideas; tailor-made Are you being too sensitive? What are you tailoring to suit your needs?
Tommy ruff	**Catching tommy ruffs:** Prosperity; being productive **School of tommy ruffs:** Learning from your experiences; group inflexibility **Dead tommy ruff:** Lacking willpower.	Abundance; fertility; inflexible; strong-willed Where have you got fertile ideas? Are you being determined?
Trevally	**Eating trevally:** Receiving spiritual wisdom; uncontrolled desires **Dead trevally:** Limited supply **School of trevally:** Group insights.	Ravenous; insatiable; streamlined; significant insights; group consciousness; abundance (big schools) What do you need to streamline? Do you need to rationalise?
Tropical fish	**Admiring tropical fish:** Valuing yourself or others **Tropical fish in an aquarium:** Modifying your values **Dead tropical fish:** Lack of individuality.	Distinctive; valuable; unique; refined Where are you being exceptional? What are you valuing?
Trout	**Catching trout:** Being opinionated **Dead trout:** Discarding opinionated views **School of trout:** Group temptation.	Temptation (can be enticed); blemished; flawed (spotted); uncompromising (resists vigorously); tout for ideas Where are you resisting change? What are you attracted to?
Whale	See Swimming mammals at the end of this chapter.	

Symbol	Symbol In Action	Possible Life Issues
Whiting	**Choosing whiting on the menu:** Exercising your power of choice **Gutting whiting:** Self-analysis; looking deeper **Several whiting:** Selective group.	Desirable; high ideals (highly rated); selective; discriminating (choosy feeders) Are you being selective? What notions are you finding seductive?
Yabby	**Eating yabbies:** Being a victim; protecting yourself **Catching yabbies:** Receiving abundance **Dead yabbies:** Lacking options.	Number ten (10 legs); new beginnings; abundance; bait; self-protection (thick shield) Are you being manipulated? Are you being defensive?

Swimming mammals

Symbol	Symbol In Action	Possible Life Issues
Dolphin	**Dolphin swimming in bow wave:** Being manoeuvrable; adaptable; being supported in your progress **Dolphins playing:** Being spontaneous; going with the flow **Feeding dolphins:** Networking.	Good-natured; playful approach; intelligent; communicative (sonar); emotional highs and lows Where are you being intuitive? Do you need to be more playful?
Dugong	**Dugong feeding:** Giving to others **Baby dugong:** Needing support; beginning to slow down **Dead dugong:** Rejecting support.	Good provider; gentleness; grace; unconscious (ocean) Are you going with the flow? Where do you need to slow down?
Platypus	**Looking for a platypus:** Seeking inner wisdom **Seeing a platypus:** Facing your fears **Holding a platypus:** Finding your inner self; coming out; playing a more visible role.	Elusive; fearful; burrowing; obscure; concealed What are you trying to find? Are you being reserved?
Seal	**Seal performing acts:** Performing for others; fulfilling others' expectations	Playful; self-applause; intelligent; good provider; valuable; flexibility; seal of approval; sealed off

Symbol	Symbol In Action	Possible Life Issues
	Seal with no flippers: Unable to honour yourself; having no room to move **Seal playing:** Needing to be more fun loving; going with the flow.	Where do you need to acknowledge your own efforts? What's out of reach?
Whale	**Whale with calf:** Developing intuition **Beached whale:** Floundering; lost sense of who you are; needing to go with the flow **Several whales:** Group intuitive awareness.	Impressive; large; power; ancient origins; strength; oversized problem; exaggeration; intuition (sonar); communication; peaceful; wail; whale of a job; whale of a time Where are you facing a huge task? Are you being intuitive?

Common Dream Theme: Drowning

To find yourself drowning in a dream could be a warning of a possible drowning incident. It may, however, symbolise feeling overwhelmed or submerged by your emotions, unable to breathe or cope, feeling out of your depth or being dragged down. You could be finding yourself in a tricky situation or in deep water, dealing with something you can't fathom or even drowning your sorrows.

Chapter 7
Food and Drink

It is the job of the soul to seek out what feeds it.
Anne Wilson Schaef

Food can symbolise your emotional and mental nourishment—ideas, beliefs, opinions and notions that you either take in, as food for thought, or refuse to accept, or perhaps your position in the 'food chain'. Particular foods may also indicate a health warning showing what may need to be included or excluded from your diet. Consider these possible meanings with any others specifically listed.

How to get the best value from this chapter

- See if you relate to any of the key words or questions and explore your own meanings which may override those given here.
- Look at all possibilities and apply the most appropriate for your situation.
- Rephrase the Life Issue questions to broaden their personal relevance to you, if necessary, by using other words with similar meanings.
- You can also turn any question around (including those you formulate) to see if you relate to them better, by asking them in a slightly different way. For example, rephrase it as a need rather than as a desire or belief or vice versa.
- The Symbol in Action examples show how to apply context or link meaning with action.

Desires and needs as opposed to outcomes and results

If a symbol represents an issue you are currently facing, then it may be indicative of your feelings, desires, beliefs or needs. This would usually occur in the first two-thirds of a dream, which often illustrates the issue you are dealing with and how you feel about it.

If a symbol comes in the form of a resolution, outcome, insight, solution or conclusion in the climax, usually at the end of the dream, then it may indicate a consequence, result or your dream advice to you.

Symbol	Symbol In Action *Look for feelings, desires, needs, beliefs or situations, explore literal meanings, apply any puns and idioms*	Possible Life Issues *Look for where, what and who this reminds you of, apply key words to thoughts, feelings or situations, explore literal meanings, apply word plays and figures of speech*
Alcohol	**Being drunk:** Losing control; lacking responsibility; carefree approach; being destructive **Holding an oversized bottle of beer:** Needing to see the funny side; growing dependency; alcoholic addiction **Smashing a bottle of alcohol:** Rejecting dependency.	Harmful feelings and attitudes; dependency; drowning your sorrows; disease; loss of control What are you addicted to? Where are you relinquishing control?
Apple	**Eating an apple:** Health warning; guarding your health: an apple a day keeps the doctor away **Picking apples:** Feeling tempted **Tree full of apples:** Harvest; bounty; abundance; healthy attitudes.	New beginnings; forbidden fruit; temptation; apple of one's eye; she's apples Do you need to guard your health? Where are you evaluating what's right and wrong?
Bacon	**Eating bacon:** Overindulgence **Cooking bacon:** Preparing for success; presenting palatable ideas **Discarding bacon:** Not taking responsibility.	Success; fat; greasy; profitable ventures; indulgence; palatable; earning a living; fundamental principles; save one's bacon Are you bringing home the bacon? Where are you providing support?
Banana	**Eating bananas:** Health recommendation; digesting ideas **Buying bananas:** Becoming intuitive **Growing bananas:** Developing instability.	Thick-skinned; phallic symbol; moon (crescent-shaped); intuition; colour yellow; banana republic What's proving easy to digest? Where are you slipping up?
Beef	**Eating beef:** Using your power; having forceful opinions **Cutting up beef:** Analysing your strengths	Complaint; strength; strong opinions; solid thinking or arguments; vigorous; exaggeration; beefeater; beefing it up; beefs; beefy

Symbol	Symbol In Action	Possible Life Issues
	Beef sitting outside of your lunch box: Ignoring your power; lacking inner strength.	Do you need power or inner strength? Do you have weighty responsibilities?
Beer	**Drinking beer:** Releasing emotions; reducing pressure; not taking things too seriously **Making homemade beer:** Creating your own solutions **Spilling beer:** Releasing feelings.	Self-indulgence; rising issues; dependency; lightening up; unwinding; drowning your sorrows; breaking free; enjoyment; pleasure; beer up; beer and skittles What's fermenting within you? What are you addicted to?
Bread	**Taking bread from another:** Denying others an opportunity: take the bread out of one's mouth **Buttering bread:** Knowing where your interests lie: know which side your bread is buttered **Making bread:** Creating wealth; fulfilling your responsibilities; being self-sufficient.	Rising trends; uplifting feelings; transformation; foundations; principles; essentials (staple food); earning your livelihood; wealth; income: breadwinner; bread and butter What do you need? Where are you supporting yourself or others?
Butter	**Spreading butter:** Smoothing things over; crawling **Having butter on your fingers:** Letting things slip: butter-fingers **Melting butter:** Needing to be more flexible.	Flattery; smooth talk; greasy; unreliable; slippery; palatable; colour yellow Are you spreading yourself too thin? Who are you buttering up?
Cake	**Eating cake:** Seeking consolation; needing support; feeling gratified **Baking a cake:** Preparing your thoughts; showing good taste **Stale cake:** Out-of-date ideas or attitudes.	Appealing ideas; sweet tooth; prize; reward; comfort; self-indulgence; palatable ideas or presentation; good taste; celebration; piece of cake Where do you want to have your cake and eat it too? What are you taking in your stride?
Candy	**Eating candy:** Enjoying the best of life; indulging yourself; attractive ideas or options	Concentrated (boiled down); crystallised ideas; inflexibility; temptation; self-indulgence;

Symbol	Symbol In Action	Possible Life Issues
	Giving candy to a child: Offering enticements	incentive; evaporate; melts away; sweet things in life
	Bowl full of candy: Lots of appealing options.	What's enticing you? What's simmering away within you?
Cheese	**Eating cheese:** Fermenting feelings; allowing things to unfold; being cheerful	Needing to mature; gets better with age; smile; happy state of mind; nourishing ideas; healthy
	Mouldy cheese: Feelings that need to be discarded	outlook; pleased; say cheese; bored; disgruntled
	Cheese with holes in it: Haven't thought it through.	Are you feeling cheesed off? What's fermenting within you?
Cherry	**Picking cherries:** Being optimistic; needing purification; desiring excitement	Christmas; celebration; joy; cheerful disposition; bright red; energy; passion; cleansing
	Bowl full of cherries: Spiritual wisdom	attitudes (rich in iron, builds blood)
	Choking on cherries: Rejecting optimism.	Where are you thinking traditionally? Do you need to honour yourself?
Chilli	**Eating chillies:** Rising emotions	Heated, contentious issues or attitudes; colour red; passionate;
	Buying chillies: Developing strong feelings	intense; hot-tempered; unfriendly; unemotional: chilly
	Serving chillies: Dealing with heated issues.	What's too hot for you to handle? Where have you been frozen out?
Coconut	**Falling coconuts:** Decreasing productivity or creativity	Visionary (two eyes at the top of the shell); creative; prolific
	Eating coconuts: Having foresight or imagination; coming out of your shell	(produces fruit for 70–80 years); confining (encloses inner liquid); defensive (hard shell)
	Collecting coconuts: Gathering creative ideas.	Where are you being very productive? Are you thinking ahead?
Coffee	**Brewing coffee:** Festering bitterness; bitter memories; leaving an unpalatable taste	Dependency; addiction; excited; sociable; temptation; self-indulgence

Symbol	Symbol In Action	Possible Life Issues
	Broken coffee pot: Rejecting dependency **Spilled coffee beans:** Gossip.	What are you finding stimulating? Where are you feeling bitter?
Corn	**Sowing corn:** Spreading ideas; teaching **Gathering corn:** Collecting ideas; hardening your attitudes **Dead corn:** Lack of openings.	Fertility; abundance; seed thoughts; seeds of doubt; meaningless; new beginnings; hollow; vain (husk); corn: (hardening of the skin); corny idea Where are you being productive? Are you showing a tough exterior?
Crumbs	**Making breadcrumbs:** Creating divisions; trivialising issues **Spilling breadcrumbs:** Expressing your sensitivities **Stale breadcrumbs:** Past feelings; outdated ideas.	Inner sensitivities; going to pieces; small fragments; disintegrate; feeling inferior or inferior position; crummy; crumbly; crumbling Are you feeling discarded or insignificant? Where have you been offered the leftovers?
Crust	**Eating the crust:** Being firm **Cutting off the crusts:** Needing to be more flexible or open **Burnt crust:** Tough exterior; hurt feelings.	Impertinence (hard); mask; outward appearance; disguise; livelihood; foundation; holds everything together; high class; upper crust; crusted prejudice Where are you showing a tough exterior? Are you having problems earning a crust?
Date	**Picking dates:** Choosing the right time **Eating dates:** Having energy and endurance **Preserving dates:** Maintaining traditions; safeguarding memories.	Euphoric (it makes an intoxicating drink); energy; special occasion; passage of time; easily preserved; dateless; date line; dated Are you feeling up to date? Where are you out of date?
Dessert	**Eating dessert:** Indulging yourself; being irresponsible; feeling satisfied	Desires; more than you need; sweet things in life; attractive ideas; luxury; pleasure; satisfaction; life's little luxuries

Symbol	Symbol In Action	Possible Life Issues
	Baking dessert: Presenting ideas; teachings **Leaving dessert:** Having self-discipline; considering the consequences.	Are you looking for gratification? Where have you got your just desserts?
Egg	**Collecting eggs in a basket:** Taking a risk: have all one's eggs in one basket **Cracked egg shell:** Coming out of your shell; new beginnings; revealing your inner value **Throwing eggs away:** Wasting your potential.	Embryonic; immature; undeveloped; new beginnings; tough exterior; fertile; self-protection; self-defences; resourceful; productive; totality; whole; source; urge; sure as eggs, egg on; bad egg Are you hiding within your shell? Where have you got potential?
Fast food	**Ordering fast food:** Being unprepared; not thinking ahead; accepting convenience; settling for second best **Unable to be supplied with fast food:** No quick fix **Throwing out fast food:** Discarding unhealthy attitudes; changing your ways.	Health warning; quick-thinking; opportune moments; impulsive; spontaneous; unhealthy; fat; unprepared; abstinence: fast Where are you denying your needs? Are you seeking instant solutions?
Feast	**Attending a feast:** Having many options; food for thought; being creative **Having a feast in your honour:** Honouring yourself; receiving recognition **Feast with no people:** Lack of recognition; disappointment.	Religious principles; public-spirited; open; sense of community; abundance; choice; celebration; plenty; surplus; self-satisfied Are you overindulging yourself? Where are you making choices?
Food	See Introduction in this chapter.	
Foreign food	See Foreigner in Chapter 17.	
Fresh food	**Selecting fresh food:** Choosing a fresh approach; natural choice **Cooking fresh vegetables:** Tampering with or using good ideas **Growing your own vegetables:** Creating an original idea.	Innovative ideas; relevant issues or experiences; pure; attractive; original; up-to-date What are you finding refreshing? Where have you got new ideas?

Symbol	Symbol In Action	Possible Life Issues
Frozen food	**Freezing food:** Protecting your position; being cold; hardening your attitude **Cleaning the freezer:** Making a fresh start **Thawing frozen food:** Being more flexible; warming to an idea; recounting the past.	Preserving; cold; unfeeling; unwelcoming; frozen with fear; inaccessible What have you put on hold? Where are you being inflexible?
Fruit	**Eating fruit:** Being tempted; adopting natural alternatives **Picking fruit:** Reaping the rewards of your efforts; selecting healthy options **Rotting fruit:** Unproductive outcomes.	Fertile ideas; productive; successful outcomes; forbidden fruit Are your endeavours proving fruitful or fruitless? Where are you enjoying the fruits of your labour?
Garlic	**Eating garlic:** Stinging comments; taking responsibility **Growing garlic:** Increased sense of wellbeing; developing healing powers **Plate full of garlic:** Unpalatable situation; unpleasant option.	Overpowering; pungent; wellbeing; overbearing; curative powers; repelling others What stinks? Where have you been offensive?
Grape	**Harvesting grapes:** Yielding the fruits of your labour; reward; abundance **Treading grapes:** Changing a situation; transforming yourself or others **Tasting sour grapes:** Discrediting something you value: sour grapes.	Network; alcohol; change of state; altered point of view; transformation; group of ideas (forms in bunches); grapevine What's fermenting within you? What are you doing unofficially?
Groceries	**Shopping in a supermarket:** Considering your options **Can't decide between different items:** Being indecisive or hesitant **Taking home shopping:** Acquiring new ideas.	Options; decisions; nourishing the mind; resourceful; gathering ideas; replenishment Are you taking stock of your resources? Where are you making choices? (Also see Supermarket in Chapter 4.)
Gum	**Chewing gum:** Mulling over ideas	Attachment; obstruction; interference; meddling habits or

Symbol	Symbol In Action	Possible Life Issues
	Buying chewing gum: Making connections	person; united; secured; gummed up
	Gum on the bottom of your shoe: Feeling bound; restricted mobility; discarding feelings.	What are you adhering to? Are you in a sticky predicament?
Health food	**Eating health food:** Valuing your self; healthy lifestyle **Fridge stocked with health foods:** Looking after your own interests; healthy diet; making healthy choices; good values **Throwing health food out:** Rejecting support; choosing unwise options.	Beneficial thinking or practices; constructive; wholesome attitudes or diet; health; vigorous; nourishing; conducive; sustaining Do you need to nurture yourself? Where do you need to make healthy choices?
Herbs	**Picking herbs:** Accepting natural alternatives **Eating herbs:** Taking remedial action **Cooking with herbs:** Presenting alternative options.	Health warning; therapeutic qualities; fragrant; spiritual refreshment (herbal teas); medicinal; adds flavour; good taste; herbalist; herbage Are you 'herbing along'? Where do you need assistance?
Honey	**Bees collecting honey:** Being endearing **Honey in a honeycomb:** Feeling organised **Candied honey:** Set in your ways; crystallised thinking; needing to be more flexible or adaptable.	Bribe; endearment; self-indulgent; sweetened; palatable options; soothing; tastes good; pleasure; enjoyment; honeymoon Are you enjoying the sweet things in life? Where have you got good taste?
Ice-cream	**Eating ice-cream:** Indulging yourself **Buying ice-cream:** Choosing palatable options **Serving ice-cream:** Offering rewards.	Adds flavour; treating yourself; desires; indulgence; cold; inaccessible feelings; suspended judgments; palatable options; good taste Where are you treating yourself? Who are you feeling cold towards?
Ingredients	**Mixing ingredients:** Brainstorming **Measuring ingredients:** Weighing up the facts	Components; mixture of views, talents, experiences or people Where are you playing a vital part?

Symbol	Symbol In Action	Possible Life Issues
	Selecting ingredients: Sorting out details.	Are you being a team-player?
Jelly	**Making jelly:** Forming ideas; needing to be flexible **Jelly that won't set:** Wavering; feeling uncertain; can't stand up for yourself **Jelly crystals:** Needing to materialise your plans.	Solidifies; transparent; obvious; shaky; undecided; unbalanced (wobbles); jell; jelly legs Are you set in your ways? Where are you feeling insecure?
Junk food	See Fast food in this chapter.	
Lamb	See Animals in Chapter 1.	
Leftovers	**Eating leftovers:** Useful old ideas **Throwing out leftovers:** Undervaluing old ideas; discarding what's no longer necessary **Leaving leftovers:** Rejecting the old; no longer relevant.	Obsolete; undesirable; outdated ideas; unnecessary; expendable; rejected; radical position; unwise choice; left-winged; left-handed What ideas have you discarded? Where have you been made redundant?
Lemon	**Eating a lemon:** Sour manner **Serving lemon drinks:** Cold remedy; being conciliatory **Rotting lemons:** Bad situation; deteriorating circumstances.	Softening up; disarm (softens water); smoothing over; cleansing; purifying; zest (adds flavour); defective: lemon What's leaving you with a bitter taste? What's turned bad or is proving useless?
Lettuce	**Eating lettuce:** Purifying your motives **Growing lettuce:** Cleansing your thinking **Throwing out lettuce:** Rejecting healthy attitudes or options.	Cleansing attitudes; clarity; healthy lifestyle Are you looking for fresh ideas? Where are you making healthy choices?
Main course	**Choosing a main course:** Prioritising your values **Eating a main course:** Fulfilling your desires; meeting your needs	Crucial ideas; foundation; central or dominant issues: mainly; impacting What are you digesting? What's giving you the most satisfaction?

Symbol	Symbol In Action	Possible Life Issues
	Leaving some of your main course: Feeling unsatisfied; had enough; unpalatable principles, reasons or issues.	
Meat	**Eating meat:** Living off another; dealing with heavy issues **Bad meat:** Making unhealthy choices **Refusing meat:** Choosing vegetarianism; exercising self-control; rejecting basic urges; showing compassion.	Animal nature, appetites or instincts; physical body; confront; flesh; heavy emotions or issues; sturdy; meaty; meet; meeting Where are you dealing with issues of substance? What are you getting your teeth into? (Also see Steak in this chapter.)
Milk	**Feeding a baby milk:** Nurturing an idea or project **Drinking milk:** Needing to look after yourself; gaining sustenance **Upset at spilling milk:** Needing detachment: crying over spilt milk.	Female energies; compassion; tenderness; caring; sustenance; encouragement; nutritious; baby; colour white; wholesome; milk teeth Are you nurturing yourself or others? Who or what are you supporting?
Nuts	**Cracking nuts open:** Solving a problem: nut it out **Unable to crack open a nut:** Facing a difficult problem: hard nut to crack **Standing on a pile of nuts:** Being enthusiastic: being nuts on.	Defensive (hard-casing); self-defences; embryonic idea; beginning; essence; in a nutshell Where have you got potential? What's proving hard to crack?
Oil	See Oil in Chapter 14.	
Olive	**Picking olives:** Choosing peace **Processing olives:** Working towards peace **Cutting down olive trees:** Undermining peace; dealing with your problems.	Holy Land; peace; wholeness; unripe (green olives); oil; weed; olive branch Where are you offering peace and reconciliation? What's unpalatable and leaves a bitter taste?
Onion	**Peeling an onion:** Getting to the essence of an issue; revealing your deeper emotions	Distinctive qualities or ideas; strong flavour; evokes emotion; emotional; tears; purifying; therapeutic; something smells

Symbol	Symbol In Action	Possible Life Issues
	Selecting one type of onion: Having expertise: know one's onions **Saute onions:** Taking the sting out of a situation.	What are you unravelling? Where are you causing upset?
Orange juice	**Drinking orange juice:** Being positive; needing vitamin C **Squeezing orange juice:** Learning from your experience **Spilling orange juice:** Losing optimism.	Juicy; interesting; colour orange; joy; optimism; vitality; communication Where do you need cooperation? What are you absorbing?
Peanuts	**Eating peanuts:** Limited thinking or opportunities **Growing peanuts:** Receiving little for your efforts: working for peanuts **Shelling peanuts:** Uncovering hidden beliefs or talents; revealing your inner self.	Pittance; trifling issues; inadequate; insufficient; limited; found wanting; unconscious beliefs (ripens underground) Are you feeling undervalued? What do you need to uncover?
Pear	**Eating pears:** Seeing similarities **Growing pears:** Fertile endeavours; doubling its size; joining forces **Spraying a pear tree:** Taking remedial action; things going wrong.	Pair up; twin ideals; partnership; couple; double; twice as much; haywire; going amiss; pair; prepare What's going pear-shaped? Where do you need to consider both sides?
Pepper	**Sprinkling too much pepper:** Overdoing it; going overboard **Using sweet pepper:** Being seductive **Empty pepper container:** Needing passion.	Spicy; enliven; sharpness; bite; quick-tempered; fiery; touchy; peppery What needs spicing up? What's irritating you?
Pineapple	**Eating pineapple:** Having a sweet manner **Cutting a pineapple:** Analysing your feelings **Rotting pineapple:** Unacceptable attitudes or options; undesirable feelings.	Sweetness; affectionate; sweet things in life; palatable; good for constipation and poor digestion; pine; pining What are you longing for? Where are you being sweet and endearing?

Symbol	Symbol In Action	Possible Life Issues
Plum	**Tree full of plums:** Abundance **Ripening plums:** Maturing rewards **Rotting plums:** Irrelevant rewards.	Effortless; well paid; reward; plum job What have you got the best of? Who or what has got the best part of you?
Pomegranate	**Picking pomegranates:** Fertile ideas **Eating pomegranates:** Being open **Rotting pomegranates:** Narrow-mindedness.	Female energies (resembles female reproductive organs); colour red; blood; fertility; productiveness Where are you being receptive? Are you being passive or submissive?
Pudding	**Baking a pudding:** Looking at new ideas **Eating a pudding:** Testing something: proof of the pudding is in the eating **Leftover pudding:** Undesirable outcomes or consequences.	Mixture of ideas; indulgence; just desserts Where are you feeling mixed up? Are you brainstorming with others?
Raisin	**Eating raisins:** Upholding your values **Spilling raisins:** Loss of prosperity **Drying raisins:** Achieving closure: all dried up.	Elevated; preserving the status quo; abundance; increase in size; awakening talents; raise; raising Are you raising the stakes? What are you trying to preserve?
Rice	**Buying rice:** Choosing your values **Cooking rice:** Abundance; increasing your efforts; enhanced opportunities; gaining from your experiences **Spilling rice:** Eroding prosperity.	Fundamentals; foundation; principles (staple food); wealth; abundance; increase in size; putting on an appearance (polished) Where do you need to double your efforts? Are you standing on your principles?
Salad	**Preparing salad:** Having mixed feelings; brainstorming **Serving salad:** Presenting a fresh approach; being cold or unemotional **Tossing salad:** Discarding feelings or ideas.	Wholesome attitudes; feeling cleansed and refreshed; cleansing thoughts; inexperienced youth; salad days Are you looking for fresh ideas? Where are you making healthy choices?

Symbol	Symbol In Action	Possible Life Issues
Salt	**Sprinkling salt on the ground:** Feeling valued: salt of the earth **Salting your food:** Needing to spice up your life; being more passionate **Adding too much salt:** Unusable ideas; contaminated; being too cynical.	Bitter taste or experience; bite; wit; adding flavour; passion for life; cynical attitudes; experience (sailor); stockpiling ideas or resources; salty, salt away, add salt, salt mine Are you being sceptical? What do you want to preserve?
Soft drink	**Drinking soft drink:** Feeling excited or enthusiastic **Shaking a soft drink bottle with the fluid overflowing:** Unable to contain your excitement; releasing your emotions; letting yourself go **Feeling sick after drinking soft drink:** Harmful repressed feelings; recovery.	Bottled-up thoughts and emotions; lighten up (aerated); sparkle; repressed issues; enthusiasm Are you suppressing your emotions? Where do you need to be more bubbly?
Soup	**Making soup:** Combining ideas; having mixed feelings **Serving soup:** Presenting digestible ideas; offering healthy choices **Spilling soup:** Wasted effort.	Association of feelings or ideas; supporting; conducive to health; wellbeing; sustenance; in the soup, soup kitchen Where are you blending with others? Are you in difficulty?
Spice	**Adding spice to your cooking:** Enjoying life; being creative; needing more passion **Adding too much spice:** Needing to settle down; overdoing it **Adding a bit of this spice and a bit of that spice:** Taking the best of what's on offer.	Savouring an experience; excitement; zest; passion; doing things differently; spicy Do you need to spice up your life? What are you attracted to?
Steak	**Ordering steak:** Dealing with heavy issues **Holding a steak up:** Increasing your risk: raise the stakes **Bad steak:** Unwise choice; bad risk.	Substantial matters; meaty issues; your share; your role; risk; finances; stake What have you got a stake in? What's at stake? (Also see Meat in this chapter.)

Symbol	Symbol In Action	Possible Life Issues
Sugar	**Adding sugar to your baking:** Making options more palatable **Adding too much sugar:** Overdoing it **Buying sugar:** Wanting to be liked.	Flattery; bribery; junk food; sweet words; sweet things in life; sweet manner; attraction; sugar daddy; sugar-coat; sugar and spice Are you being endearing? Where are you sweetening others up?
Tea	**Making a pot of tea:** Blending with others; absorbing feelings and ideas **Pouring tea to others:** Offering comfort or compassion; taking time **Offering strong tea:** Forceful opinions.	Caring attitudes; communication; social; soothing ideas; restorative; dependency; addictive feelings or habits; taking time out What's brewing within you? Where are you relating to others?
Vegetables	**Growing vegetables:** Cultivating healthy ideas, approach or lifestyle **Picking vegetables:** Making healthy choices **Cooking vegetables:** Making healthy options more palatable; interfering.	Universal principles (eaten by all); wholesome thinking; fertile ideas; loss of mental faculties: vegetable Have you got fertile ideas? Where aren't you being rational?
Water	**Drinking water:** Cleansing yourself; needing more transparency; purifying your emotions; health warning **Impure water:** Undesirable thoughts or emotions **Spilling water:** Scattering your energies.	Flow of ideas; going with the flow; essence of life; transparency; spiritual refreshment; emotional; urinary system; impervious; unreceptive; watertight; waterworks Where have you reached your high watermark? Are you being emotional?
Wheat	**Reaping wheat:** Yielding results **Cooking bread:** Transforming yourself or your situation; satisfying your needs; needing something **Large wheat crop:** Abundance; successful outcomes.	Foundations; principles (staple food); sustaining; nourishing ideas; fundamentals; crucial issues; wheat belt Where are you being productive? Are you reaping results for your efforts?

Symbol	Symbol In Action	Possible Life Issues
Yeast	**Using yeast in your cooking:** Expanding your thinking; transforming yourself or situation; gaining from your experiences **Failure of yeast to leaven bread:** Unproductive efforts **Spilt yeast:** Lost opportunities.	Transformation; change; lighten up; rise; expansion; abundance; prosperity; enhancement Where are you rising to a challenge? What's fermenting within you?

Common Dream Theme: Eating your favourite food

Enjoying your favourite food can symbolise digesting or analysing your preferred choice or viewpoint. It may also represent a desire or craving for emotional comfort and support or perhaps your need to feel good about yourself.

Chapter 8
Flowers, Plants and Trees

Embrace the purity of the Lotus.
Its soul untainted by the mud.
Meng Haoran

Plants, trees, shrubs or flowers can symbolise growth, renewal, health and healing, cycles of life, timing or the seasons. They can also represent your roots and values, family tree, branching out, attaining heights, abundance, prosperity, love, knowledge or spiritual wisdom. Consider these possible meanings along with any others specifically listed.

How to get the best value from this chapter

- See if you relate to any of the key words or questions and explore your own meanings which may override those given here.
- Look at all possibilities and apply the most appropriate for your situation.
- Rephrase the Life Issue questions to broaden their personal relevance to you, if necessary, by using other words with similar meanings.
- You can also turn any question around (including those you formulate) to see if you relate to them better, by asking them in a slightly different way. For example, rephrase it as a need rather than a desire or belief or vice versa.
- The Symbol in Action examples show how to apply context or link meaning with action.

Desires and needs as opposed to outcomes and results

If a symbol represents an issue you are currently facing, then it may be indicative of your feelings, desires, beliefs or needs. This would usually occur in the first two-thirds of a dream, which often illustrates the issue you are dealing with and how you feel about it.

If a symbol comes in the form of a resolution, outcome, insight, solution or conclusion in the climax, usually at the end of the dream, then it may indicate a consequence, result or your dream advice to you.

Symbol	Symbol In Action	Possible Life Issues
	Look for feelings, desires, needs, beliefs or situations, explore literal meanings, apply any puns and idioms	*Look for where, what and who this reminds you of, apply key words to thoughts, feelings or situations, explore literal meanings, apply word plays and figures of speech*
Acacia	**Receiving acacias:** Self-acceptance **Acacias under your pillow:** Cover up; hiding your true feelings **Planting acacias:** Developing freedom.	Enduring and endless love; devotion; boundless enthusiasm; everlasting values; unlimited possibilities; revered person or idea Do you need to love and accept yourself? Who do you have feelings for?
Ageratum	**Picking ageratums:** Seeking affection **Ageratums in your kitchen:** Harmonious domestic relationships **Dead ageratums:** Lacking compassion.	Purple; mixed feelings (thick clusters of flowers); affection; attachment; harmony; compassion; harmlessness; allegiance; dedication; serenity What are you devoting yourself to? Are you seeking peace or inner peace?
Alyssum	**Planting alyssums:** Cultivating kindness **Giving alyssums to another person:** Giving to others **Alyssum in a vase at your office:** Giving measured support to your colleagues.	Receiving blessings; charm; kindness; sympathy; imaginative; resourceful Where are you being creative? Do you need forgiveness?
Amaranth	**Buying amaranth seeds:** Wanting enthusiasm; valuing keenness and commitment **Extra large amaranths:** Big issue that won't go away **Dead amaranths:** Apathy.	Stable emotions; survival instincts; incessant problems; dynamic; energetic What recurring issues are you dealing with? Where have you got endurance?
Anemone	**Growing anemones:** Embracing change **Anemones in your bedroom:** Revitalising your relationship **Dead anemones:** Stagnation.	Self-transformation; changing feelings; rehabilitation; self-rehabilitation Do you need a make-over? What are you restoring?

Symbol	*Symbol In Action*	*Possible Life Issues*
Apple tree	See Apple in Chapter 7.	
Ash tree	**Planting ash trees:** Developing flexibility; cultivating an image; independence **Several ash trees:** Group image **Dying ash tree:** Neglecting your image.	Flexibility (adaptable to wide climate range); image; keeping up appearances (ornamental); detachment (deciduous); residue; leftovers; ash Where are you picking up the pieces? What do you need to release?
Aster	**Planting aster:** Sowing love and understanding **Cutting back aster:** Loving conditionally **Oversized aster:** Lopsided development; needing to be more practical.	Unconditional love; blessings; charity Where are you showing kindness and goodwill? Are you giving or receiving support?
Azalea	**Picking azaleas:** Taking opportunities; limiting your growth **Azaleas in your bedroom:** Flourishing relationship; small misunderstandings **Dead azaleas:** Stagnation; apathy.	Inner beauty; blooming; thriving; small talk; surface issues (shallow root system); lacking substance; loss of energy (likes humid conditions) Are you being superficial? Do you need to look deeper?
Baby's breath	**Planting baby's breath:** Cultivating inner peace **Vase of baby's breath in your bedroom:** Enriching your relationship **Dead baby's breath:** Feeling unsettled.	Serene; appealing situations or people; sweet character Where are your motives pure? Are you being sweet and endearing?
Banksia	**Planting banksias:** Developing flexibility **Cutting banksias:** Damage control; limited resilience **Banksias in your kitchen:** Difficult domestic circumstances; maintaining family integrity.	Tolerance; ability to bounce back (withstands salty winds); adaptable (grows in sandy soils); tension; difficult circumstances; being firm (stiff flowers); upholding your values (erect canes) Are you being resilient? Where are you holding strongly to your principles?

Symbol	Symbol In Action	Possible Life Issues
Birch tree or shrub	**Planting a birch tree:** Prosperity; developing independence **Several birch trees or shrubs:** Group wealth **Birch tree with no leaves:** Letting go; releasing your feelings.	Abundance (gold autumn foliage and silvery bark); looking inward (thin peeling bark); narrow-mindedness; hard-headed; hard-hearted (hard, close-grained wood); detachment (deciduous) Are you being rigid or inflexible? Do you need to look within?
Bottlebrush	**Picking bottlebrush flowers:** Selecting options; being flexible **Admiring a bottlebrush flower:** Approving of an idea **Dead bottlebrush:** Lacking courage; no rewards.	Adaptable; resilient (salt-tolerant); solid values; sound ideas; simple-minded approach (dense foliage); red; rewards; bottle cleaner; bottle-fed; bottle out; brush off; brush aside; bottle Where are you showing courage? What do you need to brush up on?
Burning bush	**Planting a burning bush:** Seeking new awareness **Being fearful of a burning bush:** Distrusting your intuitions **Dead burning bush:** Rejecting intuitions.	Bright red; inner wisdom: burning bush (bush that burned without being destroyed when God spoke to Moses) Have you experienced a realisation? Do you need to be more spiritual?
Buxus	**Planting buxus:** Becoming creative; gaining authority or influence **Oversized buxus:** Small matters blown out of proportion **Dead buxus:** Stagnation; loss of control.	Fresh and invigorating (evergreen); narrow-mindedness (small); manageable; control (can be trimmed) Where have you got a new sense of purpose? Are you dealing with trivial matters?
Cactus	**Touching cactus:** Feeling hurt **Oversized cactus:** Being too defensive **Dead cactus:** Stagnation; being inflexible.	Self-defences (tough stems and thorns); spring; adaptable (exists in arid regions); perseverance (sticky) Are you being defensive? Where are you facing difficult circumstances?

Symbol	Symbol In Action	Possible Life Issues
Carnation	**Growing carnations:** Feeling gratitude; being content **Receiving carnations:** Experiencing joy **Dead carnations:** Feeling negative; reluctant.	Sparkle; exuberance; happiness; pleasure Where are you being cheerful? Do you need to be more fun-loving?
Carob	**Picking carob:** Abundance; choosing palatable outcomes **Planting carob trees:** Promoting yourself **Dead carob tree:** Unpalatable options.	Digestible ideas (edible pod); sweetness; immune (drought-resistant); self-exposure (likes full sun); fresh and invigorating (evergreen) What are you enduring? Are you enjoying the sweet things in life?
Cedar tree	**Standing under a cedar tree:** Being overshadowed **Climbing a cedar tree:** Using your strength and influence **Dead cedar tree:** Lack of perseverance.	Strength and influence; endurance; mellowing with age (trunk divides after 20-30 years) Are you becoming more flexible? Where do you need to be strong?
Cherry tree (Japanese flowering cherry)	**Climbing a cherry tree:** Making a new beginning **Admiring a cherry tree:** Liking your self image **Dead cherry tree:** Neglecting your image; end of unproductive enterprises.	Appearances; self-image (decorative bark and ornamental); detachment (deciduous); fruitless endeavours (produces no fruit); unused; virginity: cherry What are you doing for the first time? Do you need to let go?
Christmas tree	**Decorating a Christmas tree:** Honouring the spirit **Gifts under a Christmas tree:** Spiritual gifts within you; giving of yourself **Christmas tree that has fallen over:** Questioning your faith; unbalanced views; needing more love and compassion.	Christmas; December; giving and sharing; celebrating; love and compassion; Christ; Christianity Are you thinking of others? Have you had a spiritual awakening?
Chrysan-themums	**Planting chrysanthemums:** New growth	Autumn: fall; autumn of life; rewards; abundance;

Symbol	Symbol In Action	Possible Life Issues
	Receiving chrysanthemums: Accepting rewards	appearances; pretence (showy flowers)
	Dead chrysanthemums: Unacceptance; lack of growth.	Are you reaping results? What's blooming within you?
Citrus tree	**Planting a citrus tree:** Purifying yourself	Medicinal or therapeutic; cleansing thoughts or attitudes;
	Picking fruit off a citrus tree: Needing citrus; being a sour puss	needs attention (some varieties won't crop unless pruned);
	Cutting down a citrus tree: Letting go; cutting loose.	refreshing and invigorating (evergreen) Have you bought a 'lemon'? What's left you with a bitter taste?
Clover	**Picking clover:** Choosing the best options	Good fortune; favourable circumstances; humility; ease and
	Counting clover: Feeling blessed	luxury: in clover Are you being presented with
	Mowing clover: Cutting back.	opportunities? Where are you feeling optimistic?
Columbine	**Planting columbines:** Sowing peace and goodwill	Number five (five spurred petals); serene; peaceful; harmless
	Picking columbines: Choosing inner peace	motives or actions Are you being compassionate?
	Dead columbines: Lack of peace; negativity.	Do you need to calm down?
Cosmos	**Buying cosmos:** Accepting a higher purpose or calling	Recognition (brightly coloured flowers); enjoyment; satisfaction;
	Planting cosmos: Seeking fulfilment	ordered system or process: cosmos
	Dead cosmos: Feeling dissatisfied or unsettled; unable to see the sense in things; feeling anonymous.	Where are you receiving acknowledgment? Are you finding a deeper purpose?
Crabapple tree	**Crabapple tree with no leaves:** Letting go; releasing feelings	Impatient (flowers before leaves emerge); detachment (deciduous); blending of ideas
	Picking crabapples: Choosing fruitful outcomes	(hybrid) Are you being impulsive?
	Crabapple tree with no fruit: Fruitless endeavours.	Where are you being productive?

Symbol	Symbol In Action	Possible Life Issues
Crocus	**Planting crocus:** New growth **Oversized crocus:** Being too ambitious **Dead crocus:** Stagnation; lack of progress.	Developing talents; growing ambitions; new opportunities Where are you thriving? Are you experiencing inner growth?
Cypress tree	**Planting cypress trees:** Putting up defences; developing immunity **Cutting down a cypress tree:** Opening up **Several cypress trees:** Group creativity; collective secrets.	Grieving (branches symbolise mourning); concealed feelings; obscure issues (used for screening); self-defences; protection; fresh and invigorating (evergreen); Cyprus: the island Are you putting up emotional barriers? What are you regretting?
Daffodils	**Daffodils in your office:** Showing your talents at work **Cutting daffodils:** Limiting your development **Dead daffodils:** Feeling negative or despondent.	Colour yellow; brilliant and clever; sunny disposition; radiant; personal growth; pleasure; Wales (national emblem) Are you happy and content? Where are you experiencing inner growth?
Daisy	**Planting daisies:** New ideas **Cutting daisies:** Restricting progress **Dying daisies:** Neglecting details.	Fresh approach; insignificant issues (small, low-growing plant); straightforward and uncomplicated; fresh as a daisy Are you being original? Where are you feeling renewed?
Delphinium	**Planting delphiniums:** Forming attachments; being dedicated; developing reverence **Oversized delphinium:** Being fanatical **Dead delphinium:** Disloyalty; indifference.	Devotion; affection; loyalty; paying homage Are you seeking admiration or acclaim? Where are your allegiances being tested?
Dogwood	**Planting dogwood:** Developing endurance; promoting transparency **Cutting back dogwood:** Limited perception; lacking perseverance	Loveliness; stamina; clarity; purity; naturalness What are you feeling attracted to? Are you showing inner strength?

Symbol	Symbol In Action	Possible Life Issues
	Overgrown dogwood: Neglecting or overemphasising your natural gifts.	
Eucalyptus	**Planting eucalyptus:** Developing inner strength **Climbing a eucalyptus:** Overcoming difficult circumstances **Very old eucalyptus tree:** Tried and tested; well established.	Healing; smoothing things over (produces medicinal oil); sticky situations (generates gum); tough and enduring Where do you need to take remedial action? What are you trying to bring together?
Evergreen alder	**Planting an evergreen alder:** Opportunities for growth **Fallen evergreen alder:** Not meeting your expectations **Chopping an evergreen alder:** Limited growth.	Fresh ideas (evergreen); spring; personal growth; stimulated development (fast-growing); dampened enthusiasm (requires high-moisture environment) Are you making rapid progress? Where are you relevant and up to date?
Fern	**Watering a fern:** Nurturing your creativity **Standing under a giant tree fern:** Aspiring to higher ideals; feeling overshadowed **Being in a fern forest:** Group acceptance.	Discharging your responsibilities; expressing your feelings; generating ideas (reproduces by spores); tranquillity; poise; acquiescence What are you releasing? What do you need to accept?
Fig tree	**Planting figs:** Sowing seeds of success **Collecting figs:** Reaping the fruits of your labour **Fig tree with no fruit:** Fruitless outcomes.	Prosperity; things going pear-shaped (flowers are inside a pear-shaped receptacle); concealment; fig leaf; don't care a fig for your opinion Are you hiding your feelings? Where are your efforts bearing fruit?
Flowers	See Introduction in this chapter.	
Forest	See Buildings and Places in Chapter 4.	
Forget-me-not	**Planting forget-me-nots:** Creating memories	Neglected feelings, obligations or relationships; attachment;

Symbol	Symbol In Action	Possible Life Issues
	Giving forget-me-nots: Wanting to be remembered **Dead forget-me-nots:** Blocking out feelings; being in denial; neglecting relationships.	mateship; nurturing; affection; devotion; forget; forgettable Who or what are you forgetting? What are you leaving behind?
Frangipani tree	**Planting a frangipani:** Developing self-confidence; becoming intuitive **Pruning a frangipani:** Eliminating negativity **Overgrown frangipani tree:** Neglecting your best interest or your health.	Harmful attitudes; health warning (poisonous sap); self-exposure (likes full sun); sense (overpowering scent) Are you promoting yourself? Where are you feeling drained or depleted?
Fuchsia	**Receiving fuchsias:** Welcoming solutions **Fuchsias in your bedroom:** Repairing your relationship **Dead fuchsias:** Being in denial; feeling unsettled; incompatibility.	Peace; compatibility; unity; acceptance; self-resignation; reconciliation Where are you seeking stability or balance? Do you need recognition or approval?
Gardenia	**Planting gardenia:** Increasing distractions; seeking renewal **Cutting gardenia:** Damage control; sharpening your focus; restricted creativity **Dead gardenias:** Rejecting condemnation; lack of innocence.	Invading thoughts and feelings; criticism; inflicting injury (subject to attack by root nematodes); white; purity; fresh ideas; renewal (evergreen) Where are you weak and vulnerable? Are you feeling offended and hurt?
Geranium	**Repotting geraniums:** New growth **Oversized geraniums:** Exaggerating your importance; glamour **Dead geraniums:** Loss of power and influence.	Forging the trail (trailing plant); appealing (attractive flowers); new ideas (grows from cuttings); retaining power and strength (remains in its prime for a few years) Are you trailing behind? Where are you thriving?
Gladiolus	**Planting gladiolus:** Developing optimism **Cutting gladiolus:** Repressing your talents; denying happiness	Joyous; sunny disposition; brilliant and clever (brightly coloured flowers); glad Where are you standing out?

Symbol	*Symbol In Action*	*Possible Life Issues*
	Dead gladiolus: Feeling negative or despondent.	Do you need to cheer up?
Gum tree	**Climbing a gum tree:** Showing power and determination; overcoming obstacles **Very old gum tree:** Enduring; well established **Dead gum tree:** Giving up.	Smoothing things over (yields oil); Australia (most well-known tree); strength and endurance (hard, durable timber); fresh ideas (evergreen); gummed up; up a gum tree Are you seeking renewal? Where are you showing inner strength?
Hedge	**Planning where to plant a hedge:** Self-discipline **Pruning a hedge:** Managing your limitations **Dying hedge:** Neglecting your security; bringing things out into the open.	Boundaries; confining circumstances; frontiers; immunity; cover; self-defence; concealment Are you putting up emotional barriers? Do you limit yourself?
Hibiscus	**Planting hibiscus:** Developing skills **Hibiscus in your office:** Showing great potential; needing to pace yourself at work **Dead hibiscus:** Neglecting your gifts.	Exceptional talent; glamour (exotic blooms); ornate; self-confidence; China (country of origin); nurturing (requires warmth and humidity); short-lived goals or aspirations (flowers die quickly) Do you need to take care of yourself? Where are you being showy or flamboyant?
Holly	**Decorating a Christmas tree with holly:** Honouring your spirit; putting things in a positive light **Wearing holly:** Coming out; owning your sexuality **Giving away holly:** Letting go; being open.	Imitation; pretence (used as decoration); self-defences (prickly edges); stinging comments; Christmas; gender issues (male and female flowers develop on separate trees) Do you need to be true to yourself? Are you being defensive?
Horse chestnut	**Planting horse chestnuts:** Gaining wisdom or understanding	Unpalatable (inedible nuts); rhythm; vitality (treatment for respiratory disease in horses);

Symbol	Symbol In Action	Possible Life Issues
	Picking horse chestnuts: Unpleasant options; unacceptable outcomes **Dead horse chestnut:** Lack of enthusiasm; apathy.	enlightenment (candle-like flowers); fanning your passions (fan-like leaves) What can't you accept? Do you need to catch your breath?
Hydrangeas	**Watering hydrangeas:** Continued abundance; feeding your idiosyncrasies **Cutting hydrangeas:** Damage control **Dead hydrangeas:** Lack of abundance.	Abundance (large flower clusters); flourishing; eccentric qualities; breaks down easily (flaky, wooden canes) Where are you thriving? Are you experiencing growth?
Impatiens	**Growing impatiens:** Growing impatience; developing determination **Receiving impatiens:** Being focused; adopting goals; someone being impatient towards you **Dead impatiens:** Having patience; lacking purpose.	Resolve; purpose; feeling restless; easily irritated; impatience Do you need to show unconditional love? Are you being impulsive?
Iris	**Receiving irises:** Using discrimination **Irises in your bedroom:** Strong relationship **Dead irises:** Ignoring your instincts; accepting people on face value.	Communicating; go-between (Goddess of the Rainbow, messenger in myth); strength; skill; vision; discerning; foresight; insight Where are you being perceptive? Are you being intuitive?
Jacaranda tree	**Planting a jacaranda:** Slowing down; being fair and reasonable **Shading under a jacaranda:** Avoiding issues; taking time out **Upturned jacaranda:** Reacting too strongly; going over the top; feeling exposed or vulnerable.	Relaxation (lavender); moderation; gentle; self-restraint (lives in temperate regions) What do you need to release? Where are you exercising self-control?
Japanese maple	**Planting a Japanese maple:** Being tolerant; open-minded **Upturned Japanese maple:** Unable to defend yourself; feeling exposed or vulnerable **Dead Japanese maple:** Having	Grace; diverse views or opinions (many different colours); feeling saturated (needs moist conditions); self-protection (needs to be sheltered from full sun); Japan; Japanese

Symbol	Symbol In Action	Possible Life Issues
	a closed mind; intolerant; lack of decorum and tact.	Are you accepting of others? Do you need to look after yourself?
Jasmine	**Planting jasmine:** Finding inner peace **Wearing jasmine:** Being poised and composed **Dead jasmine:** Being unco-operative; conflict.	Therapeutic; beneficial; corrective actions; tranquillity; harmony; cooperation Do you need to take remedial action? Where are you choosing healthy options?
Larkspur	**Receiving larkspur:** Being acknowledged or accepted **Larkspur in your office:** Anomalies at work **Dead larkspur:** Feeling discouraged; trapped; being cautious.	Irregularities (irregular spurred flowers); elation; appreciation; encouragement; impulsive; spur, spur of the moment Where are you spurring yourself, or others, on? Are you being spontaneous?
Laurel	**Looking at a laurel:** Defending your position: look to one's laurels **Cutting a laurel:** Not using your talents **Deal laurel:** Feeling bored; stagnating.	Fresh ideas; renewal (evergreen); feeling satisfied; fame or victory; protection Are you resting on your laurels? Where are you standing out?
Lavender	**Growing lavender:** Feeling calm; inner peace **Drying lavender:** Defending your values **Dead lavender:** Feeling unsettled.	Soothing; tranquillity; relief; provider (source of oil); ambitions; hopes; purity; innocence; virtue Do you need to be more relaxed? Are you smoothing things over?
Lemon-scented verbena	**Drinking lemon-scented verbena tea:** Health recom-mendation to aid digestion and blocked sinuses; digesting ideas **Cutting lemon-scented verbena:** Cutting loose **Dying lemon-scented verbena:** Ignoring irrelevant matters.	Trivial issues (insignificant flowers); pungent comments (very aromatic); tenuous position; slim chance (slender, rough foliage) Are you being overlooked? What looks unlikely?

Symbol	Symbol In Action	Possible Life Issues
Lilac tree	**Planting a lilac tree:** Being intuitive **Oversized lilac tree:** Acting aloof **Dead lilac tree:** Rejecting others' opinions.	France (country of origin); diverse views (multi-stemmed); sense of something (scented flowers); being reserved (prefers cool climate); detachment (deciduous); colours purple and white What do you need to release? Where are you respecting others?
Lily	**Receiving lilies:** New opportunities **Giving lilies to another:** Showing goodwill **Dead lilies:** Rejecting your values.	Convictions; acting in good faith; innocence; new beginnings; alert (bell-shaped flowers); female name: Lily Are you standing on principle? What's ringing alarm bells?
Lilly pilly tree	**Planting a lilly pilly tree:** Showing love and kindness **Picking fruits from a lilly pilly tree:** Reaping rewards **Dead lilly pilly tree:** Not learning; no growth.	Love (new growth is pink); fresh ideas; renewal (evergreen); gaining from your experience (grown from seed developed from ripe fruits) Where are you showing love? What's evolving?
Lotus	**Buying a lotus flower:** Balancing inner awareness with outer responsibilities **Glowing lotus:** Soul **Pool of lotuses:** Collective spiritual awareness; abundant spiritual gifts.	Forgetfulness (in Greek myth); sacred knowledge; inner strength; soul (roots in the mud, flower on the surface); unfolding awareness; lotus position Are you seeking inner wisdom? Where do you need to keep your poise and stay focused?
Magnolia tree	**Planting a magnolia tree:** Being flexible **Several magnolia trees:** Group versatility **Dying magnolia tree:** Rejecting others' opinions.	Protracted issues; delays (fairly slow growing); diversity of views (assorted shapes, sizes and habitats); adaptable Where are you making slow progress? What's proving time-consuming?
Maple tree	**Planting a maple tree:** Developing stamina **Being unable to pick up maple leaves:** Can't get a grasp on things	Strength; endurance; inflexibility (hard wood); detachment (deciduous); twin issues; new partnership (winged seeds borne in pairs); handout (leaves are

Symbol	*Symbol In Action*	*Possible Life Issues*
	Dead maple tree: Lack of determination.	shaped like an open hand) Are you showing inner strength? What do you need to release?
Marigold	**Planting marigolds:** Seeking acceptance or acknowledgment **Giving marigolds to another:** Showing love or inner strength; accepting others **Dead marigolds:** Being overlooked; negativity.	Recognition; sweetness (strong fragrant scent); affection; boldness; fortitude Where are you building bonds? Are you standing out?
Mistletoe	**Mistletoe in a gum tree:** Depleting your energy; weakened resolve **Hanging mistletoe on a Christmas tree:** Presenting yourself in a good light; honouring the spirit **Dead mistletoe:** Rejecting undesirable qualities; keeping an old belief system.	Feeding off others; sapping your strength (parasite); fresh ideas (evergreen); Christmas; Druidism; non-appearances (decoration) Where are you taking without giving? What are you trying to make more appealing?
Morning glory	**Planting morning glory:** Creating new openings; new growth **Buying morning glory:** Taking new opportunities **Dead morning glory:** Lack of progress.	Announcement (trumpet-shaped flowers); new beginnings (flowers close in the afternoon); daily occurrences; cyclic events; morning; morning after What's happening on a regular basis? Where are you making plans?
Mulberry	**Picking mulberries:** Reaping rewards **Mulberry tree with no leaves:** Letting go **Dead mulberry tree:** Being open.	Dark purple; emotional; protection; self-defences (good canopy of heavy shade); detachment (deciduous) What's proving fruitful? Where are you protecting yourself?
Narcissus	**Miniature narcissus:** Beginnings of vanity or pride **Oversized narcissus:** Very arrogant or self-satisfied **Dead narcissus:** Rejecting conceit.	Self-centredness; pride; arrogance; flattering yourself (in Greek myth, a youth fell in love with his own reflection) Have you got an inflated sense of self-importance?

Symbol	Symbol In Action	Possible Life Issues
		Are you being conceited or arrogant?
Nasturtium	**Wild nasturtiums:** Simple pleasures **Oversized nasturtiums:** Not taking things seriously **Dead nasturtiums:** Feeling unfulfilled; needing to express yourself.	Pleasure; satisfaction; light-heartedness; announcement (trumpet-shaped flowers) Where are you happy and content? Are you blowing your own trumpet?
Oak tree	**Standing under an oak tree:** Seeking refuge; taking time out **Climbing an oak tree:** Overcoming difficulties; mounting resilience **Dead oak tree:** Running away from difficulties; unable to prevail.	Strength; endurance (hard, durable timber); demanding situations; being held back; protracted negotiations; slow progress (slow-growing); male gender issues (showy male catkins) Are you being inflexible? What's proving to be time-consuming?
Olive tree	See Olive in Chapter 7.	
Orchid	**Receiving orchids:** Feeling valued; making amends **Giving orchids to another:** Being supportive **Dead orchids:** Underestimating the importance of something.	Delicate issues; diplomacy; compassion; serene; exceptional circumstances; significant moments Are you dealing with something out of the ordinary? What needs handling with care?
Palm tree	**Planting a palm tree:** Sowing the seeds of success; developing deceit **Standing under a giant palm:** Being overshadowed or intimidated **Dying palm tree:** Turning your back on success.	Success; beating the odds; gaining merit (symbol for victory); single-mindedness (unbranched trunk); deception; palm; palm off Who do you have in the palm of your hand? Do you need to branch out?
Pansies	**Admiring pansies:** Smoothing things over **Buying pansies:** Expressing your feminine side (communication; intuition and feelings)	Sweet-tempered; merciful; quiet (velvety petals); feminine qualities or energies; progressing smoothly; homosexuality: pansy

Symbol	*Symbol In Action*	*Possible Life Issues*
	Dead pansies: Lack of progress.	Are you being passive or compliant? Where are you dealing with gender issues?
Pear tree (Manchurian)	**Planting a pear tree:** Cultivating appearances; developing tolerance **Cutting back a pear tree:** Cutting your losses; limited flexibility **Dead pear tree:** Neglecting your image.	White; purity; innocence; broad-minded (tolerates poor soil); embellishing the facts (ornamental tree); image without substance; fruitless endeavours (produces no fruit) Are you being unproductive? What's going pear-shaped?
Pepper tree	**Planting a pepper tree:** Getting involved with others **Several pepper trees:** Group complexities **Dead pepper tree:** Stagnation; simplicity.	Grace; fresh ideas; renewal (evergreen); sorrow (weeping foliage); entangled relationships (rough and twisted trunk) What are you regretting? Where are you feeling renewed?
Petunia	**Planting petunias:** Feeling optimistic **Giving petunias:** Getting on with others **Dead petunias:** Incompatibility; conflict.	Tranquillity; compatibility; friendliness; reconciliation; bright Are you cooperating with others? Where are you showing goodwill?
Pine tree	**Planting pine trees:** Being flexible **Giant pine tree:** Well established; tenacious **Dead pine tree:** Stagnation; intolerance; giving up.	Digestible ideas (edible pine nuts); fresh ideas; renewal (evergreen); endurance (tolerates coastal conditions); pine Are you being resilient? What are you pining for?
Pittosporum	**Planting pittosporum:** Being defensive **Cutting back pittosporum:** Being open **Dead pittosporum:** Feeling vulnerable.	Protection; cover up; concealed feelings (screening shrub); immune; tough-minded (salt-resistant) Are you putting up emotional barriers? Where are you standing firm?
Plane tree	**Planting a plane tree:** Developing independence; open-mindedness	High ideals (grows to 30 metres); appealing (attractive park tree); detachment (deciduous); tolerant

Symbol	Symbol In Action	Possible Life Issues
	Plane tree with no leaves: Releasing your feelings; feeling exposed **Dead plane tree:** Intolerance; narrow-mindedness.	(to pollution); plain; plane; aeroplane Are you being adaptable? Where are you smoothing things over?
Plants	See Introduction in this chapter.	
Plumbago	**Planting plumbago:** New goals and plans **Receiving plumbago:** Self-discipline **Dead plumbago:** Being way off the mark; emotional instability; ignoring your intuition.	Inner alignment; sense of direction; inner purpose; straightforward issues; controlling your desires (needs pruning); plum Do you need to straighten yourself out? Do you know where you're going?
Pomegranate	See Pomegranate in Chapter 7.	
Poplar tree	**Poplar tree without leaves:** Feeling exposed; releasing your feelings; autumn of your life **Cutting down poplar trees:** Self-discipline **Dead poplar tree:** Rejecting negativity or popularity.	Sensitivities (light, soft wood); autumn; twilight years; sapping energy (suckering root system); aggressive; appearances (specimen tree for parks); sought after; popular Where are you feeling drained? Are you taking from others?
Poppies	**Planting poppies:** Growing dependence **Poppies floating in the air:** Discarded addictions **Dead poppies:** Rejected dependencies.	Sapped energy (produces milky sap); addictive tendencies (opium poppies); stimulation Where are you feeling dependent? Do you need inspiration and motivation?
Privet	**Planting privets:** Showing leadership **Cutting privets:** Limiting yourself **Dead privets:** Rejecting negativity.	Fresh ideas (evergreen); pest; negativity (seeds congest natural bushland); white (flowers); managing situations (used as clipped hedges); hedging your bets; doing an about-face; important role; pivot What's annoying you? Are you in control?

Symbol	Symbol In Action	Possible Life Issues
Pulling weeds	See Common Dream Theme at the end of this chapter.	
Redwood tree	**Standing under a giant redwood tree:** Feeling overawed **Redwood forest:** Group wisdom; collective poise **Dying redwood tree:** Lacking integrity.	Big obstacles or opportunities (huge tree); strength of character; endurance (durable timber); ancient knowledge Are you facing an enormous challenge? Where are you showing moral fibre?
Roots	**Digging up roots:** Questioning your value system; looking into the unconscious **Exposed roots:** Feeling exposed and vulnerable **Luminous roots:** Spiritual beliefs or values; spiritual connections; brilliant ideas; awareness.	Belief; value system; family origins; background; inner self; unconscious connections; links to others; interdependence; take root; rooted out Where are you trying to establish yourself? What's fixed or inflexible?
Rose	**Planting roses:** Sowing love and forgiveness **Receiving roses:** Being loved; needing to love yourself **Roses in your bedroom:** Loving relationship.	Comfort; secret affection; attachment; devotion; radiance; loveliness; beauty; inclusiveness; irritable (prickly stems); bed of roses; under the rose Who or what do you have feelings for? Do you need to show unconditional love?
Sassafras	**Planting sassafras:** Finding solutions **Fallen-over sassafras:** Unsuccessful healing outcomes **Dead sassafras:** Dishonourable motives; causing problems; apathy.	Therapeutic; remedial action; dignified; zest; spirit (used as flavouring essence); reducing friction or conflict (produces oil) What's impressive or imposing? Are you smoothing things over?
Shrubs	See Introduction in this chapter.	
Snapdragon	**Picking snapdragons:** Cutting yourself off; being reserved **Vase of snapdragons in your office:** Relying on your instincts at work	Intuition; communication; psychic awareness Do you need to express yourself or open up? Are you being intuitive?

Symbol	Symbol In Action	Possible Life Issues
	Dying snapdragon: Waning intuition; poor communication.	
Star of Bethlehem	**Planting star of Bethlehem:** Developing strength of character **Vase of star of Bethlehem in your kitchen:** Teaching values at home **Dying star of Bethlehem:** Lacking innocence or purity.	Innocence; honourable; distinguished; star Where are you standing out? Do you need integrity?
Sunflower	**Paddock full of sunflowers:** Abundance; group goodwill **Vase of sunflowers in your office:** Ironing out tensions at work **Cutting a sunflower:** Feeling negative; seeking positivity.	Sunny disposition; digesting ideas (edible seeds); smoothing things over (produces oil); wealth; yellow What's looking hopeful and positive? Where do you need to be optimistic?
Thistle	**Walking through thistles:** Tackling adversity; group maliciousness **Pulling thistles:** Overcoming obstacles **Oversized thistle:** Exaggerated problem.	Impenetrable situation; simple-minded approach or outlook (dense flower heads); stinging comments; Scotland (national emblem) Are you being prickly and defensive? What's proving difficult and challenging?
Thorn bush	**Being hurt by a thorn bush:** Being upset by difficulties; hurting yourself **Planting a thorn bush:** Creating problems **Dead thorn bush:** Overcoming difficulties; releasing emotional pain; rejecting criticism.	Complicated issues; difficult situations; inhibitions; emotional blocks; stinging comments; thorn; thorn in your side Are you feeling irritated or annoyed? What are you getting tangled up in?
Trees	See Introduction in this chapter.	
Tulip	**Planting tulips:** Cultivating fairness and tolerance **Buying tulips:** Acquiring confidence or faith	Open-minded (broad, pointed leaves); contentment; pleasure; trust; confidence; benevolence Where are you giving to others

Symbol	*Symbol In Action*	*Possible Life Issues*
	Dead tulips: Being narrow-minded; rejecting openness.	or giving of yourself? Are you confident and optimistic?
Violet	**Receiving a bunch of violets:** Broadening your thinking **Violets in your office:** Avoiding issues at work; needing to speak up **Dead violets:** Being conventional; narrow-minded.	Timid; avoidance; warm-hearted; unconventional (irregular showy petals); colour violet Where are you being different? Are you being passive or compliant?
Waratah tree	**Planting waratahs:** Becoming self-defensive **Flowering waratah:** Enlightenment; inner wisdom **Fallen over waratah:** Unreliable feelings.	Deep red; wisdom with age (flowerhead opens and broadens with age); covering; protective (large canopy) What are you concealing? Are you suppressing your feelings?
Water hyacinth	**Water hyacinth in a stream:** Feeling obstructed; emotional blockages **Giant water hyacinth:** Growing vanity or negativity **Dead water hyacinth:** Rejecting arrogance.	Drifting along (floats); self-importance (swollen leaf stalks); stifling or contaminating others (takes over) What ideas are you floating? Are you dominating others?
Waterlily	**Admiring waterlilies:** Wanting to take life as it comes; seeking stillness and acceptance **Waterlilies covering the surface of a pond:** Taking things on face value **Buying waterlilies:** Finding inner peace and contentment.	Surface issues; superficial approach (floats on the surface); calmness Do you need to go with the flow? Are you looking for inner peace?
Wattle	**Flowering wattle:** Success; thriving **Several wattle trees:** Group uncertainty **Dead wattle:** Lacking tact or diplomacy.	Delicate issues; subtle concepts; high quality (fine timber); adaptable (flexible branches); vulnerable (prone to attack by wood-boring insects); yellow Are you being cultured? Do you feel insecure?

Symbol	Symbol In Action	Possible Life Issues
Wildflowers	**Picking wildflowers:** Using your natural talents **Walking through wildflowers:** Suppressing your gifts or talents **Wildflowers dying out:** Ignoring your instincts.	Being spontaneous; intuition; unconscious beliefs; random occurrences; nature's gifts; disordered thinking; wild What's coming to you naturally? What can't you contain?
Willow	**Planting willow trees:** Being intrusive **Pruning a willow tree:** Limiting distractions; cutting back **Dead willow tree:** Rejecting corruption.	Grace; slender hopes; intruding thoughts; violation (large invasive root system); distorted words; corrupt motives (twisted stems); weeping willow; weep; willowy Are you grieving or regretting? What's getting distorted?
Yew	**Planting yew:** Having power and influence **Wood chopped up from yew tree:** Supporting others; lacking strength **Uprooted yew:** Feeling exposed or vulnerable.	Give and take; adaptable; quick to recover (elastic wood); strength; endurance; you Are you stretching yourself? Where are you being flexible?
Zinnia	**Planting zinnias:** Feeling happy and cheerful **Buying zinnias:** Gaining satisfaction and fulfilment **Dying zinnias:** Being reserved; feeling dissatisfied; lack of perception.	Brilliant and clever; showy; radiant; attractive; contentment; pleasure (brightly coloured flowers) Are you standing out or being unique? Where are you being optimistic?

Common Dream Theme: Pulling weeds

Dreaming of pulling weeds can symbolise weeding out undesirable thoughts, feelings or habits. It may indicate your wish to pull out of areas of your life where you are struggling, or your need to stop depriving others.

Chapter 9
Gemstones and Metals

Gems are ... energy in crystalline form.
Harish Johari

Gemstones and metals can symbolise particular energies that you need to work with to achieve balance, growth and healing in your life. Their colours can also be significant (see Chapter 5 on colours). They can also represent something pure and precious, intrinsically valuable or the transmission, or need for transmission, of energies. Consider these possible meanings with any others specifically listed.

How to get the best value from this chapter

- See if you relate to the questions or healing qualities associated with each gemstone or metal. Explore your own meanings which may override those given here.
- Look at all possibilities and apply the most appropriate for your situation.
- Rephrase the questions to broaden their personal relevance to you, if necessary, by using other words with similar meanings.
- You can also turn any question around (including those you formulate) and see if you relate to them better, by asking them in a slightly different way. For example, rephrase it as a need rather than a desire or belief or vice versa.

Desires and needs as opposed to outcomes and results

If a symbol represents an issue you are currently facing, then it may be indicative of your feelings, desires, beliefs or needs. This would usually occur in the first two-thirds of a dream, which often illustrates the issue you are dealing with and how you feel about it.

If a symbol comes in the form of a resolution, outcome, insight, solution or conclusion in the climax, usually at the end of the dream, then it may indicate a consequence, result, or your dream advice to you.

Symbol	Questions to Ask Yourself	Symbolises These Healing Qualities
	You can rephrase these questions, if necessary, using other words with similar meanings to expand their personal relevance	*Look for needs, where you express these qualities, or their presence within you (even if not fully recognised)*
Agate (Moss Agate) Agate with branching forms included	Are you feeling discordant or out of tune?	Grounding yourself Linking with nature.
Alexandrite Translucent, changes colour from green to red under different light	Do you need to change?	Spiritual insight Physical and spiritual rejuvenation.
Amazonite Translucent blue-green	Are you getting irritated and annoyed?	Calmness Improve communication.
Amber Resinous; translucent golden yellow	Are you struggling and being resistant?	Acceptance, calmness and compliance.
Amethyst Clear to translucent purple	Do you feel powerless and impotent?	Strength and transformation Peace and poise.
Angelite Opaque pale blue	Are your feelings getting the better of you?	Clear communication Open and self-expressive.
Aquamarine Clear to translucent light blue-green to blue	Are you tempted to indulge your feelings and desires?	Courage and moderation Assists eyes and throat chakra.
Aventurine Opaque, medium to dark green	Where are you lacking confidence?	Centred and independent Connecting with others.

Symbol	Questions to Ask Yourself	Symbolises These Healing Qualities
Azurite Rich, deep, ultramarine blue	Where are you being indecisive?	Creativity Intuitive awareness.
Black tourmaline Solid black crystal with striped texture	Are you feeling negative?	Positive outlook Guarding against outside negative influences.
Bloodstone Opaque green with red spots and markings	Are you scared and intimidated?	Courage and determination.
Blue lace agate Light blue with white bands in lacy pattern	Are you being intolerant and inflexible?	Patience, compassion and composure Assists thyroid gland and throat chakra.
Calcite Clear and subtle pink or green gemstone	Are you feeling aimless and lacking purpose?	Directing your energies Connecting with your source.
Carnelian Red to rich red-orange	Are your feelings getting out of hand?	Calmness Promoting love and interaction with others.
Cat's eye Chrysoberyl Clear to yellow, yellow-green	Where are you being open or taking others' problems to heart?	Emotional protection Assists eye and nervous system disorders.
Celestite Various translucent colours; pale blue more valued	Where are you afraid to speak up?	Speak the truth Being true to yourself.
Charoite Opaque, rich purple often mixed with white swirling texture	Are you confused?	Staying focused Cleanses the liver.

Symbol	Questions to Ask Yourself	Symbolises These Healing Qualities
Chrysocolla Opaque, swirling blue and green	Are you feeling blocked and uninspired?	Joy and creative self-expression Communication Aids digestion.
Chrysoprase Opaque to translucent bright apple green	Are you suppressing your feelings or feeling unloved?	Being open and loving Open-mindedness.
Cinnabar Bright orange-red	Do you submit and comply readily to others?	Persuasiveness Self-assertive.
Citrine Translucent golden yellow quartz	Are you feeling fearful and negative?	Attuned to your source Dwell on abundance.
Copper Metallic orange-pink	Do you feel inhibited and restricted?	Going with the flow Being sensual.
Copper pyrite Brassy metallic yellow	Are you feeling lost?	Intuitive awareness.
Diamond Usually brilliant clear	Are you questioning your true worth?	Valuing yourself and inner strength Personal integrity.
Dioptase Rich deep green with hint of blue	Are you feeling emotionally insecure?	Courage and strength Stabilises the nervous system.
Emerald Bright transparent green	Are you confused or undecided?	Intelligence Discernment.
Fire agate Semi-translucent dark orange with iridescent flashes	Are you frustrated and underachieving?	Expressing your full potential Transforming undesirable qualities.

Symbol	Questions to Ask Yourself	Symbolises These Healing Qualities
Fluorite Bright clear translucent colours in the same stone	Are you confused or distracted?	Concentration, focus and decisiveness Aids meditation.
Fuchsite Silvery pale green	Have you got rigid views and opinions?	Clarity and flexibility Open-mindedness.
Garnet Very dark red	Do you feel sapped of energy and strength?	Vitality and enthusiasm Connect with your source Stimulates pituitary gland.
Gold Bright metallic golden yellow	Have you got ulterior motives?	Purity and perfection Aim for universal goals.
Heliodor/ Golden Beryl Bright golden translucent yellow	Are you feeling fearful or insecure?	Confidence and initiative Intuitive awareness.
Hematite Shiny metallic dark grey, high iron content	Are you solving problems?	Clarity, will and courage Assists blood disorders and bone strength.
Herkimer Diamond Short, clear, double-ended quartz crystal	Are you feeling disconnected and uninspired?	Intuitive awareness Looking within.
Iolite Translucent blue violet	Where can't you see your way forward?	Vision and foresight.
Iron Dark iron grey	Are you being inefficient and ineffective?	Practicality and strength Encouraging masculine energies.
Jade Usually solid green, also white	Are you feeling confused and agitated?	Inner peace and wisdom.

Symbol	Questions to Ask Yourself	Symbolises These Healing Qualities
Jasper Opaque, rich, red-orange to orange-brown	Are you being negative?	Positive thoughts and self-protection Assists liver, gall bladder and bladder.
Kunzite Semi-translucent pale pink	Are you feeling unsettled or agitated?	Inner peace and love Calmness and tranquillity.
Kyanite Translucent to clear blue-violet with turquoise flash	Are you having trouble connecting with others?	Clear and open communication.
Labradorite Semi-translucent grey with blue iridescence	Are you facing a transition?	Clarity, trust and vision Keep your poise.
Lodolite Clear quartz with inclusions 'growths'	Are you being negative?	Emotional and mental protection.
Magnetite (Lode stone) Metallic iron black, often magnetic	Where are you stuck or facing emotional barriers?	Endurance and perseverance Strive for openness.
Malachite Bright, banded green	Are you dissatisfied and unsettled?	Contentment or transformation Show or develop gratitude.
Moonstone Translucent milky sheen. Blue-white to pale golden tinge	Do you seek guidance and direction?	Calm awareness Enhance communication and reflection.
Obsidian Usually solid shiny black	Are you being imaginary or visionary?	Ground yourself Link with nature.

Symbol	Questions to Ask Yourself	Symbolises These Healing Qualities
Opal Encompassing all colours	Do you have worldly goals and ambitions?	Broad awareness Intuition.
Pearl Usually white-cream, also iridescent grey	Are you being irritated?	Purity and wisdom Encourage feminine energies.
Peridot Clear to translucent yellow-green	Are you feeling caught in a rut?	Accepting and growing through transitions.
Prehnite Semi-translucent resinous, pale yellow-green	Are you condemning or judging others?	Forgiveness, compassion and acceptance.
Pyrite Metallic pale gold	Do you feel uncertain or are you faltering in your purpose?	Determination, confidence and optimism Courage.
Rhodonite Pink to rose-red with black veins throughout	Do you expect love in return for your actions?	Unconditional love Connecting with your source.
Rock Crystal Clear, transparent quartz	Do you feel vulnerable and misunderstood?	Power, strength and communication Purification.
Rose quartz Light pink	Are you angry or feeling under-valued?	Compassion, tranquillity and poise Building a sense of self and self-esteem.
Ruby Transparent, vivid red	Are you bored or feeling uninspired?	Stimulation, motivation and power Assists blood circulation.
Rutilated quartz Clear quartz with needle-like inclusions	Are you lacking or needing inspiration?	Intuitive awareness Assists brain function and the immune system.

Symbol	Questions to Ask Yourself	Symbolises These Healing Qualities
Sapphire Usually clear, brilliant, deep blue	Are you feeling negative or open to negative influences?	Intuition, awareness and joy Prosperity and wellbeing.
Sardonyx Bands of tan and reddish brown–cream layers	Are you feeling inferior or inadequate?	Virtue, honour and devotion Developing stability.
Selenite Clear to white, silky texture	Do you feel bewildered or confused?	Clarity, intuition and awareness.
Silver Shiny, pale grey metal	Have you expressed your feelings openly without due regard for others?	Integrity, honesty and modesty.
Smoky quartz Clear, light smoky grey to dark smoky grey and black	Are your appetites getting out of balance?	Stabilising or adjusting sexual energies Harmonising body and mind.
Sodalite Opaque blue with white streaks	Are you feeling tense and fearful?	Clarity, courage and composure Lighten up.
Staurolite Metallic red-brown to yellow-brown	Where are you dealing with past issues?	Acceptance and resolution.
Sugilite Opaque dark purple to purple-pink	Are you restricted or isolated?	Freedom, cooperation and inspiration.
Sunstone Dark orange with glittering reflections	Where are you grieving or feeling despondent?	Joy, enthusiasm and vitality.

Symbol	Questions to Ask Yourself	Symbolises These Healing Qualities
Tanzanite Transparent pale blue to purple	Do you have worldly goals and ambitions?	Intuitive awareness Assists the throat and 'third eye'.
Tiger iron Silky dark warm red	Are you lacking endurance?	Physical stamina and strength Strengthens the blood.
Tiger's eye Silky yellow and golden brown	Are you feeling inadequate or ineffective?	Grounding yourself Discernment.
Topaz Blue topaz or golden topaz	Do you feel powerless and undervalued?	Success, creativity and strength Love and inspiration.
Tourmaline Clear to translucent red, pink, green, blue	Do you feel rejected or regretful?	Love, understanding and compassion.
Valuables	See Common Dream Theme.	

Common Dream Theme: Finding or losing valuables

Finding valuables in your dreams can symbolise discovering, uncovering or regaining hidden talents, spiritual qualities within you, treasured memories, profitable ventures or desired solutions. Looking for valuables could represent your desire or search for these. Losing valuables could indicate their absence, disappearance or your hunger for them. Perhaps you're feeling diminished in some way, losing ground or status, feeling vulnerable and insecure or needing to re-evaluate an issue.

Chapter 10
Human Actions

To see your drama clearly is to be liberated from it.
Ken Keyes

Actions are very revealing because they show what you are doing in a dream and how you are responding to the unfolding dream story. They provide context by showing how you react to the symbol, whether you welcome it, choose to run away from it, feel threatened by it or explore it further. Ask yourself the questions listed in this chapter that relate to the action in your dream.

How to get the best value from this chapter

- See if you relate to any of the questions and explore your own meanings which may override those given here.
- Look at all possibilities and apply the most appropriate for your situation.
- Rephrase the questions to broaden their personal relevance to you, if necessary, by using other words with similar meanings.
- You can also turn any question around (including those you formulate) to see if you relate to them better, by asking them in a slightly different way. For example, rephrase it as a need rather than a desire or belief or vice versa.

Desires and needs as opposed to outcomes and results

If a symbol represents an issue you are currently facing, then it may be indicative of your feelings, desires, beliefs or needs. This would usually occur in the first two-thirds of a dream, which often illustrates the issue you are dealing with and how you feel about it.

If a symbol comes in the form of a resolution, outcome, insight, solution or conclusion in the climax, usually at the end of the dream, then it may indicate a consequence, result or your dream advice to you.

Action	Symbolism	Questions to Ask Yourself
	Look for feelings, desires, needs, beliefs or situations, explore literal meanings, apply any puns and idioms	*Look for feelings, desires, needs, beliefs or situations. You can rephrase these questions, if necessary, by using other words with similar meanings*
Abandoning	Avoiding responsibilities; letting go.	Where are you being irresponsible? What are you giving up?
Abducting	See Kidnapping in this chapter.	
Aborting	Killing off a part of yourself; miscarriage of justice; eliminating negativity.	What are you terminating? What's proving futile or unsuccessful?
Acting	Wanting to be noticed; pretence; putting on appearances; roles you play. (Also see Common Dream Theme in Chapter 13.)	Are you putting on an act? Where are you being misleading?
Announcing	Declaring your intentions; making yourself clear; seeking recognition.	What are you representing or standing for? What do you want others to know?
Applauding	Receiving acknowledgment; encouraging others.	What are you approving of? Who are you admiring or what are you aspiring to?
Arguing	Venting hidden feelings; opposing others; needing to convince yourself or others.	Are you questioning yourself? What do you need to prove?
Asking	Being open and receptive; questioning yourself.	Where are you looking for answers? Do you need to make further enquiries?
Backing up	Unable to move forward; past; memories; keeping a record; backing out of a situation.	Where are you going backwards? What do you need to revisit or review?
Bathing	Cleansing, soothing feelings; releasing emotions; vulnerability; rebirth; purifying yourself.	What are you immersing yourself in? Where do you need renewal?

Action	Symbolism	Questions to Ask Yourself
Bearing up	Being patient; having endurance; exposing your feelings: baring.	Are you finding your bearings? Where are you holding up under pressure?
Bed–wetting	Fear; releasing your feelings; letting go too soon; lacking control.	Are you being a wet blanket? Where are you feeling insecure or uncertain?
Being pregnant	Fertile; abundant; potential; indication of pregnancy; meaningful issues; weighty concern; feeling responsible; inventive.	Have you got exciting hopes and expectations? What are you developing or creating?
Bending	Flexibility; picking up the pieces; eager to please: bends.	Where are you bending over backwards? Who are you bowing down to?
Birth	See Giving Birth in this chapter.	
Bleeding	Being fleeced; paying a heavy price; danger.	What are you losing? Where are you feeling drained?
Bookkeeping	Recording lessons; being prepared; attending to details; evaluating yourself.	Are you feeling accountable? Where do you need balance?
Bowing	See Kneeling in this chapter.	
Boxing	Self-protection; being defensive; wrapping up issues and situations.	Where are you confronting yourself or others? Are you defending your values?
Branding	Taking ownership; categorising yourself; personal identity; own brand; individuality.	Are you leaving your mark? Where have you been branded or stigmatised?
Breaking	Breaking up; shattered plans; malfunction.	What's falling apart or not working? Where are you going to pieces?
Brushing	See Combing in this chapter.	
Building	Making a new start; prioritising; laying foundations; working with others.	Are you creating new plans? What's building up?

Action	*Symbolism*	*Questions to Ask Yourself*
Bumping	Being pushy; disrespectful; undiplomatic; impulsive; bump into; bump up; bump off.	Are you stepping on others' toes? Where are you being assertive?
Burning	Shedding light on an issue; purification; transformation; comfort.	Have you got a burning ambition? Are you being destructive?
Burying	Suppressing your feelings; ending; finalising; hiding; needing to unearth.	What are you laying to rest? What can't you face?
Buying	Taking ownership; acquisition; being decisive.	Are you fulfilling your needs? Where are you paying a high price?
Capsizing	Warning; losing direction; feeling overwhelmed.	What's been overturned? Where can't you cope?
Car racing	Driving yourself; being competitive; going round in circles.	Are you competing with others? Where are you rushing or being impulsive?
Censoring	Cover up; blocking your feelings; deceiving yourself.	What can't you face? What don't you want others to see?
Ceremony	Following procedure; being rigid or inflexible; showing allegiance.	Are you being formal? What are you honouring?
Chanting	Personal mantra; repetition; getting in tune with yourself; spiritual renewal.	What are you celebrating? What's proving repetitious?
Chasing	Pursuing goals; fear; guilt.	Who are you driving away? What are you running away from?
Cheating	Deceiving yourself or others; not being true to yourself.	Where are you breaking your own principles or the rules? What are you taking from others?
Chewing	Getting your teeth into something; dwelling on things.	What's eating away at you? What are you chewing over?

Action	Symbolism	Questions to Ask Yourself
Climbing	Making progress, ambitions; facing challenges; being motivated; uphill battle.	Where are you overcoming obstacles? Are you climbing the social ladder?
Closing	Closure; isolation; having a closed mind; refusing to consider; blocking out.	Where are you closing doors? Are you shutting yourself off?
Coaching	Being told what to do; can't think for yourself; being guided.	Where are you instructing others? Are you offering encouragement and support?
Colliding	See Crashing in this chapter.	
Combing	Searching; straightening out your thinking.	What are you rummaging through? Are you being groomed?
Committing adultery	Balancing desires and responsibilities; lacking loyalty or commitment.	Where are you experiencing a conflict of interest? Are you deceiving yourself or others?
Committing suicide	Lack of commitment; surrender; self-sabotage, self-sacrifice; unable to cope, can't see a way out; hopelessness; giving up; martyr.	Where are you acting against your own self-interest? What do you want to end?
Conducting business	Worldly values or concerns; organised; work or career; being decisive: none of your business.	Where are you taking control? Are you fulfilling your responsibilities?
Confusion	Feeling disorganised; lacking clarity; misunderstandings.	Are you muddling your way through? What can't you see or haven't acknowledged?
Constipation	Pent-up feelings; can't let go; being held back.	What have you been holding onto for too long? What do you need to release?
Cooking	Assimilating ideas; falsifying	Are you presenting ideas?

Action	Symbolism	Questions to Ask Yourself
	information: cooking the books.	What are you making palatable and easy to digest?
Covering	Cover up; feeling repressed; disguising issues; self-defences; self-protection.	What are you hiding? Are you suppressing your feelings?
Crashing	Danger; falling prices, finances or hopes; going too fast; being impulsive.	What's collapsing or tumbling around you? Are things piling up?
Crawling	Finding your way; making a start; inching your way forward; being childish or immature.	Where have you got potential? Who are you grovelling to?
Cremating	Feeling consumed; ending; mortality; closure; purification; simplicity.	What are you disposing of? What are you transforming?
Crossing	Making decisions; turning point; crossing the line.	Are you making a transition? Have you gone too far?
Crowding	Feeling anonymous; can't be yourself; no room to move.	Are you feeling hemmed in? Where don't you know yourself? (Also see Crowd in Chapter 17.)
Crying	Not coping; releasing feelings; cleansing yourself.	Do you need support? Where are you seeking attention?
Cultivating	See Harvesting in this chapter.	
Cutting	See Pruning in this chapter.	
Cycling	Right timing; motivation; fast-tracking; repetition.	Where are you putting in a lot of effort? Do you need balance?
Dancing	Harmony; partnership; right timing; joint goals or activities; keeping in step.	Where are you establishing a rhythm? Do you need to enjoy life or be more spontaneous?
Dating	Prioritising; attraction of opposites; appointment: date.	What's out of date? Are you making a commitment?

Action	Symbolism	Questions to Ask Yourself
Dealing	Making deals; organising; entrepreneur; profiteering: wheeling and dealing.	What do you need to deal with? What are you handling or coping with?
Diarrhoea	Unable to wait; can't hold on; releasing your feelings; requires immediate attention.	Where are you losing control? What do you need to release urgently?
Dictating	Abusing your authority; dominating others; arrogance; pride; self-importance.	Are you exercising your power and influence? Where can't you think for yourself?
Digging	Looking deeper; hiding; undermining yourself or others; exposing.	What are you searching for? What are you suppressing?
Dining	Connecting with others; sharing ideas.	Where are you digesting new ideas? Are you considering your options?
Disabling	Self-sabotage; feeling ineffective; unable to progress; crippling circumstances; ill-health.	Where have you changed your mind? What needs fixing?
Diving	Needing to cool off; being immersed; exploring the depths of your psyche; in too deep.	What's taking a nosedive? Where are you plunging in and getting involved? (Also see Drowning in Common Dream Theme in Chapter 6.)
Divorcing	Disowning parts of yourself; confronting others; conflict; making a new start.	What are you disassociating from? Where are you breaking a commitment?
Dodging	Side-stepping issues; poor communication; being indirect.	What can't you face? What are you avoiding?
Dozing	Unaware; inattentive; unconcerned; lacking motivation.	What are you in danger of missing? Do you need to be better informed?

Action	*Symbolism*	*Questions to Ask Yourself*
Drafting	Setting goals; needing a framework; building up your skills.	Are you making plans? Where are you changing your mind?
Drinking	Celebration; feeling refreshed; dependency.	Are you denying your feelings? What are you trying to avoid?
Driving	Being motivated; driving force; ambitious; decisive.	Where are you in control? Are you setting goals and making plans?
Drowning	See Common Dream Theme in Chapter 6.	
Eating	Fulfilling your needs; being supported; desires; indulgence; avoidance; compulsions; someone feeding off you.	What are you taking in? Where are you feeling satisfied and fulfilled? (Also see Dining in this chapter.)
Exercising	Exerting your willpower; maintaining control; healthy attitudes.	What do you need to practise? Where are you making an effort?
Failing	Feeling insecure or inadequate; lack of self-worth; being unprepared.	Are you feeling like you don't measure up? Where are you scared of failure?
Falling	Drop in status, prices or finances; loss of face; insecurity; fall through; fall behind.	Are you losing ground or have fallen from grace? Where have you lost power and influence?
Fasting	Inner cleansing of mind, body or spirit; self-discipline; purification.	Are you abstaining from something? What are you refusing to accept?
Fertilising	Nurturing yourself or others; favourable circumstances; providing encouragement.	Where are you giving back? Are you experiencing good growth or productivity?
Fighting	Defending your principles; facing opposition; confronting obstacles or others.	Are you struggling? Where are you being competitive?

Action	*Symbolism*	*Questions to Ask Yourself*
Fishing	Catching opportunities; aloof; being cold or unemotional; seeking spiritual guidance.	Are you fishing for ideas? What seems fishy or suspicious? (Also see Fish in Chapter 6.)
Floating	Letting go; going with the flow; lacking direction; floating an idea.	Are you feeling buoyant and happy? Where are you drifting along?
Flying	Rising to new heights; wanting freedom; spiritual aspirations; astral experience or lucid dream.	Are you being a high-flyer? Where do you need a higher perspective? (Also see Birds in Chapter 2.)
Folding	Categorising yourself or others; halving a problem; being organised.	What needs wrapping up? What are you storing or recording?
Foolish	Not taking things seriously; being misled; showing pretence; entertaining others; being ridiculous.	Are you playing the fool or clowning around? Where are you being irresponsible?
Forgiving	Accepting yourself and others; healing; letting go; releasing pain and the past.	Do you need to forgive yourself? What are you overlooking?
Freezing	Hard feelings; preserving values or relationships; isolating yourself.	Have you been frozen out? What are you feeling cold toward? (Also see Preserving in this chapter.)
Fuming	Feeling frustrated; suppressed feelings; emotional tensions.	Are you blowing your stack? What could flare up?
Gambling	Taking your chances; being too trusting or naive; risking your reputation.	What are you risking? Where are you facing uncertainty?
Gardening	Eliminating negativity; promoting yourself; spiritual development.	Where are you experiencing personal growth? What are you nurturing?
Giving	Supporting others; giving but not receiving; giving up; giving in.	What are you giving out? Where do you need to be more generous?

155

Action	*Symbolism*	*Questions to Ask Yourself*
Giving birth	Bringing into manifestation; responsibilities; confinement.	What have you created? What are you labouring over?
Going home	Protection; family roots or ties; self-identity; belief system; revisiting the past; needing acceptance.	Are you reconnecting with a part of yourself? Where do you need closure or completion?
Going in circles	Unable to find a solution; avoiding issues; business or social circle; circle of friends.	Are you getting the run-around? Where aren't you making progress?
Golf	Coordinating others; overcoming difficulties; setting targets; right timing; going the distance; relaxation; social status; wealth.	Where are you making social connections? Do you need to keep your eye on the ball?
Gouging	Obliging others; being aggressive; feeling coerced.	Where are you making things happen? Are you forcing things or exerting pressure?
Grasping	Holding on too tightly; can't let go; manipulative.	What's within your grasp? Where are you taking control?
Grumbling	Unable to accept; frustration; discontent.	Are you feeling disappointed or disgruntled? Where do you need to make a change?
Harvesting	Sowing ideas; right timing; abundance; satisfaction; fruitful outcomes or rewards; karma: effects of past deeds.	Where are you reaping results or the fruits of your labour? Are you gathering your energies or taking stock of your resources?
Healing	Health issues; being out of balance; restoring healthy attitudes.	Are you taking remedial action? Where do you need renewal?
Hemming	Tying up loose ends; feeling besieged; wrapping up; attending to details.	Are you feeling hemmed in? Where are you looking for closure or are completing a task?

Action	Symbolism	Questions to Ask Yourself
Hiding	Feeling repressed; cover up; beating; hide; hiding.	Where are you being secretive? What are you avoiding or suppressing?
Holding	Being possessive; resentments; holding back; hold out; hold off.	Where are you holding onto your feelings? What can't you let go of?
Hopping	Energetic and enthusiastic; needing balance; lack of completion.	Where do you need to hop to it? Are you hopping from one thing to another?
Hugging	Expressing feelings; offering compassion; love and affection.	What are you embracing? What are you valuing?
Hunting	Hounding; wounding; offending; being destructive; relentless.	What are you pursuing? Where are you being ruthless?
Hurrying	Feeling unprepared; being reckless; having no time.	Are you being impulsive? Where do you need to speed things up?
Immunising	Release from obligations; being unresponsive; insensitive; protection; self-defences; vaccination.	What are you resisting? Where are you enjoying immunity?
Imprisoning	Suppressed feelings; feeling trapped; self-imposed restrictions.	Where are you feeling confined or restricted? Are you putting up emotional barriers?
Insulting	Low self-esteem; putting others down; showing disrespect; feeling violated; being undiplomatic.	Where have you been offensive? Have you been hurt?
Interviewing	Taking opportunities; following procedure; assessing a situation; formalities; employment prospects.	What are you questioning? Are you trying to impress?
Jogging	Running away; fit for the task; self-discipline; jogging your memory.	What are you running after? Where are you pushing yourself?

Action	Symbolism	Questions to Ask Yourself
Judging	Being an authority; your inner critic; being cynical; conscience; looking down on others.	Are you judging or misjudging others? Are you judging yourself too harshly?
Juggling	Trouble coping; prioritising; too many commitments.	Where are you doing more than one thing at a time? Are you juggling your responsibilities?
Jumping	Being enthusiastic; energetic; right timing; jump to it.	Where are you jumping up and down or making a fuss? Are you jumping at an opportunity?
Kidnapping	Feeling vulnerable; demanding; being helpless.	What have you taken that you shouldn't have? Are you sabotaging yourself?
Killing	Denying yourself; eliminating habits; being aggressive; past-life recollection; destructive feelings or habits; making a killing.	What are you doing away with? Has part of you died?
Kissing	Feeling desirable; wanting to be loved; desire; passion; sensuality.	What are you attracted to? Where are you feeling connected?
Kneeling	Ability to bend; being respectful; flexibility.	Where are you showing humility or reverence? What's brought you to your knees?
Knitting	Nurturing yourself; coordinating others; patching up differences.	What are you bringing together? What's unravelling before you?
Knocking	See Common Dream Theme in Chapter 16.	
Labouring	Enduring; taking great pains; grinding away.	What are you finding a struggle? Where are you making a big effort?

Action	Symbolism	Questions to Ask Yourself
Laughing	Being light-hearted; mocking others; seeing the ridiculous or absurd; not taking things too seriously.	Do you need to laugh at yourself? What are you laughing at?
Launching	New beginnings; setting high ideals; needing to let go.	What are you embarking on? What's taking off?
Lifting	Setting higher goals; inspiration; receiving guidance; lift off.	Where are you supporting others? Are you raising your standards?
Lining up	Alignment; respecting authority; waiting your turn; balance; following procedure.	Are you being patient? Where do you need to fall into line?
Locking	Security; lack of trust; attachment.	What have you shut out? Where are you protecting yourself?
Mailing	Sending messages; communicating; intuitive awareness.	Are you seeking information? What are you advertising or promoting?
Making love	Seeking wholeness or union; balancing opposites; unfulfilled desire; making connections.	Are you being creative or passionate? What do you need to balance?
Making a U-turn	Retracing your steps; going backwards; being too hasty.	Where are you doing an about-face? Are you changing your direction?
Marching	Following others; conforming; lack of individuality; keeping in time.	Are you making steady progress? Where are you taking things in your stride?
Marriage	Alliance; sharing common goals; partnership; being faithful; spiritual union; showing loyalty.	What do you need to live with? Where have you made a commitment?
Massage	Soothing your feelings; indulging yourself; relaxation; calmness.	Who or what are you manipulating? Where are you putting your needs first?

Action	*Symbolism*	*Questions to Ask Yourself*
Masturbating	Selfishness; self-indulgence; self-satisfaction; self-serving.	Are you seeking self-gratification? Where do you need stimulation?
Mending	Making restitution; improving; correcting imbalances: on the mend.	What do you need to restore? Where are you making amends?
Menstruating	Releasing your feelings; letting go; new possibilities.	Where do you need rhythm? Are you entering a new cycle?
Miscarry	Warning; mishap; lacking potential; failure; fruitless endeavour; mismanagement; exclusion; injustice: miscarriage of justice.	Where have you aborted your plans? What have you lost?
Missing	Lost opportunities; being unprepared; feeling unworthy.	What can't you find? What have you had to give up?
Mixing	Socialising; trying new things; unity in diversity.	Are you feeling confused or mixed up? Where have you got mixed feelings?
Operating	Major adjustment; detachment; receiving support; internalising problems; losing part of yourself.	Where are you performing? Who or what are you manipulating? (Also see Surgeon in Chapter 17.)
Moving	Change and transition; keeping things moving; stirring; inspirational: moving.	Where are you making progress? Do you need to move on?
Mowing	See Pruning in this chapter.	
Ordaining	New opportunities; higher purpose; following your conscience.	Are you being promoted? Where are you answering to a higher authority?
Orgy	Needing to impose limits; rebellious attitude; stretching boundaries; free thinking; uninhibited.	Are you wishing to break free or be spontaneous? Are you overindulging yourself?

Action	Symbolism	Questions to Ask Yourself
Pacing	Taking things in your stride; being put through your paces; keep pace; need for peace and calm.	Where are you worried or anxious? Do you need to pace yourself?
Packing	Wrapping up a situation; feeling unsettled; going to the pack; send packing; pack in; pack up.	What are you leaving behind? Do you need to move on?
Painting	Cover up; suppressing your feelings; expressing yourself; restoring feelings, relationships or situations.	Where are you being creative? What are you representing?
Parading	Promoting; moving forward; acknowledgment or recognition; receiving approval.	Are you showing off? What do you need to inspect?
Parking	Finding where you belong; temporary setback; new views; relaxation.	Where have things come to a standstill? Are you taking time out?
Participating	Being a team-player; sharing responsibilities; getting the most out of life.	Where do you need to be more actively involved? Are you relating to others?
Partying	Being spontaneous; conforming; alliances; loyalties; party; towing the party line.	Have you got cause for celebration? Are you uniting with others?
Paying	See Buying in this chapter.	
Peddling	Making progress; making an effort; selling or promoting yourself.	What are you pushing? Where have you gained momentum?
Perching	Enjoying respect and authority; precarious position; being out of touch.	Are you looking down on others? Where have you been elevated?
Petting	Showing your feelings; being kind to yourself; feeling desirable.	Are you being affectionate? What's arousing or stimulating?
Photographing	How you think others see you; feeling detached; the past; seeing the bigger picture.	Where do you need to put things in focus? Are you dealing with memories?

Action	*Symbolism*	*Questions to Ask Yourself*
Planting seeds	Developing new talents; having potential; new beginnings; laying foundations.	Are you sowing new ideas? What are you cultivating or nurturing?
Playing	Enjoying yourself; being spontaneous; balancing your life.	Are you playing with an idea? What aren't you taking seriously?
Plotting	Conspiring against others; charting your course; intrigue; setting goals.	Are you making plans? Where are you colluding with others?
Ploughing	Reinvesting your energies or finances; having expectations; new cycle or beginnings.	Where are you making preparations? What are you ploughing your way through?
Plunging	Uncovering repressed emotions; feeling overwhelmed; falling from grace; drop in status.	Where are you in too deep? Are you diving into things too soon?
Poverty	Low self-esteem; feeling deprived; resenting.	Are you feeling dissatisfied? Where are you lacking opportunities?
Praying	Respecting a higher authority; needing comfort; solitude; contemplation; spiritual aspirations.	Where are you seeking guidance? Do you need to surrender?
Preserving	Rescuing; saving; stockpiling.	Are you defending your values? Where are you reinvesting? (Also see Freezing in this chapter.)
Promising	Being convincing; loyalty; swearing allegiance.	Where are you making a commitment? Are you being honourable?
Prostituting	Comprising your principles; lack of self-respect; impersonal; loss of dignity.	Have you been dishonoured or degraded? Are you selling yourself short or making concessions?
Prowling	Fears; suppressed feelings; intruding; being sneaky; taking from others.	What are you afraid of? What part of you seeks recognition? (Also see Attacker in Chapter 17.)

Action	Symbolism	Questions to Ask Yourself
Pruning	Fashioning ideas; promoting growth; eliminating negativity; favourable circumstances.	What are you bringing into shape? What are you cutting back on?
Pulling	Power of accomplishment; attracting others; having pulling power.	Where are you struggling? Are you pulling together with others?
Punishing	Needing to stand up for yourself; being bullied; hurting yourself.	Where are you judging yourself or others? Are you making things harder than they need to be?
Pushing	Struggling to achieve; setting your own agenda; being pushy.	Where are you driving yourself hard? Are you forcing matters?
Push-ups	Self-discipline; being assertive; pushing others; inner strength; pushy.	Where are you supporting yourself? What are you pulling into shape?
Racing	See Car racing in this chapter.	
Rallying	Common goals; mocking others; being competitive; steep increase in prices; rallied; rally.	Are you mobilising support? Where are you recovering?
Rampaging	Forcing issues; feeling disturbed or agitated; lacking restraint: rampant.	Where are you lacking control? Are you being destructive?
Raping	Warning; feeling powerless; being exploited.	Are you violating your principles? What are you doing against your will?
Reaching	Satisfying your needs; connecting with others; going within.	What are you holding out for? What do you need to give to yourself?
Reading	Needing more information; intuitive awareness; having a reading; self-improvement.	Are you looking for answers? Where are you reading a situation?
Rehearsing	Seeking perfection; scared of failure; building your confidence; honing your talents.	What are you going over again and again? Where are you feeling prepared?

Action	Symbolism	Questions to Ask Yourself
Risking	Feeling exposed; dealing with uncertainties; considering consequences.	Are you making changes? Where are you taking chances?
Rowing	Making progress; working hard; coordinating efforts; right timing.	Where are you working closely with others? Do you need to establish a rhythm?
Running	Driving yourself hard; being hasty; making rapid progress. (Also see Chasing in this chapter.)	What are you running after? Who or what are you running away from?
Searching	Making enquiries; self-analysis; questioning who you are.	What are you looking for? Do you need answers?
Seducing	Persuading others; lack of self-control; uncontrolled desires; being led astray.	Are you enticing or tempting others? Where are you being manipulated?
Singing	Harmonious feelings; being in tune; letting your feelings out; expressing yourself.	Where are you feeling happy and content? What's fulfilling you?
Skiing	See Snow in Chapter 14.	
Smiling	Joy; excitement; amusement; friendly manner; acceptance.	What are you approving of? Where have you got a positive outlook?
Spying	Having suspicions; feeling guilty; being deceiving; not being true to yourself.	Are you being secretive? What do you need to keep an eye on?
Stealing	Feeling impoverished; insecurity; lacking permission; underhanded dealings.	Are you misappropriating your energies? What are you taking from others?
Strangling	Clinging on; fighting for survival; out of breath.	What are you suppressing? Where are you feeling crushed or squeezed?
Stripping	Feeling deprived; being uninhibited; flaunting yourself.	Do you need to deal with essentials? Where are you feeling exposed?

Action	Symbolism	Questions to Ask Yourself
Surfing	Mastery; handling situations; coordinating your efforts; fear and elation; precarious position.	Do you need balance? Where are things going up and down?
Swimming	Progressing; exploring unconscious beliefs; rebirth and renewal; swimmingly.	What are you dipping into? Where do you need discipline or training?
Swinging	Being left hanging; simple pleasures; childhood memories.	Are you doing a complete turn-around? Where are you fluctuating?
Taking the sacraments	Making a promise to yourself; observing procedure; Christianity; formalities; stereotyped views.	Are you making a commitment? Where are you taking a significant step?
Tying	Obligating others; complications; making connections.	Where are you feeling bound? Are you getting tied up in knots?
Untying	Releasing ties; simplifying your life; loosening emotional bonds.	Where do you want to free yourself up? Do you need to tie up loose ends?
Walking a tightrope	Needing discipline and focus; no room for mistakes; taking a risk.	Where haven't you got room to manoeuvre? Are you under extreme pressure?
Washing	See Bathing in this chapter.	
Weaving	Creating; patience and persistence; linking ideas; relationships.	What are you dodging or trying to avoid? Where are you putting a positive spin on things?
Weeding	See Pruning in this chapter and Common Dream Theme in Chapter 8.	
Weeping	See Crying in this chapter.	
Weighing	Having an influence; feeling weighed down; oppressed: weighty.	What are you evaluating or weighing up? Where do you need to change the balance?

Action	Symbolism	Questions to Ask Yourself
Yoga	Looking within; inner strength; finding yourself; self-discipline; needing poise and composure.	Are you stretching yourself? Where do you need to be more flexible?

Common Dream Theme: Being naked in public

To find yourself naked in public can symbolise feeling exposed, vulnerable, unprotected, unprepared or defenceless. It may also represent having a poor self-image, trying to find your role in life or dealing with essentials.

Chapter 11
Insects and Reptiles

Among boulders of immovable dignity,
the insects of subconscious scheming roam.
Chögyam Trungpa

Insects can symbolise insignificant issues or problems, irritations, impatience, interruptions, intrusions or your obsessive tendencies. They can also represent feeling pestered or undervalued, creepy feelings and suspicions or the undesirable qualities in yourself and others. Consider these possible meanings along with any others specifically listed.

How to get the best value from this chapter

- See if you relate to any of the key words or questions and explore your own meanings which may override those given here.
- Look at all possibilities and apply the most appropriate for your situation.
- Rephrase the Life Issue questions to broaden their personal relevance to you, if necessary, by using other words with similar meanings.
- You can also turn any question around (including those you formulate) to see if you relate to them better, by asking them in a slightly different way. For example, rephrase it as a need rather than a desire or belief or vice versa.
- The Symbol in Action examples show how to apply context or link meaning with action.

Desires and needs as opposed to outcomes and results

If a symbol represents an issue you are currently facing, then it may be indicative of your feelings, desires, beliefs or needs. This would usually occur in the first two-thirds of a dream, which often illustrates the issue you are dealing with and how you feel about it.

If a symbol comes in the form of a resolution, outcome, insight, solution or conclusion in the climax, usually at the end of the dream, then it may indicate a consequence, result or your dream advice to you.

Symbol	Symbol In Action *Look for feelings, desires, needs, beliefs or situations, explore literal meanings, apply any puns and idioms*	Possible Life Issues *Look for where, what and who this reminds you of, apply key words to thoughts, feelings or situations, explore literal meanings, apply word plays and figures of speech*
Ant	**Ant being stepped on:** Losing your individuality; self-sacrifice; being a martyr **Ant carrying heavy load:** Dedicated; feeling burdened **Ants devouring something:** Group destructiveness.	Team-player; hard-working; staying power; irritation; organisation; petty annoyances; patience; diligence; foresight (stores food) Are you feeling small and insignificant? Where are you following others?
Aphids	**Spraying aphids:** Eliminating unhealthy attitudes **Aphids attacking your plants:** Something eating away at you; having suspicions **Large scale aphid attack:** Feeling depressed; under attack.	Harmful habits; negativity (transmits disease); parasitic tendencies; feeding off others What is sapping your energy? Are you taking without giving?
Bee	**Being stung by a bee:** Being hurt by a comment or event **Bee on a hat:** Being obsessive: bee in your bonnet **Bee on a clothesline:** Fast-tracking: making a beeline.	Ordered; disciplined; industrious; group cooperation; inner sweetness; busy bee Where are you giving maximum effort? Are you losing your individuality?
Beetle	**Scarab beetle in dung:** Resurrecting your plans **Lots of beetles:** Strong negativity **Beetle on its back:** Feeling helpless; needing support.	Destructive thoughts and forces; eternal life; regeneration Where are things changing? What's been resurrected?
Blowfly	**Trying to swat a blowfly:** Trying to diffuse difficulties **Blowfly on your food:** Tainted motives; being put off **Blowfly laying eggs:** Festering emotions; emotional wounds.	Emotional pain (lays eggs in rotten meat and open wounds); insight (large eyes); pestering; harassment; irritation; contemptible Where are you spreading negativity? Are you offending or provoking others?

Symbol	Symbol In Action	Possible Life Issues
Bug	**Seeing a bug near someone else's ear:** Lack of privacy; gossip; revealed secrets **Looking at bugs under a microscope:** Ill-health; self-analysis; discovering what's bothering you **Dead bug:** Overcoming negativity or bad habits.	Unhealthy attitudes or feelings (micro-organisms responsible for disease); eavesdropping; irritation; fixation; contemptible attitude or person; waste of time; bug bear; being bugged; bugger What's bugging or irritating you? Where are you being obsessive or can't let something go?
Butterfly	**Butterfly emerging from a cocoon:** Plans taking off or changing; coming out of yourself **Butterfly flying around:** Being vain or fickle: social butterfly **Lots of butterflies:** Feeling nervous: having butterflies; transforming your life.	Beauty; gentleness; grace; new beginnings; brilliant colours; self-transformation Are you making a new start? Where are you showing your inner beauty?
Caterpillar	**Caterpillar eating your plants:** Destructive; being undermined **Spraying caterpillars:** Stamping out negativity or corruption **Caterpillar in your bed:** Needing to renew your relationship.	Metamorphosis; change of character; mobility (numerous pairs of legs); feeds off others (parasite); power; having means; vehicle: caterpillar What's being transformed? Where have you got mobility?
Centipede	**Being stung by a centipede:** Feeling hurt; hurting yourself **Centipede in your bedroom:** Not being honest in your relationship **Lots of centipedes:** Many opportunities; group of unscrupulous people.	Mobility (many legs); hidden thoughts; tainted motives; corruption (poison claws); stagnation (paralyses prey) What's come to a standstill? Where have you got mobility?
Cicada	**Cicadas making a noise:** Saying too much **Cicada in your bedroom:** Being secretive or holding back your feelings in your relationship **Treading on a cicada:** Revealing a confidence; lost secrets.	Covert actions; suppressed feelings; secret; stage of life; monotonous (males produce droning sound) What are you finding tedious? Do you need to express yourself?

Symbol	*Symbol In Action*	*Possible Life Issues*
Cockroach	**Baby cockroach:** Growing annoyance **Kitchen full of cockroaches:** Uncontrolled negativity or irritations **Killing a cockroach:** Inability to adapt; eliminating negativity.	Adaptable (ability to acclimatise); negativity; obscure notions; being kept in the dark (lives in dark environment); pest; nuisance What are you spreading? What are you concealing?
Cocoon	**Caterpillar in a cocoon:** Protecting yourself **Emerging from a cocoon:** Becoming independent; transition **Damaged cocoon:** Being unable to move on.	Stage of life; unfoldment; protective attitudes or feelings; insulating circumstances; self-defences; immunity; security; nurturing; preserving values or the status quo Where are you protecting yourself or others? Are you letting go?
Cricket	**Crickets chirping:** Being optimistic **Lawn full of crickets:** Great intuitiveness; intrusive psychic awareness **Cricket in your office:** Needing to start on a project; making best use of timing.	Intuition (long antennae); right timing (jumps); song (chirp); cheerfulness: chirpy What can you see coming? What are you jumping at?
Crocodile	**Wrestling a crocodile:** Confronting difficulties **Being attacked by crocodile:** Feeling threatened or vulnerable; being misunderstood **Sensing a crocodile:** Something you haven't seen; more to an issue.	Lurking threat; vulnerability; obscure; concealed; watchfulness; evolution; crocodile tears What have you overlooked? Where are things not as they seem?
Dragonfly	**Dragonfly on your window pane:** False perceptions **Several dragonflies:** Group uncertainty or misconceptions **Dead dragonfly:** Ignoring your dreams; resisting change.	Change; appreciation of dreams; illusion (according to myth); summer; predatory What needs changing? Where do you need clarity?
Dung beetle	**Dung beetles in your bedroom:** Needing to	Recycling thoughts; processing information; regeneration;

Symbol	Symbol In Action	Possible Life Issues
	rejuvenate your relationship **Several dung beetles:** Group renewal **Dead dung beetle:** Having a closed mind; stagnation.	considerng new ideas (soil fertilisers) What issues are coming up for you again and again? Are you giving back or reinvesting?
Dust mite	**Being allergic to dust mites:** Health warning; reacting to insignificant issues **Protecting yourself from dust mites:** Defending yourself against negativity **Overrun by dust mites:** Lots of irritations.	Health warning; small or trivial annoyances (microscopic invaders); grim scenarios; disturbances; dust; mite; dust down; dust up What do you have an aversion to? What can't you see or have over-looked?
Earwig	**Earwig in your office:** Spreading gossip at work; reprimanding work colleagues **Lots of earwigs:** Finding fault with others **Dead earwig:** Being private.	Eavesdropping; spreading negativity (infects fruit); scolding; earwigged; earwigging Who are you trying to influence? Have you got access to private information?
Fire ants	**Fire ants in the kitchen:** Taking a stand on domestic issues **Large fire ants confronting you:** Facing big issues; important principles **Dead fire ants:** Backing down.	Colour red; hurtful words or situation (painful sting); standing up for yourself; standing on principle; rising challenges (stands up and bites); aggressive; commu-nity minded (lives in colonies) Are you defending yourself or others? Where are you being aggressive?
Fireflies	**Trying to capture fireflies:** Needing to be versatile **Group of fireflies:** Brilliant ideas; clever people **Dead fireflies:** Being inflexible; lacking creativity.	Changeable; adaptable (colour alters with habitat); intuition; bright ideas (luminous properties); fiery energy; fire Are you standing out? Where do you need to be flexible?
Fleas	**Flea in your ear:** Receiving a dressing down: flea in one's ear **Fleas on your dog:** Health warning for your pet; nagging negative feelings	Consistent irritations; leaping from one thing to another (jumping insect); shabby appearance; decrepit; freeloading (parasite); harbouring grudges

Symbol	Symbol In Action	Possible Life Issues
	Having fleas in your bed: Annoyances in your relationship.	(host for tapeworms); flea-bitten; flea market; flea pit Are you taking without giving? What's eating away at you?
Fruit fly	**Fruit fly in your fruit:** Negative influences; tainted motives **Wide fruit fly infestation:** Group ineffectiveness; widespread corruption **Spraying for fruit fly:** Eliminating negativity.	Contaminated motives; unhealthy attitudes; sinking values (drooped wings when flying); unproductive endeavours Are you being destructive? What's been fruitless?
Furniture borer	**Finding holes in your wood:** Feeling undermined **Fumigating your office for furniture borers:** Eliminating negative influences at work **Breeding furniture borers:** Spreading negativity; encouraging deeper investigation.	Destructive thoughts, feelings or habits; elusive ideas (inconspicuous head); bore: probing issues Where are you undermining yourself or others? What's eating away at you?
Glow-worm	**Holding a glow-worm in your hand:** Feeling inspired **Group of glow-worms:** Group intuitions **Dead glow-worm:** Lacking inspiration or joy.	Talent; bright ideas; inspiration; loving feelings; happiness; rekindled motivations Are you seeing the light? Where are you standing out?
Goanna	See Lizard in this chapter.	
Grasshopper	**Several grasshoppers:** Group intuitions **Plague of grasshoppers:** Many irritations; overwhelming negativity **Dead grasshoppers:** Being rigid or inflexible.	Self-protection (camouflaged); adaptability; giving and receiving of impressions (makes a ticking sound) Where are you leaping ahead? Are you blending into the background?
Hornet	**Being stung by a hornet:** Feeling hurt **Extra-large hornet:** Being extremely critical; exaggerating criticism	Wounded pride; cutting remarks (stings); unfavourable reactions Where are you stirring up a hornet's nest?

Symbol	Symbol In Action	Possible Life Issues
	Dead hornet: No backlash.	Are you hurting yourself or others?
Insect	See Introduction in this chapter.	
Lace bug	**Lace bug in your hand:** Handling delicate issues **Lace bug in your office:** Feeling lethargic or apathetic at work **Dead lace bug:** Choosing simplicity; rejecting negativity or selfishness.	Sapped vitality (drinks sap and leaves lacy leaf structure); feeding off others; lack of mobility (poor fliers); entwined relationships; weaving; lace Where are you feeling drained? Are you taking from others?
Lice	**Infestation of lice:** Intruding selfish motives **Having head lice:** Corrupted thinking **Dead lice:** Rejecting selfishness.	Freeloading (blood sucker); taking things easy; contemptible person Are you taking and not giving? What are you finding irritating?
Lizard	**Lizard sunning itself:** Warming towards something **Alert lizard:** Being intuitive **Lizard defending itself:** Holding onto outdated ideas or practices.	Dreamtime; dreams; prehistoric; intuition (acute hearing, senses vibrations); survival; detachment (loses its tail); lounge lizard Are you taking it easy? What have you been associated with from its beginnings?
Maggot	**Seeing maggots breeding:** Festering emotional wounds **Oversized maggots:** Overemphasising emotional problems **Killing maggots:** Rejecting negativity.	Decaying principles or relationships; breaking down barriers; cowardice (limbless larva) Where are things deteriorating? Are you making unhealthy choices?
March fly	**Being bitten by a march fly:** Feeling hurt **Swarm of march flies:** Group antagonism **Dead march fly:** Lack of progress.	Feeding off others (blood suckers); sarcastic comments (biting); discipline; time marching on; dismal situations or outcomes; month of March; marching Have you received your marching orders? Are you making progress?

Symbol	Symbol In Action	Possible Life Issues
Mealy bug	**Mealy bug in your office:** Hassles at work; needing to let go; temporary setbacks **Spraying for mealy bugs:** Eliminating annoyances **Infestations of mealy bugs:** Overwhelming negativity.	Irritation; annoyance (pest); attachment; holding onto feelings (sticks to plants); short-lived (male dies after mating); discharge; discharging responsibilities (produces secretion); reserved: mealy-mouthed Are you afraid to speak up? Where have you got sticking power?
Midges	**Midges attacking you:** Invading annoyances **Oversized midges:** Exaggerating trivial matters **Dead midges:** End of unpleasantness.	Aversions (can inflict allergic reactions); painful situations; driving others away (repels people from beaches); offensive attitudes; small: midget What are you underestimating? Where are you thinking small?
Millipede	**Being overrun with millipedes:** Unconscious influences **Spraying for millipedes:** Stagnating; confronting apathy **Oversized millipede:** Exaggerating a harmless situation.	Harmless; ability to move (many legs or feet); twisted way of looking at things (coils when disturbed); lethargic (sluggish); unconscious beliefs (remains beneath the soil to avoid predators) Where have you got mobility? What are you hiding?
Mosquito	**Being bitten by a mosquito:** Feeling used or hurt; drained **Can't kill a mosquito:** Unable to control negativity **Killing a mosquito:** Rejecting negativity.	Disease; domineering female energies (female sucks blood); feeding off others; emotional wounds; hurtful gossip (piercing sting); concealed; hidden (comes out at night) Are you taking what you can get? Where have you been stung?
Moth	**Moth eating a curtain:** Discarded feelings: moth-eaten **Moth ball in drawer:** Repressed feelings: mothballed **Moths around a light:** Being obsessive.	Perseverance; driving ambitions; seeking spiritual awareness (driven to the light); nocturnal; can see what others can't Are you being irrational? What's been eating away at you?

Symbol	Symbol In Action	Possible Life Issues
Mud dauber	**Mud dauber digging:** Throwing mud at someone **Oversized mud daubers:** Interfering female influence **Dead mud dauber:** Emotional clearing.	Earthy values; impure motives; negative female energies (female builds nests of clay); emotional blockages (plugs holes); embracing ideas (folded wings); muddle What are you repressing? Are you being a stick in the mud?
Praying mantis	**Praying mantis in a church:** Seeking inspiration **Several praying mantis:** Group aspiration or isolation **Dead praying mantis:** Narrow-mindedness; lack of inspiration.	Female dominance (female eats the male after mating); wider picture (swivel head); prayer (adopts a praying posture); private (solitary existence) Are you seeking guidance? Where are you being used?
Reptiles	See Snake in this chapter.	
Scorpion	**Hidden scorpion:** Unseen difficulties **Scorpion in the bedroom:** Hurting your partner or hurting each other **Many scorpions:** Group irritations or betrayal.	Stinging comments (poisonous tail); undesirable feelings; rapid death; zodiac sign of Scorpio Where have you been hurt? Are you feeling threatened?
Silverfish	**Silverfish eating:** Something eating away at you **Infestation of silverfish:** Many irritations **Dead silverfish:** Emotional isolation.	Relating to others (lives among other insects); foresight (long antennae); rapid progress (fast-running insect); leaving things behind (long tail appendage) Where do you need to cooperate with others? Are you being intuitive?
Snake	**Being bitten by a snake:** Hidden danger; feeling tempted **Snake in long grass:** Deception: snake in the grass **Holding onto a snake skin:** Unable to change or progress; needing to make a transition; holding onto the past.	Danger; poisonous; limbless; healing (caduceus); transformation (sheds skin); snaky Are you facing temptation? Where are you changing?

Symbol	Symbol In Action	Possible Life Issues
Spider	**Getting caught in a web:** Feeling trapped or controlled; being deceived **Spider spinning a web:** Spinning a yarn; being creative **Spider in the bedroom:** Using your partner.	Web of intrigue or deceit; manipulation; control; interconnection; ensnared; industrious; negative female energies or influence (female eats her mate); world wide web Are you being influenced by a dominant female? What are you getting entangled in? (Also see Common Dream Theme at the end of this chapter and Cobweb in Chapter 14.)
Stick insect	**Just being able to detect a stick insect on a leaf:** Seeing resemblances **Stick insect next to you:** Needing to be supportive: stick by **Trying unsuccessfully to lift a stick insect off a leaf:** Tenacity: stick at.	Adaptable (camouflaged); sticky predicaments; hiding your feelings; self-protection; stick to; stick up; stick around What haven't you seen? Are you being self-defensive?
Termite	**Termites in your house:** Feeling vulnerable or threatened; being undermined; self-sabotage **Spraying for termites in your office:** Rejecting the status quo at work **Oversized termite:** Bigger problem than expected.	Big impact (leaves visible mounds); unrefined; unsophisticated (primitive insect); status; social order; privilege (colonies are divided into castes) Are you undermining yourself or others? What have you overlooked?
Thrip	**Infestation of thrips:** Losing energy or enthusiasm; overwhelming negativity **Thrips attacking plants:** Feeling used; being undermined **Spraying thrips:** Rejecting control or negativity.	Backward-thinking (throws head back when disturbed); unhealthy attitudes (spreads disease); wounding words (piercing mouth parts); feeding off others (sucks sap); can't go the distance (flies short distances) What's sapping your energy or strength? Are you taking without giving?

Symbol	Symbol In Action	Possible Life Issues
Turtle	**Turtle burying its eggs:** Suppressing your feelings; grounding yourself **Turtle on its back:** Feeling vulnerable or defenceless; reversal of circumstances; loss of dignity **Turtle swimming:** Making steady progress; being in your element.	Slow progress; withdrawn; protection; self-defensive; turn turtle; turtle-necked; turtledove Where are you making slow progress? Do you need to come out of your shell?
Wasp	**Wasp in your bedroom:** Damaging your relationship; hurting each other **Destroying a wasp nest:** Rejecting criticism or negativity **Under attack by many wasps:** Threatening group.	Colours yellow and black; wounding words (powerful sting); irritable feelings; slender waist; waspish Where have you been hurt? Are you feeling threatened?
Weevil	**Weevils in your food:** Unacceptable ideas **Large weevil in your office:** Major problem at work which could prove lengthy **Dead weevil:** Previous problem; rejecting negativity.	Extended negotiations (elongated snout); unrefined thoughts or emotions (rough scaled body); menacing influences (serious pest to crops) What's being spoiled? Are you being undermined?

Common Dream Theme: Seeing a big black spider

To dream of being in danger or attacked by a big black spider can symbolise feeling manipulated or controlled by a dominating, overbearing female influence. It could also symbolise feeling vulnerable, scared, being in danger or possible entrapment.

Chapter 12
Mythical Animals, Characters and Cultural Images

Imagination is more important
than knowledge.
Albert Einstein

Mythical creatures and images can symbolise your wild imaginings, your unknown talents, unexplored parts of yourself or concepts that you find mysterious or unrealistic. They can also have a significance based on folklore and legend which extends beyond your own personal experience. Consider these possible meanings along with any others specifically listed.

How to get the best value from this chapter

- See if you relate to any of the key words or questions and explore your own meanings which may override those given here.
- Look at all possibilities and apply the most appropriate for your situation.
- Rephrase the Life Issue questions to broaden their personal relevance to you, if necessary, by using other words with similar meanings.
- You can also turn any question around (including those you formulate) to see if you relate to them better, by asking them in a slightly different way. For example, rephrase it as a need rather than a desire or belief or vice versa.
- The Symbol in Action examples show how to apply context or link meaning with action.

Desires and needs as opposed to outcomes and results

If a symbol represents an issue you are currently facing, then it may be indicative of your feelings, desires, beliefs or needs. This would usually occur in the first two-thirds of a dream, which often illustrates the issue you are dealing with and how you feel about it.

If a symbol comes in the form of a resolution, outcome, insight, solution or conclusion in the climax, usually at the end of the dream, then it may indicate a consequence, result or your dream advice to you.

Symbol	Symbol In Action *Look for feelings, desires, needs, beliefs or situations, explore literal meanings, apply any puns and idioms*	Possible Life Issues *Look for where, what and who this reminds you of, apply key words to thoughts, feelings or situations, explore literal meanings, apply word plays and figures of speech*
Angel	**Seeing an angel:** Help is at hand; needing to purify yourself; being compassionate; the extraordinary; looking beyond **Reaching out to an angel:** Seeking guidance; needing healing **Angel lifting you up:** Feeling inspired, guided or loved; receiving help from beyond.	Intuition; inner communion (divine messengers); hierarchy; making the grade; afterlife; healing; innocence; heaven; higher self or purpose Are you seeking guidance and inspiration? Where are you being pure, virtuous or helpful to others?
Basilisk	**Baby basilisk:** Developing problem; potentially harmful situation; insidious **Basilisk holding you in its gaze:** Needing to be vigilant against danger or temptation **Fighting a basilisk:** Confronting your fears or shadow.	Shadow side of yourself (undesirable qualities within you or unacknowledged parts of yourself); being manipulated; evil (deadly serpent's gaze); lust; preserver of values (guards treasure); health warning Are you considering a potentially damaging course of action? What could be causing you harm or producing ill-health?
Centaur	**Centaur visiting you:** Receiving guidance; needing poise **Riding centaur:** Controlling your desires; balancing needs and responsibilities **Tying a centaur up:** Confining your power; lacking judgment.	Wise teacher (such as Achilles, in Greek myth); animal-man; male energies; balance (half-horse half-man) Are you feeling conflict between your desires and responsibilities? Where do you need to combine strength and wisdom?
Cerberus	**Meeting Cerberus:** Fearing the unknown **Confronting Cerberus:** Confronting your fears; resisting change **Cerberus won't let you past:** Not your time; being unable to move forward.	Fear of death (dog with three heads who guards the entrance to the underworld or afterlife); transition; right timing Are you questioning whether to move on? Are you fearful of what lies ahead of you?

Symbol	*Symbol In Action*	*Possible Life Issues*
Chimera	**Being chased by a chimera:** Running away from your fears; feeling threatened **Confronting a chimera:** Dealing with your fears; facing your shortcomings **Killing a chimera:** Overcoming your fears; transforming negativity.	Unrealistic dreams (fire-breathing monster); evil; danger; enduring; strong; temptations; fears (lion's head, goat's body, serpent's tail); shadow side of yourself (undesirable qualities within you or unacknowledged parts of yourself) Where are your fears running away with you? Are you acting like a monster?
Cinderella	**Meeting Cinderella:** Acknowledging a denied part of yourself **Being Cinderella:** Feeling manipulated; needing to wait for the right moment; having a sense of destiny **Cinderella dying:** Lost hopes and dreams; losing part of yourself.	Heroine; triumphing over adversity; believing in yourself; make-over; jealousy; happy ending; rags to riches Where are you feeling used or neglected? Are you transforming yourself?
Cyclops	**Running from a Cyclops:** Retreating from challenge; feeling threatened or intimidated **Confronting a Cyclops:** Facing your fears; fighting prejudice; standing up for yourself **Dead Cyclops:** Previous challenge or threat; overcoming your fears.	Single-minded; prejudiced (one-eyed giant); enormous challenge; brute strength or force Are you being pressured or overpowered? Are you being biased?
Dragon	**Being chased by a dragon:** Running away from your fears **Fighting a dragon:** Confronting yourself; facing a challenge **Dragon guarding treasure:** Difficulties that have their own rewards.	Fears; legendary reputation; good fortune; being a dragon Where have your fears been imagined? Have you been unfair or unreasonable?
Dwarf	**Being a dwarf:** Feeling overshadowed; being overlooked **Shaking hands with a dwarf:**	Mysterious (magical powers); underestimating yourself or a problem; hoarding tendencies;

Symbol	Symbol In Action	Possible Life Issues
	Accepting your limits **Standing over a dwarf:** Dominating others; being intimidating.	greedy; small, menacing influence; won't achieve full potential; undeveloped; feeling insignificant or undervalued Are you stunting your own growth? Where aren't you achieving your full potential?
Elves	**Elves teasing you:** Feeling frustrated or tormented **Elves hiding:** Lost causes; don't want to disclose your feelings or intentions; can't find what you're looking for **Several elves:** Group maliciousness.	Power to create (has magical powers); elusive; mysterious (believed to be imaginary and shy); link to nature Are you being disruptive? Where do you need to be creative?
Fairy	**Seeing fairies in your garden:** Needing to take a closer look; not being taken seriously; sense of disbelief **Stepping into a fairy ring:** Being out of touch with reality; fanciful imaginings; delusions; feeling like you don't belong; exploring other levels of consciousness **Sick fairies:** Blocked creativity.	Can't rely on what you see; spiritual nature; delicate issues; link to nature; elementals; power to create (aids nature and has magical powers); male homosexual; elusive; mysterious (believed to be imaginary and shy); fairly; fairytale; fairy godmother What's having a happy ending? What seems unbelievable?
Garuda	**Flying with Garuda Airlines:** Indonesia; travelling; taking a journey; moving on **Capturing a garuda:** Being reserved; keeping information to yourself; being secretive or cautious **Dead garuda:** Feeling unsupported; lack of information.	Conquest; being supportive; communication (bird which transports Vishnu, a Hindi deity) What are you delivering? Where are you making progress?
Genie	**Seeing a genie:** Good fortune; wishes coming true; realised hopes and dreams; receiving assistance **Several genies:** Multiple opportunities; energies out of your control	Realms of fantasy; imagination; resourceful; power of the mind; willpower What's fantastic and hard to believe? Are you using your creativity?

Symbol	Symbol In Action	Possible Life Issues
	Dead genie: Disappointment; dashed hopes; lacking support.	
Giant	**Giant stepping on you:** Being overpowered or intimidated; feeling powerless **Confronting a giant:** Being assertive; taking on the powers that be **Dead giants:** Previous obstacles; overcoming your fears.	Big possibilities; using excessive force; needing a superhuman effort; feeling like you can take on the world Are you overstepping the mark? Where are you facing a massive task?
Griffin	**Facing a griffin:** Confronting yourself; acknowledging your fears **Being chased by a griffin:** Running away from your fears; feeling threatened or vulnerable **Being in the grips of a griffin:** Fears or forces gaining power and strength.	Observant; determined (winged monster with eagle-like head); power (body of a lion); vindictiveness; protection (guards sacred treasure); fears; shadow side of yourself (undesirable qualities within you or unacknowledged parts of yourself) Do you need to defend your values? Where are you seeking power or revenge?
Harpies	**Harpies after you:** Feeling threatened; being manipulated **Confronting harpies:** Transforming your negative side **Oversized harpies:** Increasing resentment or vindictiveness; exaggerating your fears or shortcomings.	Seizes from others (birds with women's faces and sharp claws who torment humans without killing them); spite; malicious-ness; menacing female; harp on What are you going on incessantly about? Are you being selfish or self-serving?
Hydra	**Meeting a hydra:** Confronting your shortcomings **Turning into a hydra:** Dangerous or obsessive habits **Confronting a hydra:** Overcoming dependency or addiction.	Number nine (monster with nine heads, which when struck, each head grows two more); constant negativity; addictive harmful attitudes Where are you dealing with habitual maliciousness? Are you having trouble controlling your shortcomings?

Symbol	Symbol In Action	Possible Life Issues
Lamia	**Running from a lamia:** Feeling threatened; running from your fears **Confronting a lamia:** Facing your shortcomings **Dead lamia:** Overcoming your fears; rejecting injustice.	Beauty only skin deep; shallowness; devourer of children; envy; ruthlessness (beautiful legendary queen who was transformed into half an animal because of her wickedness) Do you need to nurture your inner child? Where could you be more understanding?
Medusa	**Running from Medusa:** Unwilling to face a dreadful situation; feeling persecuted or targeted **Confronting Medusa:** Facing your fears; needing to face your problems **Dead Medusa:** Overcoming your fears; previous threat.	Hideous sight; horrendous circumstances (woman who was transformed into a three-winged monster and whose gaze turns you into stone); can't look at an issue or situation; menacing female influence Are you facing adversity or adversaries? What can't you face?
Mermaid	See Siren/Mermaid this chapter.	
Minotaur	**Running from a minotaur:** Fearful of your desires **Slaying a minotaur:** Controlling your natural impulses **Baby minotaur:** Developing strengths; potential problems.	Power without intelligence (head of a bull, body of a man); basic urges and appetites (animal-man) Are you letting your instincts and impulses get the better of you? Where aren't you thinking?
Monster	See Common Dream Theme at the end of this chapter.	
Mythical	See Introduction in this chapter.	
Pandora	**Opening Pandora's box:** Situation getting away from you; lacking control; having regrets **Trying to close Pandora's box:** Unable to go back; holding onto hope	Curiosity (opened a forbidden box releasing the ills of the world, leaving only hope inside); lack of self-discipline; foolishness Is your curiosity getting you into difficulties?

Symbol	Symbol In Action	Possible Life Issues
	Looking at several Pandora's boxes: Several situations that could get out of hand	Where is your independence limiting you?
Pegasus	**Feeding Pegasus:** Upholding your integrity **Riding Pegasus:** Having the power to achieve; receiving assistance; successful endeavours or outcomes **Dead Pegasus:** Loss of power or self-respect.	Enduring; indestructible (immortal winged horse who carries hero to victory over evil); dignity of the spirit; integrity Where are you achieving victory? Are you doing good?
Phoenix	**Rising phoenix:** Growing through change; new beginnings **Turning into a phoenix:** Personal transformation **Sick phoenix:** Refusing to change; feeling stuck; stagnation.	Rebirth; transformation (legendary bird that sets fire to itself and rises again); purification of character; inner beauty (rare beauty, long, exotic feathers); evolution; mythical; spiritual energies Do you need to reinvent yourself? Where are you enduring and overcoming challenges?
Prince/ Princess	**Being a prince or princess:** Feeling blessed or chosen; believing in your right or prerogative **Being a reluctant prince or princess:** Having doubts about the role expected of you; fears about being able to live up to others' high expectations **Abusing your position as prince or princess:** Denigrating a position; lack of self-belief; letting others down; feeling unworthy.	Emerging fate or fortune; subject to envy; liberation of love; heroism; being in a good position; make-believe; right person for the job; predestined; vision of perfection; living in an ivory tower; out of touch with reality; privilege and responsibility; princely sum Do you have a sense of destiny or are you growing into a role? Where are you showing outstanding qualities or are feeling valued and respected?
Prometheus	**Meeting Prometheus:** Discovering conceit **Prometheus urging you on:** Needing to serve self-interest **Confronting Prometheus:** Challenging authority.	Power (stole fire from the gods, was punished cruelly but remained unrepentant); pride; theft; arrogance Have you been treated unfairly? Where don't you regret your actions?

Symbol	Symbol In Action	Possible Life Issues
Serpent	See Snake in Chapter 11.	
Siren/ Mermaid	**Hearing sirens singing:** Attraction; being manipulated **Discovering a mermaid:** Being fascinated; out of the ordinary **Slaying a siren:** Overcoming temptation; self-control.	Female power; seduction; distraction; deception; dangerous; alluring; unobtainable Are you feeling tempted? Where are your desires over-riding your responsibilities?
Sleeping Beauty	**Sleeping Beauty waking:** Having a second chance; new beginnings; overcoming obstacles **Sleeping Beauty falling asleep:** Being manipulated; unable to express yourself **Kissing Sleeping Beauty:** Initiating change; power of love.	Biding your time; make believe; wishful thinking; being swept off your feet Have you got hidden potential? What opportunities are you waiting for?
Sphinx	**Admiring the Egyptian sphinx:** Seeking power and wisdom **Confronting the Greek sphinx:** Rejecting control and manipulation **Damaged sphinx:** Lacking courage or inner strength.	Strength and intelligence (body of a lion with head of a man, in Egyptian tradition); devouring mother (monster with woman's head and lion's body, in Greek myth); ancient; ancient history Are you being overpowering and dominating? What's mysterious and incomprehensible?
Three fates	**Seeing the three fates:** Facing transition **Running away from the three fates:** Denying your wisdom; fear of ageing **Slaying the three fates:** Overcoming your fear; lack of vision.	Mortality (childhood, maturity, old age—maid, matron and hag); prediction; wisdom; visionary What's evolving? Are you losing track of time?
Unicorn	**Riding a unicorn:** Using your intuition or inner strength; fulfilling your dreams **Leading a unicorn:** Being a good example **Injured unicorn:** Damaged reputation; unable to achieve the impossible.	Being intuitive (has special powers); purity; grace; chastity; legendary reputation; visionary Where are your motives honourable? What's elusive and unattainable?

Symbol	Symbol In Action	Possible Life Issues
Vampire	**Vampire biting you:** Feeling used; lacking energy or vitality; being violated **Being chased by a vampire:** Feeling intimidated; needing to protect your rights **Breeding vampires:** Exploiting others; increasing self-interest.	Exploitation; self-interest; disease; fears; feeling deprived; needing others Are you taking advantage of others? Where are you feeling drained or depleted?
Witch	**Being under a witch's spell:** Being manipulated **Witch after you:** Being persecuted: witch hunt; feeling targeted **Being a witch:** Manipulating others; being envious; causing trouble; being a bad influence.	Wise woman; power; able to cure or harm; menacing influence; being spiteful or hostile; jealousy; trickery; ugly; witchy; witch-doctor Where do you feel left out or like an outsider? Who's bringing out the worst in you?

Common Dream Theme: Being chased by a monster or seeing a ghost
*Running from a monster or seeing a ghost can symbolise fears or memories.
Perhaps you're feeling intimidated or not wanting to face a hideous or
frightening situation. Your fears may not be real or they could be
haunting and possessing you. You could be embarrassed by feeling jealous
(a touch of the 'green-eyed monster') or perhaps you're shying away
from facing enormous odds that may be stacked against you.*

Chapter 13
Names

Names are more than mere labels.
Your name is a very important key
to understanding yourself as well as
the first element of your identity.
Laureli Blyth

Names can represent people you know or symbolise an attribute, sentiment, memory or experience you've had, or that you associate with them. Some names like those listed in this chapter can also have embedded meaning, or be used as word puns, to represent qualities within you. Explore all these possibilities before settling on the most feasible meaning.

How to get the best value from this chapter

- Look at the meaning or symbolism of the name and ask yourself the associated question.
- You can rephrase the questions to broaden their personal relevance to you, if necessary, by using other words with similar meanings.
- You can also turn any question around (including those you formulate) to see if you relate to them better, by asking them in a slightly different way. For example, rephrase it as a need, rather than a desire or belief or vice versa.

Desires and needs as opposed to outcomes and results

If a symbol represents an issue you are currently facing, then it may be indicative of your feelings, desires, beliefs or needs. This would usually occur in the first two-thirds of a dream, which often illustrates the issue you are dealing with and how you feel about it.

If a symbol comes in the form of a resolution, outcome, insight, solution or conclusion in the climax, usually at the end of the dream, then it may indicate a consequence, result or your dream advice to you.

Name	Name Meaning or Symbolism *Look for needs, where you express these qualities or their presence within you (even if not fully recognised)*	Ask Yourself *You can rephrase these questions if necessary, using other words with similar meanings to expand their personal relevance*
Aaron	Dignified	Where are you raising your standards or being elevated?
Abbott	Religious order	Are you acting in good faith?
Adam	Adam and Eve	Where are you being original or founding something?
Alan	Good-looking	What are you finding attractive in yourself or others?
Alastair	Protector	What values are you preserving?
Alexander	Supporter of humankind	Where are you offering or receiving assistance?
Alice	In Wonderland	Where are you out of touch with reality?
Amanda	Lovable	Do you need to love yourself?
Angela	Angelic	Where are you searching for perfection?
Archer	Arch, accomplished	Are you achieving success?
Ball	Having a ball	Are you enjoying yourself or needing to keep things moving?
Barbara	Stranger	What feels foreign or unfamiliar?
Bird	See Introduction in Chapter 2.	
Bishop	Clergyman	Are you ministering to others?
Black	See Colours in Chapter 5.	
Border	Boundaries	Where have you reached your limits?

Name	Name Meaning or Symbolism	Ask Yourself
Boyle	Boil	What's seething within you?
Brady	Energetic	Are you being passionate and enthusiastic?
Brian	Powerful	Where are you using your inner strength or being persuasive and influential?
Burrowes	Burrow under	What are you hiding?
Butler	Head servant	Are you attending to others?
Cannon	Cannonball	Where are you on a collision course?
Caroline	Womanly	Do you need to express your feminine side?
Carpenter	Joinery	Where do your affiliations lie?
Carroll	Christmas song	Are you celebrating who you are or praising others?
Carter	Carry	Where are you being responsible?
Cassandra	Elegance	Do you need to show humility and grace?
Chad	Contester	Where are you upholding your rights?
Christopher	Supporter of Christ	Are you holding spiritual or religious values?
Claire	Bright	Are you dazzling others or wanting to shine?
Cooke	Cook	What are you preparing or needing to prepare for?
Creek	Up the creek	Where are you experiencing difficulties?
Crouch	Bend down	What's weighing heavily on you?

Name	Name Meaning or Symbolism	Ask Yourself
Cunningham	Cunning	Are you being calculating or deceiving?
Daniel	Wisdom	Where do you need to show inner wisdom or good judgment?
David	Precious	What are you valuing?
Day	Day by day	What are you doing continuously or monotonously?
Dean	Head	Are you in control or needing to take charge?
Deborah	The bee: be	Where are you being industrious and organised?
Deidre	Sorrow	Are you suffering or feeling distressed?
Desiree	Desire	What are you longing for?
Dicker	Haggle	Do you need to bargain for what you want?
Dolittle	Doing as little as possible	Where are you being lazy or apathetic?
Drake	Duck down	Do you need to take cover?
Drummond	Beating	Are you working with, or needing to find, rhythm?
Dunn	Done	Where do you need closure?
Dyke	Ditch	Where are you feeling channelled or needing to channel your energies?
Dylan	Connected to the sea	Are you out of your depth?
Edward	Affluent protector	Where are you seeking abundance or security?

Name	Name Meaning or Symbolism	Ask Yourself
Elizabeth	Pledge to God	Are you making a promise to yourself or needing to show your allegiances?
Elvis	Wise	Where are you being perceptive or needing inner wisdom?
Emma	Universal	Are you being inclusive?
Evan	Warrior	Where are you defending yourself or your rights?
Fairchild	Impartial	Are you being fair and balanced?
Fairfax	Justice	Where are you showing good judgment?
Fairweather	Bright, clear	What's going well?
Felicity	Happy	Where are you feeling content or at peace with yourself?
Fisher	Search	What are you looking for?
Florence	Blooming	Where are you thriving?
Flynn	Red	Are you fiery or passionate?
Ford	Crossing	Where are you facing a transition?
Forrester	Forest	Where you can't see the wood for the trees?
Fox	See Animals in Chapter 1.	
Frank	Independent	Are you being self-sufficient?
Gail	Lively	Where are you showing spirit and energy?
Gardiner	Gardener	What are you cultivating?
Geoffrey	Peace	Are you seeking agreement or inner peace?

Name	Name Meaning or Symbolism	Ask Yourself
George	Man of the land	Where are you being practical?
Gloria	Glorious	Are you being honoured?
Golding	Golden	Are you seeking spiritual values?
Goodman	Blameless	Where have you got honourable motives?
Grace	Graceful	Where are you showing charm and grace?
Guy	Wide	Are you being broad-minded or inclusive?
Hannah	Graceful	Where are you showing charm and grace?
Harper	Nag, pester	What are you dwelling on?
Harvey	Protector	What are you protecting or defending?
Hawkins	Hawker	Where do you need to convince others?
Hilary	Cheerful	Are you feeling happy or optimistic?
Hope	Faith	Where are you expecting results?
Ignatius	Fiery	Are you emotional or highly strung?
Ingle	Fireplace	Where are you seeking comfort?
Irene	Peace	Are you seeking harmony or inner peace?
Isaac	Humour	Do you need to laugh at yourself or take things less seriously?
Jackson	Jack	Where do you need support?
Jacqueline	Supplanter	Are you undermining yourself or others?
James	Supplanter	What needs replacing?

Name	Name Meaning or Symbolism	Ask Yourself
Jane	Divine gift	What do you value highly?
John	Benevolent	Where are you being kind to yourself or others?
Jolly	Cheerful	Do you need to be more joyful?
Jordan	Channel	Do you need to go with the flow?
Judith	Praised	Where do you need to applaud yourself or others?
Kevin	Moderate and peaceful	Do you need to be more flexible or reasonable?
King	Ruler	Where are you taking or needing to show leadership?
Lamb	See Animals in Chapter 1.	
Levi	Cooperative	Are you connecting with others or needing to be inclusive?
Lincoln	Link	Where do you need to find yourself or relate to others?
Linda	Beautiful	What do you find appealing in yourself or others?
Long	Sustained	What's proving long and drawn out?
Louise	Warrior maiden	Are you showing courage or needing to defend your principles?
Lucy	Light	Where are you sensing greater possibilities or do you need to take things less seriously?
Luke	Illumination	Are you feeling inspired or searching for the truth?
Manfred	Peace	Where are you seeking harmony or inner peace?

Name	Name Meaning or Symbolism	Ask Yourself
Marshall	Official	Do you need to take charge?
Martin	Companion	Where do you need support and understanding?
Mary	Bitter	Are you feeling resentful or discontent?
Mason	Builder	Where are you making new plans?
Meeting famous people	See Common Dream Theme at the end of this chapter.	
Michael	Comparable to God	Are you striving to be the best you can?
Moody	Disheartened	Where are you feeling disappointed?
Nathan	Contribution	What legacy are you leaving behind?
Neil	Hero	Are you overcoming great difficulties?
Newton	New	Are you being creative or original?
Nicole	Victorious	Where are you succeeding?
Oswald	Divine strength	Are you making a superhuman effort?
Parker	Park	Where are you being held back?
Paul	Small	Where are you feeling insignificant or unimportant?
Peters	Dwindle	Where are you feeling devalued or what's decreasing in importance or relevance?
Phoebe	Shining	Are you radiating success or needing to shine?
Phyllis	Shepherdess	Where are you leading and guiding others?

Name	Name Meaning or Symbolism	Ask Yourself
Pike	Piking out	Are you shirking your responsibilities?
Piper	Music	Where are you playing your part?
Power	Strength	Are you using your inner strength or being persuasive and influential?
Price	Expensive	Where have you paid the price?
Prudence	Foresight	Have you got vision or a sense of things to come?
Quentin	See Five in Chapter 15.	
Quinn	See Five in Chapter 15.	
Rachael	Cherished	What are you valuing?
Ralph	Swift	Where do you need to respond quickly or get a move on?
Ramona	Protector	Are you defending yourself or others?
Rebecca	Bound	Where are you feeling restricted?
Redden	Blush	Are you feeling embarrassed?
Robin	Outlaw (Robin Hood)	Where are you following goals regardless of the consequences?
Rogers	Roger: 'Got it'.	What are you understanding or where are you feeling understood?
Rupert	Distinctive	Are you seeking recognition?
Ruth	Beautiful friend	Where are you trusting others?
Samantha	Attentive	Do you need to be more careful or observant?

Name	Name Meaning or Symbolism	Ask Yourself
Sarah	Princess	Where have you high aspirations?
Shepherd	Escort	Are you being a guiding influence?
Smart	Refinement	Where are you switched on and up to date?
Spry	Active	Are you being dynamic and enthusiastic?
Stephen	Crown	Are you seeking power and authority or recognition?
Tankard	Vessel	Where are you being receptive?
Taylor	Tailor	Do you need to adapt or satisfy certain requirements?
Thomas	Twin	Are you noticing resemblances or repetition?
Trainer	Instructor	Where are you teaching or coaching others?
Trudgen	Trudge	Are you losing your motivation?
Turner	Turn: shift	Do you need to alter your thinking or change your position?
Underwood	Under: below	Where are you feeling inferior or what are you suppressing?
Ursula	Bear	Are you carrying responsibilities?
Victoria	Conqueror	Where are you overcoming yourself or obstacles?
Victory	Triumph	Are you achieving success?
Vincent	Conquer	Where are you overcoming yourself or obstacles?
Virginia	Pure	Are your motives virtuous?

Name	Name Meaning or Symbolism	Ask Yourself
Vivian	Alive	Where are you living life to its fullest?
Ward	Avert	What do you need to change?
Wendy	Wanderer	Where are you drifting or lacking direction?
White	See Colour in Chapter 5.	
William	Resolve	Where are you showing determination and persistence?
Winnifred	Peaceful friend	Are you being composed or needing inner peace?
Wordsworth	Importance of speech	Are you speaking the truth or being true to your word?
Wright	Right: perfect	Are you in the right place at the right time?
Xavier	Brilliant	Are you talented or seeking recognition?
Young	Youthful	Where are you young at heart or being inexperienced?
Zara	Illumination	Are you feeling inspired or searching for the truth?
Zoe	Life	Where are you fighting for survival?

Common Dream Theme: Meeting famous people

Famous people can symbolise certain qualities within you or gifts that you didn't know you had. They would be attributes you associate with that particular person such as talent, beauty, sex appeal, intrigue, violent tendencies, ability to plot and scheme. They could also represent your ambitions to be rich and famous, the different roles you play, the various sides of your personality or your character changes. Perhaps you're out of touch with reality at times or simply hamming it up.

Chapter 14
Nature

Healthy feet can hear the
very heart of holy Earth.
Sitting Bull

Natural phenomena or features in your dreams can symbolise your environment, external or supporting influences, conditions or people. They may also represent general characteristics; essential qualities; your innate character; natural tendencies, forces or feelings and circumstances beyond your control. Consider these possible meanings along with any others specifically listed.

How to get the best value from this chapter

- See if you relate to any of the key words or questions and explore your own meanings which may override those given here.
- Look at all possibilities and apply the most appropriate for your situation.
- Rephrase the Life Issue questions to broaden their personal relevance to you, if necessary, by using other words with similar meanings.
- You can also turn any question around (including those you formulate) to see if you relate to them better, by asking them in a slightly different way. For example, rephrase it as a need rather than a desire or belief or vice versa.
- The Symbol in Action examples show how to apply context or link meaning with action.

Desires and needs as opposed to outcomes and results

If a symbol represents an issue you are currently facing, then it may be indicative of your feelings, desires, beliefs or needs. This would usually occur in the first two-thirds of a dream, which often illustrates the issue you are dealing with and how you feel about it.

If a symbol comes in the form of a resolution, outcome, insight, solution or conclusion in the climax, usually at the end of the dream, then it may indicate a consequence, result or your dream advice to you.

Symbol	Symbol In Action	Possible Life Issues
	Look for feelings, desires, needs, beliefs or situations, explore literal meanings, apply any puns and idioms	*Look for where, what and who this reminds you of, apply key words to thoughts, feelings or situations, explore literal meanings, apply word plays and figures of speech*
Air	**Looking into the air:** Can't see what you're looking for; seeking inspiration; aspiring to greater things **Breathing in the air:** Needing to calm down **Floating in the air:** Drifting along; gaining a higher perspective; needing to ground yourself.	Atmosphere; distinctiveness; communication; disappearing; mind; airing Do you need to air your grievances? Where are things still up in the air?
Ashes	**Burying ashes:** Putting the past behind you **Putting ash on the garden:** Taking the best of what the past can offer **Covered in ash:** Engulfed by the past; nothing left to offer.	Cleansing; feeling burnt out Are you dealing with what's been left behind? Where are you experiencing transformation?
Avalanche	**Hearing an avalanche coming:** Warning; impending threat; needing to be on your guard **Covered by an avalanche:** Danger; feeling out of control; feeling overcome **Running from an avalanche:** Wanting to escape; avoiding issues; can't face your feelings.	Can't cope; feeling devastated or vulnerable; danger; frozen out What's fallen or where have you let things slide? Are you feeling overwhelmed or inundated? (Also see Landslide in this chapter.)
Bacteria	**Looking at bacteria under a microscope:** Self-analysis; looking deeply; something you could miss **Having tests done:** Health warning; looking at causes **Breeding bacteria:** Health warning; developing unhealthy habits; strengthening harmful influences; unhealthy environment.	Self-sabotage; eroding confidence; underestimated problems; health warning What's undermining you? What do you need to take a deeper look at?

Symbol	Symbol In Action	Possible Life Issues
Biosphere	**Seeing a book with biosphere on the cover:** Cooperating with others; needing to be more open-minded **Lecturing on the biosphere:** Supporting and valuing others; being a team-player **Receiving high marks for biosphere exam:** Enjoying healthy relationships; accepting diversity.	Full of life; right to life; diversity of views and opinions; unity in diversity Where are you being supportive? Are you looking for an inter-dependent relationship?
Bubble	**Being in a bubble:** Insulating yourself; feeling isolated **Blowing bubbles:** Speaking without thinking **Bubble bursting:** End of good times; unfulfilled hopes and dreams.	Simmering issues; matters that lack substance; hopes; thoughts; thought bubble Are you daydreaming or fantasising? Are you bubbling over with excitement and enthusiasm?
Cave	See Cave in Chapter 4.	
Cliff	See Cliff in Chapter 4.	
Clouds	**Head up in the clouds:** Daydreaming; fantasising; out of touch with reality **Reaching for a cloud:** High aspirations **Approaching storm clouds:** Impending threat or difficulty.	Gloomy feelings; threatening situations; under suspicion; nebulous What's taking shape? What's clouded your judgment?
Cobweb	**Cobwebs throughout your house:** Neglecting yourself or your beliefs; needing to update **Cobwebs in your bedroom:** Letting your relationship slide; ignoring your need for rest **Being caught in a cobweb:** Can't see a way out; complications; being dominated.	Transparent motives; delicate issues or feelings; confusion; female dominance; world wide web Are you feeling trapped or manipulated? Where do you need greater transparency? (Also see Spider in Chapter 11.)
Compost	**Building compost:** Fertile endeavours or outcomes; sustaining yourself	Recycling; recurring feelings or situations Are you using all your resources?

Symbol	Symbol In Action	Possible Life Issues
	Scattering compost: Sharing or dispelling productive ideas; giving back **Huge pile of compost:** Lots of energy; valuable resource; overemphasising a recurring problem.	Where do you need to save time and energy?
Constellation	**Looking up at the constellations:** Considering your future; feeling in awe **Studying the constellations:** Considering group issues; seeing the bigger picture **Seeking a book featuring the constellations:** Needing a philosophy of life.	Astrological influences; astronomy; mystery; related ideas Where are you showing brilliance or promise? Do you have a sense of fate or destiny?
Cycle	**Cycling fast:** Making rapid progress; being impulsive **Day followed by night:** Things will change; pattern to unfolding events; inevitable; predictable **Wheel turning:** Progression of events; karma; reaping what you sow.	Repetitive behaviour or situations; sequence of events; phase of life What's recurring? What's taking a long time? (Also see Cycling in Chapter 10.)
Cyclone	**Trapped in a cyclone:** Warning; feeling emotionally stuck; being intense **Hearing a cyclone warning:** Stormy times ahead; difficult emotional issues **Cyclone blown off course:** Previous emotional threat.	Depression; emotional pressures; warning of impending danger Are you being destructive? Are you subject to violent outbursts?
Dam	**Building a dam:** Suppressing yourself; saving yourself or your energy; investing in the future **Letting water out of a dam:** Releasing emotions; outpouring of feeling **Heart-shaped dam:** Holding back love.	Suppressed feelings; emotional release; liberation Where are you feeling blocked? Are you conserving your energy?

Symbol	Symbol In Action	Possible Life Issues
Damp	See Humidity in this chapter.	
Darkness	**Darkness descending upon you:** Developing obscurity or complications; feeling unsure **Being lost in the dark:** Can't find your way; feeling confused **Darkness fading:** Coming to light; increasing clarity; feeling more confident; sensing a way forward.	Mysterious; obscure; hidden; meaningless Where are you feeling fearful or depressed? Are you being kept in the dark or out of the loop?
Desert	See Desert in Chapter 4.	
Ditch	**Jumping over a ditch:** Leaping over problems **Ditching your bag:** Offloading emotional baggage **Falling into a ditch:** Succumbing to difficulties.	Feeling drained; channelling energies; difficulty to overcome; offloading; ditching What do you need to abandon or let go? What are you avoiding or rejecting?
Earth	**Seeing earth revolving around the sun:** Playing your part; sensing a purpose **Crumbling handfuls of earth in your hand:** Worldly values that have no substance **Seeing the earth from outer space:** Gaining a sense of perspective; seeing the bigger picture.	Physical plane; mundane matters; worldly goals or values; interdependence Do you need to keep your feet on the ground? Are you being down to earth?
Earthquake	See Common Dream Theme at the end of this chapter.	
Ecology	**Reading a book on ecology:** Desiring interdependence **Receiving a high mark for an ecology exam:** Relating to others; enjoying quality relationships **Lecturing in ecology:** Taking responsibility.	Repercussions; extent of your influence What are you relating to? Do you need to adjust to your environment?
Electricity	**Light coming on:** Seeing the light	Energy; power; drive; nervous system

Symbol	Symbol In Action	Possible Life Issues
	Laying electrical wires: Channelling your energies **Being electrocuted:** Being highly strung; overanxious.	Where are you dealing with emotional tension or excitement? Do you need to connect to your source?
Environment	**Pollution:** Unhealthy mental, emotional or physical environment **Crowded planet:** Feeling anonymous; heavy competition **Chopping down vegetation:** Unsustainable position; needing to be responsible.	Integrated attitudes; right conditions; surrounding situations; context; your environment What external influences are impacting on you? Where do you feel supported or are supporting others?
Erosion	**Eroded creek bed:** Feelings eating away at you **Climbing up an eroded slope:** Regaining lost values **Landslide:** Slipping back into old habits.	Abrasive situations or people; causing friction; eroded confidence Are you feeling worn down? What's slowly deteriorating?
Excreta	**Blocked toilet:** Emotional blockage; repressed feelings **Can't go to the toilet:** Holding onto emotional pain; can't let go **Walking past an open sewer:** Issue that doesn't smell right; public negativity.	Offensive feelings, attitudes, people or situations; involuntary actions What do you need to release or eliminate? What no longer serves you?
Explosion	**Bomb exploding:** Danger; unexpected shock; uncontrolled outside influences **Volcano exploding:** Losing your temper **Implosion:** Self-harm.	Volatile situations; emotional outbursts; danger Are you unable to contain your feelings? Where are things about to erupt and boil over?
Field	See Field in Chapter 4.	
Fire	**Starting a fire:** Igniting strong feelings; purification; transforming yourself or others **Seeing a fireball:** Danger; uncontrolled emotion; passions running high	Intense feelings; passion; cleansing; transformation; playing with fire Are you being destructive? Where are you taking risks? (Also see Flames in this chapter.)

Symbol	Symbol In Action	Possible Life Issues
	Putting out a fire: Feeling discouraged; unenthusiastic; lethargic; denying your emotions.	
Flames	**Being in a burning house:** Warning; fuming feelings; being consumed by negativity **Playing with fire:** Taking risks **Using a flame-thrower:** Channelling your energies or emotions.	Spirit; mind; smouldering feelings; passion; past love; old flame What issues are flaring up? What are you all fired up about? (Also see Fire in this chapter.)
Flood	**Being caught in a flood:** Warning; feeling engulfed **Water flooding into your bedroom:** Emotional relationship **Rising flood waters:** Increasing vulnerability; inability to cope; surge of interest.	Danger; can't cope; feeling swamped; memories flooding back Are you feeling overwhelmed or inundated? Are you experiencing an outpouring of emotion?
Fog	**Being caught in a fog:** Can't see your way forward; lost your direction **Coming out of a fog:** Finding your bearings; back on track **Walking into a fog:** Losing your way; can't progress; getting confused.	Veiled issues; feeling enveloped; mysterious or obscure; smog Are you feeling confused or uncertain? Where are you being short-sighted?
Fossil	**Searching for fossils:** Looking for clues; retracing the past **Finding an important fossil:** Significant past influence; important point; missing link; finding evidence **Dropping a fossil:** Losing connections.	Past issues; fundamentals; ancient wisdom; digging up the past What needs preserving? What's outdated or behind the times?
Gas	**Cooking with gas:** Channelling your energies **A balloon filled with helium gas:** Soaring hopes; advancement; rising sales or finances; raise; economic upturn; moving faster than you thought	Explosive feelings or situations; expanding horizons; energy; drive; boasting; idle chatter; unimportant matters; gasbag What's irritating you? What's taking off or expanding without limits or restrictions?

Symbol	Symbol In Action	Possible Life Issues
	Leaking gas: Pent-up emotions; losing enthusiasm, energy or drive.	
Ghost	See Common Dream Theme at the end of Chapter 12.	
Glacier	**Exploring a glacier:** Needing to slow down; making slow progress; unavoidable **Glacier encroaching onto your house:** Circumstances that will have a family impact **Melting glacier:** Thawing feelings.	Frozen feelings; cold-hearted; preserving your values; inactivity; inevitable What's progressing very slowly? Who or what aren't you warming to?
God	**Hearing words spoken by God:** Intuitive awareness; receiving spiritual guidance **Sensing God's love:** Unconditional love; being at peace; don't need to fear **Knowing God's will:** Sensing your higher purpose; inner knowing; having faith in your spiritual convictions.	Universal principles; higher power; unconditional love; infinity; spiritual beliefs; guidance; My God; God Almighty Do you need to fulfil your higher purpose? Where are you considering the bigger picture?
Gravity	**Being pulled down:** Held back; being forced **Trying to get up but can't:** Feeling compelled or influenced **Going up into space in a rocket:** Breaking free; being independent; challenging authority; using your creativity.	Weighty issues; predictable outcomes; gravitate Who or what are you attracted to? Where are you dealing with important or serious issues?
Hailstones	**Being caught in a hail storm:** Feeling hurt by stinging comments; intense feelings **Catching hailstones:** Defending yourself against negativity **Very large hailstones:** Big difficulties; exaggerated problems.	Barrage of abuse; uncompromising difficulties Where are you being forceful or pressuring others? Are you seeking acclaim or recognition?
Heaven	**Looking toward heaven:** Seeking spiritual guidance or	Being in favour; life after death; angelic qualities; heavenly

Symbol	Symbol In Action	Possible Life Issues
	inspiration; being patient **Being in heaven:** Promising rewards; next world; afterlife; gaining perspective; seeing the bigger picture; blissful **Seeing the pearly gates of heaven:** Time's up; moving on; new awareness.	Where are you feeling happy and rewarded? Are you moving heaven and earth to achieve your goals?
Hole	**Digging a hole:** Making things difficult for yourself; progressing: making a hole in **Falling into a hole:** Danger; loss of power; losing ground or status; unable to get motivated **Hole in your heart:** Health warning; limiting your love; loving conditionally.	Openings or opportunities; leaking information; split factions or personality; getting out of something; loophole; picking holes; square peg in a round hole Where are you finding fault? Are you getting into difficulty?
Humidity	**Being lethargic in a humid environment:** Feeling discouraged; lacking energy or motivation **Perspiring in a glasshouse:** Feeling stifled **Getting off a plane and being struck by the humidity:** Being shocked; feeling oppressed.	Dampened enthusiasm; sticky situation Are you putting a damper on things? What are you getting steamed up over?
Hunger	**Being hungry:** Feeling unsatisfied; lacking power and influence; starved of love; lacking ideas **Going on a hunger strike:** Attracting attention; denying your needs **Being hungry but unable to eat:** Insatiable desires; unable to stand up for yourself; feeling helpless.	Physical, emotional and mental appetites; personal needs Where are you feeling empty or unfulfilled? What are you craving or desiring?
Iceberg	**Admiring an iceberg:** Needing more composure; being cool **Hitting an iceberg:** Hurt by bitterness; being unemotional; running into obstacles	Reserved manner; unconscious; iceberg lettuce; icebergers Where can you only see the tip of the iceberg? Do you need to break the ice?

Symbol	Symbol In Action	Possible Life Issues
	Huge iceberg in front of you: Frozen out; big difficulty ahead.	
Island	See Island in Chapter 4.	
Jungle	**Hacking your way through a jungle:** Being short-sighted; needing perspective; struggling to get ahead; making slow progress **Fighting in a jungle:** Confronting your natural impulses **Being attacked by animals in a jungle:** Overcome by your desires; lawlessness.	Impenetrable; basic instincts; survival of the fittest; concrete jungle; law of the jungle; jungle juice Are you facing strong competition? Where do you need to prove yourself?
Landscape	**Being a landscape gardener:** Following your soul's purpose; cultivating inner beauty **Planning a new garden:** Charting your course; setting goals **Destroying an old garden:** Making way for the new.	Planning your life; taking in the bigger picture Are you improving or trying to develop your natural talents? What are you imitating?
Landslide	**Running from a landslide:** Things getting on top of you or out of hand **Being trapped under a landslide:** Feeling stuck; swamped; snowed under or overpowered **People cheering at a landslide:** Landslide victory or overwhelming success.	Letting things slide; misjudging a situation; out of control feelings or situation; being on the run; slipping away Where are you feeling overwhelmed? Are you losing ground, status or position? (Also see Avalanche in this chapter.)
Light	See Light in Chapter 5.	
Lightning	**Seeing lightning in the sky:** Flashes of inspiration; being struck by an idea **Holding a lightning rod:** Averting trouble; discharging your energy; channelling your inner strength	Danger; ability to deliver a blow; power; authority; quick as lightning; lighten up Are you being destructive? Where do you need to strike quickly?

Symbol	Symbol In Action	Possible Life Issues
	Struck by lightning: Warning; unexpected affliction; not in your best interests; abusing your power.	
Magic	See Magician in Chapter 17.	
Magnet	**Holding a magnet:** Having magnetism or appeal **Being pulled by a magnet:** Being fascinated; lacking independence; being manipulated **Magnet repelling objects:** Driving others away; being held back; feeling unwelcome; overbearing influences.	Magnetic personality; seductive; irresistible; drawn in; force for healing Where are you being influenced? What are you attracting?
Manure	**Shovelling manure:** Shifting your energies **Spreading manure on the garden:** Conserving your energies; giving back; widening your influence **Selling manure:** Depleting your energies; selling yourself short.	Fertile imagination; recycling; yielding results; nurturing yourself Where are you generating new ideas? Are you being productive and efficient?
Moon	**Full moon:** Receiving insight; being foolish: lunatic **Lunar eclipse:** Fading intuition; being overlooked: being eclipsed **Landing on the moon:** Exploring new frontiers; forging the way; loneliness.	Unconscious; intuition; natural rhythms; feminine qualities; subordination; over the moon; mooning Where are you being guided? What's got its own rhythm?
Mountain	See Mountain in Chapter 4.	
Nature	See Introduction in this chapter.	
Ocean	**Sailing on the ocean:** Setting your course **Diving in the sea:** Exploring the unknown (or the unconscious) **Being washed into the ocean by a giant wave:** Danger; confused by something you	Below the surface; unconscious mind; depths of your being; mysterious; current of opinion; unfathomable; ebb and flow of life Where are you dealing with influences beyond your control?

Symbol	Symbol In Action	Possible Life Issues
	can't fathom; subconscious beliefs dominating you; feeling overwhelmed.	What seems endless?
Oil	**Striking oil:** Finding wealth; abundance; success **Oil on your tongue:** Flattering others **Oiling another's palm:** Exerting your influence; perverting the course of justice; bribing or persuading.	Reduce friction; fatty or greasy food; prosperity; harmony; cooperation; essential oils; well oiled Do you need to smooth things over? Where aren't you mixing with others?
Outer space	See Outer space in Chapter 4.	
Photosynthesis	**Seeing a book with photosynthesis on the cover:** Needing to be positive **Receiving a high mark for an exam in photosynthesis:** Achieving growth; having stamina **Lecturing in photosynthesis:** Spreading optimism.	Transformation; change; seeing the best in everything; producing goodwill Are you achieving personal growth? Where are you turning a negative situation into a positive one?
Planets	**Making a model of a planet:** Putting a good spin (or twist) on what you present **Seeing all the planets in the solar system:** Considering the bigger picture; your role in the scheme of things **Flying over Venus:** Wanting or expressing love.	Recurring issues; astrological influences; spin-off; spin doctor; spin-out Are you spinning out of control? What's out of this world?
Quicksand	**Being stuck in quicksand:** Getting dragged in; being pulled back; feeling trapped; can't cope; feeling overwhelmed **Pulled out of quicksand:** Confronting your fears; overcoming pitfalls; receiving help **Not seeing quicksand until too late:** Danger; being naive or unsuspecting; needing to be more aware.	Precarious position; hasty; impulsive; sinking into depression; quick-tempered; quick-witted; quick What are you being sucked into? What can't you get out of?

Symbol	*Symbol In Action*	*Possible Life Issues*
Rain	**Getting wet:** Being subject to outside influences; putting a damper on things **Dancing in the rain:** Ignoring consequences; liberating your feelings **Watching the rain from a sheltered position:** Protecting yourself.	Sadness; inner cleansing; downpour of feelings; regeneration; feeling saturated; determination; raincheck; right as rain; rained out; come rain or shine What do you need to release? Where do you need renewal?
Rainbow	**Looking for gold at the end of a rainbow:** Trying to find yourself; looking for rewards; imagined gains **Seeing a double rainbow:** Exceptional situation; feeling privileged; rare beauty **Admiring a rainbow:** Needing composure or poise.	Peace and tranquillity; bridge to other states of awareness; inner beauty; multicultural society; inspiration Are you finding unity within diversity? Are you chasing rainbows?
River	See River in Chapter 4.	
Road	See Road in Chapter 4.	
Rock	**Boulder in your path:** Obstacle to overcome **Rocky path:** Finding things hard going **Stacking rocks:** Building security; being defensive; defending your position.	Solid base or reputation; not showing your feelings; being stoic; tough; being changeable; rocking the boat Are you being solid and dependable? Are you between a rock and a hard place?
Sand	**Walking in the sand:** Finding it hard going; needing endurance **Rubbing sand through your fingers:** Handling friction **Shovelling sand:** Unearthing feelings; reorganising your time.	Takes time; smoothing things over; sanding; sands of time; sandpaper Where are you being worn down? Are you abrasive or irritating?
Seasons	**Seeing a chart with the seasons on it:** Importance of timing **Dressing in season:** Acting appropriately; suiting the occasion	Cycle of life; being in good condition; opportune moments; inactivity; in season; seasonal; dead season What needs to happen in its own time?

Symbol	Symbol In Action	Possible Life Issues
	Being in winter: Needing to bide your time; being serious.	Are you going through a phase?
Seaweed	**Collecting seaweed:** Setting goals **Eating seaweed:** Wholesome feelings or attitudes **Getting tangled in seaweed:** Being led or manipulated.	Healthy attitudes or habits (nutritious); easily influenced (subject to undercurrents) Are you drifting through life? Are you feeling washed up?
Shadow	**Being scared of your shadow:** Having doubts and suspicions; unable to face yourself **Large shadow:** Unable to let go; being pursued by fears; growing gloom or sadness **Having no shadow:** Leaving no trace; melting into obscurity; disappearing problems.	Shallow; fears; shady character; shadow self; attachments; projections; unsubstantial; secondary issues; phantom; imagined problems; hanging onto feelings; shadow-boxing; shadow cabinet; shadow of a doubt; shadow of yourself What's going on behind your back? What part of you seeks recognition and acknowledgment?
Shell	**Collecting shells on the beach:** Gathering resources; protecting yourself **Cracking an eggshell:** Needing to be more open; hastening your development **Finding a shell with no animal in it:** Feeling defenceless.	Self-protection; defensive attitudes; feeling targeted; framework; shell-shocked; artillery shells Are you coming out of your shell? Where are you protecting yourself or others?
Smoke	**Smoke in your eyes:** Clouded judgment; bewildered; can't see clearly **Smoking:** Addictive tendencies or habits; dependency **Breathing in others' smoke:** Absorbing others' problems; being harmed by others' actions.	Obscurity; preserving your values; driving out negativity; fuming; smoker; smokescreen Where are you being ambiguous or misleading? Are you feeling uncertain or confused?
Snow	**Skiing in the snow:** Finding balance; needing discipline; letting things slide; being on a slippery slope	Hostile reactions; icy reception; preserved values; crystallising views; feeling restricted; white as snow; snowed in; snowballing

Symbol	Symbol In Action	Possible Life Issues
	Thawing snow: Warming to something or someone **Snow falling on you:** Having cold feelings; frigid.	What's getting away from you? Are you being frozen out?
Soil	**Shovelling soil:** Shifting your support; rearranging your beliefs **Worms in soil:** Fertile ideas or ventures **No topsoil:** Unproductive enterprises.	Earthiness; grounding; productive endeavours; support; belief system What are you supporting? Are you growing and maturing?
Sound	**Breaking the sound barrier:** Blowing your own trumpet; moving quickly **Listening to sound effects:** Taking things in; making an impact **Sounding the alarm:** Warning; worrying yourself or others.	Making yourself heard; speaking and listening Are you holding sound principles? Who are you sounding out?
Spring	**Basking in spring sunshine:** Benefiting from your growth **Jumping on a springboard:** Bouncing back; using momentum; having something sprung upon you **Having a spring in your step:** Enthusiasm.	Origin or source; original ideas; beginnings; feelings that well up; new growth; time of year; rejuvenation Do you need to spring into action? Where do you need to show some flexibility?
Stalactite/ Stalagmite	**Looking up at stalactites:** Suspended judgments; emotional hang-ups **Looking at stalagmites:** Emotional outbreaks **Cave full of stalactites and stalagmites:** Unconscious beliefs.	Frigid; hardened feelings; standing up for yourself or others What are you projecting onto others? What are you hanging on to?
Storm	**Being caught in a storm:** Tense situation; feeling agitated or unsettled **Teacup rattling in a storm:** Feeling excited over a trivial matter: storm in a teacup	Violent outbursts; looming threat; commotion or uproar Are you in emotional turmoil or upheaval? Where are you forcing your way?

Symbol	Symbol In Action	Possible Life Issues
	Seeing a storm approaching: Impending difficulty or disturbance.	
Sun	**Sun shining:** Feeling blessed; enjoying life; feeling renewed; receiving insights and inspiration **Getting sunburnt:** Dangerous exposure; overdoing it; giving to others and neglecting yourself **Dying of exposure:** Warning; being unprepared; needing to protect yourself.	Sunny disposition; source of power and strength; light; wisdom Are you blessing others with joy and happiness? Where are you being supportive?
Sunrise	**Looking at sunrise:** New beginnings **Sun rising over the city:** New business opportunity or career move; renewed enthusiasm for work **Colourful sunrise:** Appealing new beginnings.	New beginnings; new opportunities; renewal Where are you looking at expanding horizons? Do you need to pick up where you left off?
Sunset	**Looking into the sunset:** Contemplating or reflecting on things **Sun setting over your business:** Ending or evaluation of your work **Colourful sunset:** Welcomed ending.	Period of review; evaluation; twilight years; beauty of accomplishment Where do you need closure? Do you need to review and reflect?
Swamp	**Being trapped in a swamp:** Getting cuaght; feeling over-whelmed; burying your feelings; withdrawing into yourself; being introverted **Being pulled out of a swamp:** Coming out of yourself; gaining confidence; receiving help; regaining control **Not seeing a swamp until it's too late:** Unaware of your insecurities or difficulties.	Being caught or trapped; complexities; shaky ground; emotional quagmire; giving way Are you feeling swamped? Where are you getting in too deep?

Symbol	Symbol In Action	Possible Life Issues
Thunder	**Not hearing thunder:** Turning a deaf ear; unaware of a developing problem **Being scared by thunder:** Feeling intimidated; vulnerable **Deafening thunder:** Serious threat; overpowering problem.	Loud manner; threatening situation; thunderous applause; startling situation; thunderbolt; thunderstruck Have you stolen someone's thunder? Where have you been a resounding success?
Tide	**Being swept away by the tide:** Being swayed by a current of thinking or emotion **Being washed up by the tide:** Feeling used; emotionally spent **Rising tide:** Surging feelings; unable to cope; getting out of your depth; danger.	Ebb and flow of life; cyclic nature of things; rising trends, opinions or feelings; holding back the tide; tide you over Have you reached your high water mark? Where are you dealing with emotional undercurrents?
Twilight	**Looking for stars:** Facing a state of transition **Seeing an increasing number of stars:** Coming out of obscurity; strengthening intuition **Can't see any stars at twilight:** Trying to find your identity.	Partial realisations; faint intuitions; declining years; strength or influence; stuck in between; waning; twilight zone Where have you glimpsed part of the picture? Are you sensing possibilities?
Underworld	**Boat with people on it travelling into the underworld:** Passing over; making a transition **Seeing underworld figures:** Issues of conscience; being tempted to act unethically **Breaking free from a gangster:** Escaping from domination; overcoming your temptations.	Criminal element; offensive acts or motives; afterlife; personal hell Where are you convicting yourself? Are you thinking of the repercussions of your thoughts and actions?
Valley	**Abseiling down into a valley:** Going backwards; descending **Walking through a steep valley:** Waning enthusiasm; situation that's hard to get out of or recover from **Climbing out of a valley:** Overcoming your difficulties.	Hollow promises or victory; feeling unfulfilled Are you falling into depression? What's going downhill?

Symbol	Symbol In Action	Possible Life Issues
Vibrating	**Sitting in a vibrating seat:** Being manipulated; feeling pressured **Feeling vibrations in a room:** Being intuitive **Appliance vibrating:** Faulty mechanism or body; feeling disturbed; being out of balance.	Atmosphere; keeping busy; constant motion; intuitive impressions; picking up vibrations Are you wavering or can't make up your mind? Where can't you settle?
Volcano	See Volcano in Chapter 4.	
Wake up	**Waking up in a bad mood:** Not wanting to face something; unenthusiastic **Jumping out of bed to the alarm:** Being enthusiastic; new awareness **Can't wake up:** In denial.	Increased awareness; catching on to an idea; recognition; understanding; stirring into action Where have you received a wake-up call? Do you need to be more switched on?
Water	See Water in Chapter 7.	
Waves	**Surfing in the waves:** Mastering a curly situation; feeling in control; experiencing heightened feelings or awareness **Small waves:** Minimal disruptions or disturbance **Being dunked by waves:** Feeling swamped; unable to cope; fears overcoming you.	Life's ups and downs; rise and fall of energies; feeling doubtful; curly questions; wavering What are you waving aside or dismissing? Are you on the same wavelength as others?
Weather	**Forecasting the weather:** Having expectations; making a prediction **Dressed geared up for the weather:** Preparing yourself for what lies ahead **Being out in the weather:** Feeling exposed; dealing with circumstances or influences beyond your control.	Emotional state; endurance: weathering Are you feeling under the weather? What are you making heavy weather of?

Symbol	Symbol In Action	Possible Life Issues
Wind	**Enjoying the wind in your hair:** Welcoming change **Strong winds:** Powerful forces against you or that you need to work with **Bag filled with wind:** Being too talkative.	Feeling unsettled or restless; turn of events; unexpected good fortune; windfall; poor digestion; windbag; get wind of; second wind Where are you sailing close to the wind and taking risks? Do you need to cast your cares to the wind and be more carefree?

Common Dream Theme: Being in an earthquake
*To dream of an earthquake can symbolise danger, being on shaky ground,
feeling as though your life has turned upside down or great upheaval.
It can represent feeling shattered, devastated, threatened, vulnerable
or symbolise that drastic measures need to be taken.*

Chapter 15
Numbers

Be at peace and see a clear pattern and plan
running through all your lives.
Nothing is by chance.
Eileen Caddy

In numerology each number emits a vibration and symbolises particular qualities with their own positive and negative aspects. If you see a number in your dream with more than one digit, reduce it to its essence, unless it has a particular meaning to you. For example, 1958 would be $1 + 9 + 5 + 8 = 23$ then $2 + 3 = 5$. Master numbers such as 11, 22 and 33 retain their own vibration.

How to get the best value from this chapter

- Ask yourself the questions that relate to your number and see which questions or qualities you relate to. Explore your own meanings which may override those given here.
- Look at all possibilities and apply the most appropriate for your situation.
- Rephrase questions to broaden their personal relevance to you, if necessary, by using other words with similar meanings.
- You can also turn any question around (including those you formulate) to see if you relate to them better, by asking them in a slightly different way. For example, rephrase it as a need rather than a desire or belief or vice versa.

Desires and needs as opposed to outcomes and results

If a symbol represents an issue you are currently facing, then it may be indicative of your feelings, desires, beliefs or needs. This would usually occur in the first two-thirds of a dream, which often illustrates the issue you are dealing with and how you feel about it.

If a symbol comes in the form of a resolution, outcome, insight, solution or conclusion in the climax, usually at the end of the dream, then it may indicate a consequence, result or your dream advice to you.

Number	Symbolises These Qualities	Questions to Ask Yourself
	Look for feelings, desires, needs, beliefs or situations, explore literal meanings, apply any puns and idioms	*Look for feelings, desires, needs, beliefs or situations. You can rephrase these questions, if necessary, by using other words with similar meanings.*
One	Initiative; action; independence.	**Positive:** Where have you got a pioneering spirit? **Negative:** Are you being selfish and competitive?
Two	Duality; lovers; sharing.	**Positive:** Where are you being cooperative and receptive? **Negative:** Are you being divisive or non-committal?
Three	Trinity; harmony; completeness.	**Positive:** Where are you being creative and dynamic? **Negative:** Are you being disruptive or disorganised?
Four	Stability; solidarity; work.	**Positive:** Where are you using intellect and discipline? **Negative:** Are you being rigid and inflexible?
Five	Freedom; independence; individuality.	**Positive:** Where are you embracing changes? **Negative:** Are you being rebellious and undisciplined?
Six	Nurturing; assistance; affection.	**Positive:** Where are you interested in serving others? **Negative:** Are you being possessive and restrictive?
Seven	Sacred; indivisible; mind and spirit.	**Positive:** Where are you showing prudence and discrimination? **Negative:** Are you isolated and arrogant?
Eight	Achievement; renewal; balance.	**Positive:** Where are you attracting success and prosperity? **Negative:** Are you being greedy and domineering?

Number	Symbolises These Qualities	Questions to Ask Yourself
Nine	Ideals; dynamic; creative.	**Positive:** Where are you being intuitive and accepting? **Negative:** Are you being impulsive and emotional?
Numbers	See Numbers in Chapter 16.	
Ten	New beginnings; completion; unity.	**Positive:** Where are you striving for perfection? **Negative:** Are you unable to accept second best?
Eleven	Visionary; mastery; revelation.	**Positive:** Where can you see the bigger picture? **Negative:** Are you abusing your power; or being fanatical?
Twelve	Cosmic order; grace; perfection.	**Positive:** Where have you got a sense of purpose and deeper meaning? **Negative:** Do you need to show forgiveness and lenience?
Thirteen	Transition; superstition; imperfection.	**Positive:** Where are you embracing change? **Negative:** Are you fearing the unknown?
Sixteen	Female energies; vulnerability; innocence.	**Positive:** Where are your motives pure? **Negative:** Are you feeling insecure and helpless?
Twenty-one	Initiation; maturity; responsibility.	**Positive:** Where are you being wise and level-headed? **Negative:** Are you avoiding responsibility?
Twenty-two	Attainment; enlightenment; completeness.	**Positive:** Where are you taking action and being productive? **Negative:** Have you set your standards too high?
Thirty-three	Spiritual potential; unselfish; sacrifice.	**Positive:** Where are you devoted to others?

Number	Symbolises These Qualities	Questions to Ask Yourself
		Negative: Are you being a martyr?
Forty-four	Turning point; obstacles; purification.	**Positive:** Where are you showing endurance and discipline? **Negative:** Have you got selfish motives?
Zero	Eternity; timeless; unlimited possibilities.	**Positive:** Where have you got untapped potential? **Negative:** Are you putting limits on yourself?

Common Dream Theme: Have I dreamt the winning Lotto numbers?

Rarely would numbers in dreams serve this function, however,
it is possible. More commonly, numbers would have a symbolic meaning
as dreams serve to move you to a point of wholeness and balance in your life.

Chapter 16
Objects and Other Things

I know I'm not seeing things as they are,
I'm seeing things as I am.
Laurel Lee

Objects and things can symbolise parts of yourself—your thoughts and feelings, areas of focus or your aims and objectives. They can represent your preoccupations, obsessions and exaggerations. They may also symbolise your status or circumstances—the predicaments, hindrances, obstacles and complications that you face. Look to the feeling behind the imagery and your relationship to the action for an indication of its significance. Consider these possible meanings with any others specifically listed.

How to get the best value from this chapter

- See if you relate to any of the key words or questions and explore your own meanings which may override those given here.
- Look at all possibilities and apply the most appropriate for your situation.
- Rephrase the questions to broaden their personal relevance to you, if necessary, by using other words with similar meanings.
- You can also turn any question around (including those you formulate) to see if you relate to them better, by asking them in a slightly different way. For example, rephrase it as a need rather than a desire or belief or vice versa.

Desires and needs as opposed to outcomes and results

If a symbol represents an issue you are currently facing, then it may be indicative of your feelings, desires, beliefs or needs. This would usually occur in the first two-thirds of a dream, which often illustrates the issue you are dealing with and how you feel about it.

If a symbol comes in the form of a resolution, outcome, insight, solution or conclusion in the climax, usually at the end of the dream, then it may indicate a consequence, result or your dream advice to you.

Symbol	Meaning or Symbolism	Ask Yourself
	Look for feelings, desires, needs, beliefs or situations, explore literal meanings, apply any puns and idioms	*You can rephrase these questions, if necessary, using other words with similar meanings to expand their personal relevance*
Accident	Bad luck; set back; unforseen obstacles; making amends; danger; warning; restoring relationships, values, status or situations.	What's happened unexpectedly or unintentionally? What do you need to repair, redress or pay attention to?
AIDS–HIV	Health warning; prone to negativity; being too open; lacking immunity; needing to cut yourself off.	Are you feeling vulnerable? Where do you need to protect yourself?
Alarm clock	Needing to be alert; timing issues; motivation; being prepared; needing to make a start; shock; precision; time running out; alarm; alarmist; warning bells.	Where are you being organised or running on time? Have you had a wake-up call?
Alibi	Rationalising your actions; measuring up; collecting evidence; your reputation; feeling secure or vulnerable; trust issues; making allowances or excuses.	Are you justifying or defending yourself? Where are you questioning your credibility?
Altar	Spiritual aspirations or practices; inner reflection; seeking guidance; honour and devotion; having or losing faith; alter.	What are you changing or altering? Are you sacrificing yourself or others?
Amnesia	Emotional or mental blockages; letting go; clear break with the past; being oblivious; split personalities; vague; inattentive.	What have you left behind or don't want to face? What have you overlooked or neglected?
Ankh	Immortality; ancient Egypt; eternal life; spirit; reincarnation.	What's enduring or resisting change? Where are you holding ever-lasting hopes and aspirations?
Anorexia	Self-deprivation; ignoring your self-interest; unhealthy attitudes; starving for attention; feeling out of balance or control; warning.	Are you lacking self-esteem or self-acceptance? Do you need to nurture yourself?

Symbol	Meaning or Symbolism	Ask Yourself
Archer	Committing to a course of action; goal driven; keeping sight of things; being direct; zodiac sign of Sagittarius; single-minded.	Where are you focusing on targets or aiming for your goals? Do you need to keep to the point or stay on track?
Arrest	Feeling guilty; questioning yourself; prevented from making progress; blocked; being challenged; justifying yourself.	Where have you been caught out? Has your conscience got the better of you?
Atlas	Finding your way; getting your bearings; taking a stance in relation to others; your position on an issue; feeling lost; gaining a different perspective; organising.	Are you trying to find yourself? Where are you mapping out your life or plotting your course?
Automatic teller machine	See Bank in Chapter 4.	
Autopsy	Being observant; morality; self-analysis; tearing yourself apart; following procedure; picking over remains; laying blame; mortality; closure; finality of a decision; official line.	Where are you uncovering causes or dealing with cause and effect? Do you need to be dispassionate or impartial?
Bagua mirror	Harmony; good atmosphere; having rapport with others; seeing yourself as you are.	Where are you protecting yourself or others? Are you rejecting negativity?
Bait	Being pressured or manipulated; feeling trapped or tricked; getting caught; being seduced or tempted; ambushing others; being naive.	Are you feeling used or targeted? Where are you being provoked or enticing others?
Ballot	Changes in attitude or behaviour; conforming; having influence; feeling powerless; having your say.	Are you making decisions or deciding on your values? Where are you being secretive?
Barcode	Counting the cost; self-worth; consequences and sacrifices you make; setting your standards; finding value.	Where are you paying a price? Are you focusing on speed and efficiency?

Symbol	Meaning or Symbolism	Ask Yourself
Big bang	Thinking big; never ending; God; philosophical perspective; beginnings; bigger picture; astronomy; enormous; causes and origins; unable to contain.	What are you grappling to understand or grasp? Where are you dealing with potentials or unlimited possibilities?
Billet	Mutual convenience; flexibility; living up to others' expectations; nurturing environment; being supported; transient; just passing through; moving on.	Where are you putting up with or accommodating others? Are you in a state of transition?
Bingo	Hinging on outcomes; got it: bingo; uncertainty; high expectations; things going your way; unexpected fulfilment or disappointments.	Are you taking risks or dealing with probabilities? Where have you been lucky?
Biopsy	Looking inward; self-analysis; looking deeper; disease; infected or tainted motives; undesirable thoughts, feelings or habits.	Where are you dealing with cause and effect? Are you reviewing your life or your goals?
Birthday	Taking ownership; growing in wisdom or maturity; ageing; self-worth; believing in yourself; anniversary; celebration.	Are you receiving acknowledgment or recognition? Do you need to honour yourself?
Bolt	Securing a relationship; being impulsive; feeling restricted; being locked in; unexpected occurrence; linking issues; bolt from the blue; bolt.	What are you running away from or is getting away from you? Where do you want to break free?
Bomb	Feeling bombarded; time ticking away; shock; emotional blow-ups or outbursts; bombshell; time bomb.	Are you making an impact or discharging your power and energy? Where are you dealing with an explosive situation?
Bonus	Financial perks or gain; emotional advances or rewards; unexpected abundance or happiness; bonus issue.	What have you received that you didn't expect? Where are you receiving additional benefits?

Symbol	Meaning or Symbolism	Ask Yourself
Book	Gaining insight; knowledge; achievement; getting to the point; self-analysis; teaching; reaching out to others; self-advancement.	What are you looking into or exploring? What are you trying to understand?
Bottle	Suppressing your feelings; courage; congestion; dependence; feeling repressed; bottleneck; bottle-fed.	Are you losing your bottle? What are you bottling up?
Bowling	Straight and narrow path; right technique; getting a grip on things; straightening out a situation; direct approach; uninterrupted course; trying not to deviate; keeping score; recreation; straight down the line.	Where are you aligning yourself? What's bowled you over or taken you by surprise?
Braces	Aligning yourself with others; being straight and honest; speaking frankly; brace.	What are you strengthening or supporting? Where are you bracing or preparing yourself?
Bucket	Containing situations; personal boundaries; dealing with limitations; supporting yourself or others.	Are you carrying responsibilities? Where are you fulfilling your needs?
Buoy	Keeping buoyant or cheerful; being optimistic; boy.	What are you bringing to the surface? Where are you charting your course? (Also see Boy in Chapter 17.)
Burglar alarm	Danger; taking precautions; feeling insecure; taking no risks; needing to secure your position.	What's disturbed you? Where have you been warned?
Business card	Your identity; responsibilities; fulfilling others' expectations; making yourself available; connecting with others.	Are you promoting yourself? Where are you adopting a business-like approach?

Symbol	Meaning or Symbolism	Ask Yourself
Button	Projected feelings or attitudes; attending to your appearances; tying up loose ends; keeping things to yourself; improving your self-image: button up.	Where are you attending to detail or concerned with finishing touches? Are you bringing things together?
Caduceus (winged staff entwined by two serpents)	Healing; communication (carried by Hermes); symbol of the medical profession.	Where are you using power or initiating action? Do you need to find balance?
Calculator	Counting the cost; maths; weighing up the facts; being precise; economising.	What are you assessing or evaluating? Where are you being calculating or devious?
Camera	Making memories; stage of life; seizing the moment; enduring record; needing or wanting to remember; recollecting the past.	What do you need to focus on? What's passing the test of time?
Cancer	Health warning; malicious influences; corruption; negativity; urgency; taking over; harmful attitudes; fighting for your survival; needing to prioritise.	What's getting out of control? Where are you being undermined?
Candle	Shedding light on a subject; soothing; seeking or receiving inspiration; peace; ritual; atmosphere; spiritual aspirations.	Where are you burning the candle at both ends? Do you need to look within?
Carnival	Going along with the crowd; celebrating; caught up in the power of the moment; light-hearted approach; need for joy; making a spectacle of yourself; being frivolous; feeling happy.	Where are you leaving your cares behind? Do you need to let off steam?
Cartoon	Imitating or mocking others; seeing the absurd or ridiculous; looking at the funny side; being sarcastic.	Do you need to laugh at yourself? What aren't you taking seriously?
Casino	See Gambling in Chapter 10.	

Symbol	Meaning or Symbolism	Ask Yourself
Ceiling	Passing or reaching thresholds; personal boundaries; standards or goals; evaluation of your experiences; expectations; limits.	Have you reached a ceiling or upper limit? What's surpassed your expectations and gone through the ceiling?
Cement	Being an adhesive force; feeling bound; strength; endurance; long-lasting effects; being tough; inflexible; uniting others; firming up support; rigid views; cementing relationships.	What are you holding together? Are you being strong and using your inner strength?
Certificate	Honour and prestige; high self-esteem; convention; ceremony; feeling proud; having rights; qualifying; power; wealth.	What have you achieved or accomplished? Where are you being acknowledged or respected?
Chainsaw	Abusing your power; being irresponsible; pressuring others.	Where are you being powerful and strong? Are you being efficient?
Chair	Official position; overseeing responsibilities; leading or organising others; taking it easy; reflection; unwinding; chairperson.	What are you presiding over? Where are you in a position of authority?
Charm	Being manipulated; seducing or tempting others; good fortune; pleasing features; endearing; making a good impression; lucky charm; charming; working like a charm.	What are you finding attractive or captivating? What's going well for you?
Childcare	Training yourself or others; delegating responsibility; developing potential; laying foundations; nurturing yourself or others; commitment; childish behaviour; feeling guilty; childhood memories; revisiting a role.	Where are you in a position of responsibility? What is proving hard to manage?
Chopsticks	Skills; talents; versatility; digesting ideas; being agile.	What are you feeding? What are you handling well?

227

Symbol	Meaning or Symbolism	Ask Yourself
Cigarette	Self-sabotage; dependence; fuming feelings; needing self-discipline.	Are you hurting yourself? Are you disrespecting others?
Circle	Wholeness; undivided; without beginning or end: vicious circle.	Are you going around in circles? Have you come full circle?
Club	Sense of belonging; abundance; gathering support; clubs: three-leafed clover.	Where are you defending yourself? Are you feeling lucky?
Coffin	Dealing with remains; memories; mortality; past; letting go; finality of a decision or outcome.	What part of you has died? What has ended or come to a close?
Compact disc	Harmonious relationships; indestructible; inspiration; joy; intuition; staying power; being on the right wavelength.	Where are you listening? What's enduring?
Condom	Being responsible; giving conditionally; considering consequences; feeling safe; avoiding repercussions.	What can't you conceive? Where are you taking precautions?
Conduit	Self-insulation; feeling dis-connected; leaking information; goal-setting; self-defensive; prioritising.	Are you being a channel or directing your energies? Where are you protecting yourself?
Conference	Formal agenda; keeping to the point; forming allegiances; common purpose; negotiation and networking; reviewing; planning; setting goals.	What are you discussing with others? Where are you gaining a wider perspective?
Credit card	Trusting yourself; fulfilling desires; being irresponsible; ignoring consequences; convenience; self-discipline.	Where are you risking the future? What are you borrowing?
Crescent	Rebirth; new moon; emblem of Islam or Turkey.	Where are you feeling renewed? Are you facing new beginnings?
Cross	Christianity; crucifixion; martyrdom; distinguished	Where have you got a cross to bear?

Symbol	Meaning or Symbolism	Ask Yourself
	service; protection; redemption; blessing; sacrifice; getting cross; cross-purposes; crossed out.	Have you got spiritual aspirations?
Crutches	Lacking independence; making slow progress; feeling inadequate; temporary setback.	Where do you need support? Are you progressing despite limitations?
Date	Feeling accepted; timing issues; expectations and obligations; meeting others; romance; ageing; date: the fruit; dated; dateless.	Where do you want more time? Have you made a commitment? (Also see Date in Chapter 7.)
Death camp	Survival instincts; determination; negativity; losing your will; bearing up; fighting the odds; against the odds; wrongdoing; injustice.	What's coming to a slow and painful end? Where are you being destructive?
Decoy	See Bait in this chapter.	
Delivery	Communication; trust; performance; fulfilling yours or others' expectations; giving birth to an idea, project or child.	Are you concerned with your presentation? Where are you delivering the goods?
Deposit	Thinking ahead; saving your energy; considering opportunities; security; having spare energy; believing in yourself; investing in yourself; commercial interests.	Are you making a commitment to your future? Where are you putting your trust?
Donor	Giving of yourself; big sacrifice; having a special bond; new lease on life; benefactor; supporter; sponsoring others.	Where are you giving to others? Are you being given a second chance?
Door	See Common Dream Theme at the end of this chapter.	
Drain	Feeling used; deprived; wasted efforts; feeling empty and unfulfilled; emotional clearing or outlets; suppressed emotions; depleted enthusiasm: down the drain.	Where are you feeling drained? Are you releasing your feelings?

Symbol	Meaning or Symbolism	Ask Yourself
Drawbridge	Self-defences; self-protection; retreating; restricting access; being inaccessible; being uncooperative.	Are you blocking or suppressing your feelings? Where are you withdrawing or isolating yourself?
Drill	Repetitive thoughts, feelings or actions; military; discipline; practice; rigorous routine; drilling or questioning yourself or others.	Are you observing correct procedure? Are you dealing with formalities?
Drugs	Taking remedial action; dependency; mental; emotional or physical addiction; being drugged; drug-user.	What are you relying on? Where do you need support?
Drum	Finding your own purpose; timing; talents; playing for time; repetitive issues or events; eardrum; drumming up support.	Where are you developing your own rhythm? What are you having drummed into you?
Dummy	Unable to be yourself; need to calm down; not the real thing; needing a crutch; putting on a good appearance; feeling stupid: dummy.	What can't you understand? Where do you, or others, need pacifying?
Earring	Intuitive awareness; listening to yourself; good listener.	Where do you need to listen? Do you like what you hear?
Easel	Revealing your talents; expressing yourself; being pushy; making yourself available.	What are you supporting? Where do you need to promote yourself?
Economy	External factors; context; economics; profiting from your actions; saving energy or time; commercial interests; opportunities.	What are you doing in an efficient and cost-effective way? Where are you being frugal or holding back from giving your fullest?
Elastic	Backtracking; likely to snap; limits to your growth or patience; changing your mind or principles.	Are you contracting or expanding? Where are you being flexible?
Emergency	Urgent remedial action; feeling compassion; needing support; danger; prioritising your values.	What needs your immediate attention? What are you concerned about?

Symbol	Meaning or Symbolism	Ask Yourself
Envelope	Wrapping up; expressing your feelings; communicating with others; being enveloped; pushing boundaries.	What have you sealed? Where are you pushing the envelope?
Equinox	Marking change; observing progress; acknowledging a significant event; need for balance and stability; symmetry; inevitability; predictable; cyclic nature of things; six months.	Where do you need to achieve balance? Are you being caught in the middle?
Explosion	See Bomb in this chapter.	
Facelift	Making a new start; having a second chance; make-over; self-transformation; wanting to impress; pretence.	What are you improving? Where aren't you being true to yourself?
Feather	Feeling happy; sharing the same fate; cowardice; self-enrichment; birds of a feather; in fine or high feather; feather your nest; feather in one's cap.	What do you need to treat more lightly? What are you achieving?
Fence	Barriers or obstacles; self-protection; defining boundaries; limiting yourself; determining values; feeling restricted.	Are you sitting on the fence and not making a commitment? Where are you feeling fenced in?
Ferris wheel	Being supported; desires; attraction; expressing your inner child; needing to be spontaneous.	Do you need a different perspective? Where are you going around in circles?
Film/Movie	Life episodes or occurrences; relaxation; memories and recollections; objectivity; life lessons; evaluating; educating or entertaining yourself.	What are you reviewing? Where do you need a different perspective?
Fireworks	Emotional blow-ups; celebration; making a spectacle of yourself; gaining attention; impressing others.	Are you creating an impact? Where are you feeling disturbed or excited?

Symbol	Meaning or Symbolism	Ask Yourself
First aid kit	Dealing with the fundamentals; following procedure; needing remedial action.	What needs immediate attention? Where do you need to prioritise? (Also see Emergency vehicle in Chapter 18.)
Flying saucer	Intrusion or interference; intelligence; novel or innovative idea; feeling insecure; fears; considering potentials; delving into the unknown.	Where are you moving boundaries? Are you dealing with the unfamiliar?
Football	Team-player; cooperation; aggression; common goals; sense of fair play; seeing things in black and white; self-discipline; playing the game.	Where are you being competitive? Are you dealing with opposition? (Also see Football oval in Chapter 4.)
Footsteps	Leading others; leaving your mark; providing an example; being led; taking step by step.	Are you following in someone's footsteps? Where are you creating an impression?
Fraction	Dealing with small details; more to come; taking things out of context; bias; pieces of the puzzle; needing to consider the whole story.	What could fracture or fragment? What are you putting back together?
Fracture	Going to pieces; giving way; feeling fragile; damage; split loyalties; warning; interruption; differing beliefs; breaking from tradition; split personality.	Where are you dealing with differences? What's breaking up?
Gallows	Hang-ups; mortality; helplessness; suspended judgments; convicting yourself; criminal behaviour; being made redundant; destructive attitudes or behaviour.	Where have you been left dangling with no support? What part of yourself are you killing off?
Game	Being fair-minded; playful approach; inconsequential outcomes; gambling; not taking things seriously; joining with others; gaming; game is up; on the game; 'It's only a game'.	Where are you playing the game or following the rules? Are you being pursued or treated as fair game?

Symbol	Meaning or Symbolism	Ask Yourself
Gate	Open or closed opportunities; obstacles; intruding thoughts or feelings; gatecrasher.	Where are you considering your options? What are you gaining access to?
Ghetto	Feeling labelled; being singled out; rigid boundaries; deprived; discrimination; limited opportunities; being coerced.	Where are you feeling isolated? Are you feeling constrained?
Glass	Need for transparency; versatility; strong and delicate; handle with care; reflection; need for sharper focus; limitations of expected possibilities; glasses; looking glass.	What are you seeing through? Have you reached a glass ceiling?
Globe	Global issues; earth; universal views; sphere of influence; worldly wise; interdependence; your environment; looking at the bigger picture; being supported.	Are you being inclusive? Where are you being philosophical? (Also see Earth in Chapter 14.)
Grade	Weighing up; sense of achievement; self-worth; learning; evaluating yourself; level of performance; qualifying; graded; making the grade.	Are you measuring yourself against others' standards? Where do you need to smooth things over? (Also see Exam in Common Dream Theme in Chapter 4.)
Gun	Self-defences; meeting opposition; feeling threatened; criminal intentions; outlaw tendencies; forcing the issue; being coerced, pressured or manipulated.	Do you need to stick to your guns? Where are you going great guns or handling things with speed and power?
Haemorrhage	Health warning; urgency; losing your feelings for someone; letting things slide; needing to prioritise.	What can't you stop? Where are you losing energy or enthusiasm?
Hair dye	Not being true to yourself; pretence; living a lie; make-over; self-transformation.	Are you changing your thinking? Where are you trying to live up to others' expectations?

Symbol	Meaning or Symbolism	Ask Yourself
Hammer	Thrashing out a problem; being hard on yourself or others; losing control; under the hammer or offered for sale; hard as nails.	Are you hammering a point or forcing your view? Are you driving yourself or others?
Hammock	Being supported; suspending your judgments; taking time out; relaxation.	What's still up in the air? Where do you need to be more laid-back?
Handbag	Fulfilling everybody's needs; feeling vulnerable; feminine energies or role.	Are you using your feminine strengths to influence others? Are you fulfilling domestic responsibilities?
Handcuffs	Being restricted; limitations; conscience; feeling guilty; being hard on yourself; judging yourself or others; self-criticism.	What are you securing? Where are you being held back?
Handle	Having control; dealing with issues; managing yourself and others; opportunities; manipulating a situation; gaining access; losing emotional control; handler; handouts.	What are you handling? Are you flying off the handle?
Hang-glider	Left hanging; being suspended; hanging on; dependency; pushing boundaries; new possibilities; hang-ups.	Where are you taking risks? Are you on the edge?
Hard disk	Way of thinking; belief system; memories; self-analysis; mind; your values; organised; Akashic records (universal hall of records); magnetic influence (magnetisable material); dealing with details, facts or evidence.	Where are you processing information? What are you recollecting?
Hard hat	Gaining access to hidden parts of yourself; emotional fallout; being responsible; taking control; rigid views; self-protection; emotional defences; demanding situations; having realistic expectations; hard; hard feelings.	Are you being hard-headed or unemotional? Where are you weighing up risks?

Symbol	Meaning or Symbolism	Ask Yourself
Harness	Exploiting opportunities; feeling burdened; hard work; exercising self-control; being manipulated; assuming authority; utilising energies.	What are you controlling or directing? What needs reigning in?
Haversack	Responsibilities; holding on; taking ownership; being responsible; thinking ahead; independence.	Are you feeling prepared? Where are you fulfilling your needs?
Heap	Things piling up; clutter; abundance; making a contribution; losing control; making a problem worse; many layers to an issue; heap of trouble.	What are you accumulating? Are you falling in a heap?
Hearth	Home; warmth; self-protection; fond memories; romance; socialising with others; relaxation.	Where are you feeling comfortable and accepted? Are you concerned with security or your personal security?
Helmet	Taking precautions; being defensive; rigid attitudes; protecting yourself or others.	Are you keeping your thoughts to yourself? Where are you being unyielding?
HIV	See AIDS–HIV in this chapter.	
Honeymoon	Feeling content and happy; marriage; holiday; high expectations; new commitment; new beginnings.	Where have you got off to a good start? Are you enjoying a period of goodwill?
Horoscope	External influences; subtle energies; potential strength and weaknesses; fate; prediction; birthday; individuality.	Where are you considering your future? What's got perfect timing?
Horse float	Being in control; weighty issues; relaxation.	Where are you seeking mobility? Are you dealing with big responsibilities?
Horseshoe	Good luck; protection; prosperity; self-defensive; fortuitous.	Do you need to do an about-face? Where do you need to look after yourself?

Symbol	Meaning or Symbolism	Ask Yourself
Hose	Taking control; directing others; home and hosed.	Where do you need to channel your energies? Are you being flexible?
Hourglass	Passing time; patience; ageing; moving on; opposing points of view; evolving issues; needing to get started.	What's unavoidable or inescapable? Where are you dealing with opposites?
Hybrid	Inclusiveness; evolution; indecision; evolving issues; lack of individuality; variety; crossbreed; best of both worlds.	What are you bringing together? Where have you got mixed feelings?
Incense	Calming effect; inner peace; meditation; atmosphere; looking inwards; spiritual aspirations; clarity.	Are you feeling incensed? Where do you need to reflect?
Infection	Disease; contagious feelings; undesirable thoughts, feelings or habits; corrupting yourself or others; contaminated motives; infectious.	Are you spreading ill-feeling? What can't you contain?
Intercom	Nervous system; family issues; close connections; tuning in; looking inwards.	Are you being intuitive? Where do you need to listen to yourself?
Jigsaw	Piece of a puzzle; important details; associated feelings or thoughts; related situations; sense of belonging; seeing where things fit together; finding your place or role.	Where are you feeling puzzled or confused? What are you pondering over or reflecting on?
Job	Career; serving others; how you see yourself; carrying out your responsibilities.	What roles are you playing? Where are you fulfilling others' expectations?
Journal	Review; contemplation; being observant; learning from your experiences.	What are you keeping a record of? Where are you evaluating your experiences?
Juice extractor	Gaining information; developing your potential; finding yourself.	What are you taking out? Where are you applying pressure or feeling pressured?

Symbol	Meaning or Symbolism	Ask Yourself
Jump	Sudden rise in status; being motivated; overcoming obstacles; deserter; jump on; jump ship; jump start.	What are you jumping at? Where are you leaping ahead?
Kennel	See Dog in Chapter 1.	
Key	Solutions; gaining access; openings; opportunities; having authority; keyboard.	Where have you got the answers? Are you keyed up or anxious?
Knot	Feeling confused; making quick progress; feeling constricted; nautical mile; getting entangled: tied in knots; at a rate of knots.	Are you tying yourself in knots? Are you dealing with difficulties?
Ladder	Rise or fall in social or financial status; personal aspirations; higher purpose; higher consciousness; feeling superior; looking down on others.	Are you climbing the corporate ladder? Have you reached the heights of your fame or career?
Leader	Dominance; self-assurance; expertise; courage; decisiveness; vision; front-runner; leadership qualities.	Where are you taking control or exercising authority? Are you inspiring or guiding others?
Legend	Legendary reputation; seeking or giving explanation; tradition; exaggeration.	Where are you trying to ascertain the truth? Are you receiving notoriety?
Lego block	Making new plans; trial run; needing to have fun; exploring new possibilities.	Where are you making things fit? Are you being creative?
Leotard	Being fit; capable; give and take; self-discipline; looking good; tight or good fit; under strain; feeling squeezed or pressured.	Are you feeling comfortable in your role? Where are you feeling challenged or stretched?
Letter	Conferring with others; message; communicating; learning something new; fulfilling your responsibilities.	Do you need to listen to others or yourself? Where do you need to know more?

Symbol	Meaning or Symbolism	Ask Yourself
Lock	Closed prospects; feeling excluded; needing a solution; being barred; rigid or inflexible outlook; denying yourself; unable to be yourself.	Are you unable to proceed? Where are you securing your position?
Mask	Disguising your feelings; putting on a front or brave face; playing different roles; your public face; fulfilling others' expectations.	Where are you shielding or protecting yourself? What are you hiding behind?
Menu	New ideas; fulfilling desires; feeling satisfied.	Where are you making choices? What are you prioritising?
Metal detector	Looking for answers; taking ownership; finding yourself; needing direction; discovering your talents.	What have you lost? Do you need inner strength?
Microscope	Self-analysis; attention to detail; looking within; seeing what others can't; exaggerating small issues; being perceptive; foresight.	What do you need to take a closer look at? Where are you looking for answers?
Microwave	Sacrificing quality; being efficient; not allowing enough time; being impulsive.	Where are you looking for convenience? Do you want quick results?
Mouse trap	Having limitations; emotional barriers; feeling trapped or repressed; unable to progress; suppressing your feelings.	Have you been caught out? Where are your fears holding you back?
Numbers	Evaluating a situation; considering the facts; selecting options; shoring up support; looking for regularity or routine; quantity; systematic approach; dealing with details; sequence of events; order of things.	What's not adding up? Where is your number up?
Objects	See Introduction in this chapter.	
Olympic	High standards; self-discipline; great achievement; four-year	Where are you striving to be your best?

Symbol	Meaning or Symbolism	Ask Yourself
	period; success; lofty goals and ambitions; making sacrifices.	Are you being very competitive?
Ouroboros (Snake consuming its own tail)	Destruction and renewal; eternal life; unity; gnosticism.	Where are endings leading to new beginnings? What's continuous or proving never-ending?
Overdraft	See Debt collector in Chapter 17.	
Paperweight	Unable to let go; applying pressure; being too responsible; being repressed; keeping things together.	Are you being responsible? Where are you controlling or dominating others?
Parade	Feeling on display; official inspection; making a good impression; public opinion; review and scrutiny; parading your talents; receiving recognition.	Where are you or others acknowledging your achievements? Are you being distracted by the passing parade?
Pen	Being creative; teaching; communicating with others; pushing boundaries.	What are you authorising? Where are you feeling confined or restricted?
Pencil sharpener	Making a good impression; needing to be more focused; being clear or definite.	Are you being sharp or astute? Who have you been sharp with?
Pendulum	Suspended judgments; fluctuating fortunes, events or prices; doing a turnaround; can't settle.	Where are you having trouble making up your mind? Are your moods swinging or changing?
Pentagram (five-pointed star)	Number five; personal status or rank; psychic power. (Also see Five in Chapter 15.)	Are you abusing your power? Where are you seeking control or domination?
Perm	Change; permanence; make-over; self-transformation; pretence; not being true to yourself.	Are you wavering? Where have you changed your thinking?
Photocopier	Committing a fraud; losing quality; forgery; communication; spreading	Who are you imitating? Where are you aware of similarities or repetition?

Symbol	Meaning or Symbolism	Ask Yourself
	wisdom; reproducing an idea; replica; copying.	
Picture	Memories; artist; beauty; imitation; someone's interpretation; creativity; fantasies; self-image; movies.	What are you visualising or imagining? What are you representing or symbolising?
Pillow	Sleep; feeling comfortable; seeking relief; being lethargic or passive.	Do you need to relax? Where are you looking for support?
Playgroup	Teaching others; being naive; being childish; childhood memories; having potential; laying foundations.	Do you need to connect with your inner child? Where are you being dependent? (Also see Baby and Children in Chapter 17.)
Playstation	Needing to react quickly; dependence; being decisive; influencing outcomes; out of touch with the real world.	Do you need to interact with others? Where do you need to be more involved?
Power board	Overdoing things; being full-on; spreading yourself in different directions.	Where are you channelling your energies? Are you pacing yourself?
Refrigerator	Chilling out with friends; frozen out; melting the ice; insulating yourself; cool; cool off.	What do you need to preserve? Where are you feeling cold or unenthusiastic?
Ring	Continuity; marriage; endless love; devotion; loyalty; ever-lasting; outclass: run rings around; ring of confidence.	Are you making a commitment or taking a pledge? Where are you being faithful to yourself or others?
Riot/Protest	Self-indulgence; disorder; dissatisfaction; confronting injustice; being principled; taking a stand; being rebellious.	What are you disapproving of? Where are you being undisciplined?
Roller-coaster	Being taken for a ride; emotional highs and lows; runaway events; lack of control; fear; impulsiveness; being reckless; fate.	What's got its own momentum or agenda? Where are you dealing with life's ups and downs?

Symbol	Meaning or Symbolism	Ask Yourself
Rosary beads	Can't let go; spiritual aspiration; guidance; personal mantra.	Where are you keeping score? What's coming around again and again?
Rubber boots	Being prepared; defending your beliefs; taking precautions; rubbing; rubber stamp.	Where are you being down to earth? Do you need to get back to basics?
Rubbish	Past attitudes or beliefs; out of date; decaying ideas; unhealthy; better disposed of.	What no longer serves you? What is festering within you?
Rug	Self-protection; defences; foundation; beliefs; admiration; exposing or betraying yourself or others; rug up.	What are you sweeping under the carpet? Are you pulling the rug out from under someone?
Rusty tools	Unused talents or skills; outmoded work practices.	Where is your thinking out of date? What do you need to discard?
Saddle	Burdens; feeling comfortable; self-discipline.	Where are you in control? What are you being saddled with?
Safe	Acceptance; contentment; trusting yourself or others; tolerance; love; support.	Where are you feeling secure? Are you at peace with yourself?
Sage	Teaching others; spreading wisdom; clearing your energies; gaining clarity.	Are you seeking inner wisdom? Where are you being wise? (Also see Sage in Chapter 20.)
Saw	Terminating; discontinuing; intervening; tearing apart; proverb or maxim; being aware; seen; seesaw; score.	What are you cutting back on? What's aggravating you?
Scales	Sense of fairness; being impartial; balance; harmony; right and wrong; zodiac sign of Libra; needing to put things right.	What are you weighing up? Where are you dealing with injustice?
Scoreboard	Scoring points; self-esteem; assessing your performance;	Where are you keeping score? Are you gaining results?

Symbol	Meaning or Symbolism	Ask Yourself
	numbers game; music: score; evaluating yourself against others; being competitive.	
Screwdriver	Needing or making adjustments; sexual intercourse; gaining leverage; screwed.	Have you 'screwed up' or made a mess of things? Where have you been taken advantage of?
Seatbelt	Protecting yourself; progressing safely; avoiding risks; feeling secure.	Are you taking precautions? Where do you want to maintain your position?
Seesaw	Opposing position; role reversal; working together; being over-ruled; life's highs and lows.	Where do you need to restore balance? Are you having emotional ups and downs?
Sensor light	Warning; foresight; premonitions; being alert; being defensive; emotional sensitivities; protecting yourself.	Where are you being perceptive? Are you being intuitive?
Shovel	Shifting loyalties or position; looking below the surface; relocating or rearranging.	What are you unearthing or trying to find? Are you undermining yourself?
Sunglasses	Can't face something on your own; coping mechanisms; talents; protecting yourself.	What are you putting your own interpretation on? Where are you being outstanding?
Shredder	No trace with the past; seeking a new start; being unaccountable for your actions; evading responsibilities.	Where are you leaving no evidence? Are you feeling guilty?
Shroud	Suppressing feelings; mystery; masking the truth; cover up; Jesus Christ; death; ending.	Where are you protecting yourself or others? What are you hiding or can't see?
Sickle	Grim reaper; death; ending; closure; zodiac sign of Leo; ritual; Druidism; sickle cell anaemia.	Where are you reaping rewards? Are you reaping what you've sowed?

Symbol	Meaning or Symbolism	Ask Yourself
Sink	Sinking your differences; losing ground, reputation or position; unawareness; suppressing your feelings; needing to settle down.	What's declining or heading down? What have you lost?
Solitary	Reflection; peace; being unsupported; trying to find yourself; feeling excluded; empty or unfulfilled; breaking free; independence; withdrawn; turning your back on society.	Where are you feeling isolated? Are you being non-committal?
Sperm	Imitation; making a copy; fathering; recreating; seed thought or idea; initiating; sperm whale; being responsible for.	What are you breathing new life into? What are you originating or creating?
Spiral	Evolving circumstances; transformation; moving on or forward.	Where are you making progressive and continual progress? What's spiralling out of control?
Sponge	Immersed in your work; having nothing left; feeling saturated; being wrung out; taking from others.	What are you absorbing or taking in? Are you sponging off others?
Square	Stability; foundation; four directions; square up; square deal; square peg in a round hole.	Are you being square or conservative? Where are you back to square one or where you started?
Stamp	Communicating with others; leaving your mark; authorising; making an impression; suppressing; stamping ground.	What do you need to stamp out? What are you giving validity to? (Also see Post office in Chapter 4.)
Stop sign	Terminated plans; obstructions; suppression; out of your control; warning not to proceed; closure; stop; stopgap.	Where have things come to a halt? What are you putting to an end?
Submarine	Feeling pressured or restricted; needing to work closely with others; seeing no way out.	Are you feeling overwhelmed? Where are you looking below the surface?

Symbol	Meaning or Symbolism	Ask Yourself
Swearing	Being disrespectful; speaking the truth; upholding your principles.	What are you promising? Where are you being offensive?
Switch (light)	Feeling connected or disconnected; controlling your energies; change; seeing the light.	Do you need to be switched on? What's on again and then off again?
Sword	Having the upper hand; facing hostilities; applying pressure; using force; violence; power; destruction; ceremony; authority; intimidating others.	Are you confronting opposition? Where are you wielding your influence?
Syringe	Needing support; lacking integrity; depleted strength; habitual responses; threatening others; feeling vulnerable.	Where are you being dependent? What are you relying on?
Telephone	Communicating with others; getting in touch with yourself; receiving intuition.	What messages are you sending to others? Do you need to listen to your inner self?
Television	Reviewing your experiences; communicating; broadcasting your feelings or views; entertaining or educating yourself; relaxation; public knowledge; picturing an outcome.	Where are you receiving or processing information? What are you visualising or imagining? (Also see Film/Movie in this chapter.)
Theatre	Different sides of your character; roles you play; make believe; putting on a performance; entertaining ideas or others; looking at life from another perspective.	Are you being dramatic or melodramatic? Are you putting on an act or showing pretence?
Things	See Introduction in this chapter.	
Timer	Being deceptive; pretence; punctuality; taking precautions; sequence of events.	What's automatic? Where are you feeling insecure?
Torch	Searching for answers; looking within; revealing the truth; devotion; torchbearer.	Are you seeing the light? Who are you holding a torch for?

Symbol	Meaning or Symbolism	Ask Yourself
Tow bar	Taking the past with you; responsibilities; emotional baggage; holding on; being guided or influenced; relaxation.	What are you taking with you? Where are you feeling tied? (Also see Wagon in Chapter 18.)
Triangle	Number three; Holy trinity; trio; threesome; mind body and spirit. (Also see Three in Chapter 15.)	Where are you reaching the apex of your career? Are you channelling spiritual energy?
Trophy	Succeeding against the odds; victory; success; self-discipline; achievement.	Are you feeling triumphant? Where are you feeling proud and satisfied?
Trunk	Recollections; reminiscing; moving on; leaving things behind; torso; transition; sorting things out; emotional baggage; swimming trunks.	Where are you repressing the past? What are you taking with you?
T-square	Being out of balance; falling into line or conforming; getting the right angle.	Are you measuring up? Where do you need a new point of view?
Umbrella	Self defences or protection; being prepared; playing it safe; anticipating problems; emotional fallout; nurturing yourself.	Are you taking cover or trying to shield yourself? What are you forecasting or predicting?
Uranium	Sending signals; power; energy and drive; irreversible effect; radiation therapy; remedial action; contaminating yourself or others.	Where are you dealing with a potentially dangerous situation? What could be long-lasting?
Vacuum cleaner	Putting your affairs in order; leaving no trace; feeling in control; housekeeping; inner cleansing; cleaning up.	Who are you sucking up to? Do you need to pick yourself up?
Vase	Good looks; self-image; appearances; appreciation of beauty; vessel for the spirit.	What are you doing for show? Where have you got good taste?
Vice	Feeling secure; being firm; holding on; having a good grip on things; corruption; shortcomings.	Who's got you in their grasp? Are you withstanding pressure?

Symbol	Meaning or Symbolism	Ask Yourself
Video tape	See Television in this chapter.	
Vocabulary	Speaking your mind; sharing information; having a voice; disagreeing; giving advice; affirming yourself; connecting with others; communicating.	Where do you need to express yourself? Are you having words with someone?
Voices	Opinions; communicating with others; expressing your feelings; others' expectations; being creative; affirming your intentions.	Where do you need to speak up? Are you listening to others?
Whiteboard	Gaining or needing clarity; presenting information; organising; education; teaching; instructing others.	Where are you learning or sharing information? What do you need to visualise?
Wig	Make-over; self-transformation; not being true to yourself; being scolded; wigging.	Are you adopting others' ideas? Where aren't you thinking for yourself?
Wound	Feeling exposed; helpless; resigning yourself to the facts; needing support; damaged reputation; emotional pain.	Where have you been hurt? Are you causing pain to others?
Yawn	Lack of motivation or interest; tired; lethargic; taking in ideas.	Where are you feeling bored? Are things opening up for you?
Yin-Yang	Reconcilable differences; positive and negative side; dual nature of things; Chinese philosophy; complementary needs; wholeness.	Are you seeking balance and harmony? Where are you dealing with opposing forces or interests?
Zip	Being open; feeling vulnerable; hiding your feelings; being quiet; shutting yourself off; zippy; zip code.	Where are you being flexible? Are you dealing with an open-and-shut case?

Common Dream Theme: Knocking on or opening a door

To dream of an open door can symbolise being offered or accepting opportunities, extending your boundaries or adopting an 'open door policy' in your home or workplace. Closed doors, on the other hand, can represent barriers, obstacles, disappointments or dilemmas that you face. Knocking on a door can illustrate your desire for help or answers, needing to make yourself heard or be noticed or your desire for admission and access. Or maybe you're being intrusive or have been 'knocked back' or 'knocked down'. If you noticed the doormat, perhaps you are feeling used, unappreciated or 'walked all over'.

Chapter 17
People, Roles and Clothing

The self-actualising person . . . is not
a normal person with something added,
but a normal person with nothing taken away.
Abraham Maslow

People can sometimes represent themselves in your dreams. It is more common, however, for them to symbolise an area of your life (such as work or relationships) or a part of yourself—gifts, skills, qualities, characteristics or features that you haven't fully recognised or owned. Consider these possible meanings with any other specifically listed.

How to get the best value from this chapter

- See if you relate to any of the key words or questions and explore your own meanings which may override those given here.
- Look at all possibilities and apply the most appropriate for your situation.
- Rephrase the questions to broaden their personal relevance to you, if necessary, by using other words with similar meanings.
- You can also turn any question around (including those you formulate) to see if you relate to them better, by asking them in a slightly different way. For example, rephrase it as a need rather than a desire or belief or vice versa.

Desires and needs as opposed to outcomes and results

If a symbol represents an issue you are currently facing, then it may be indicative of your feelings, desires, beliefs or needs. This would usually occur in the first two-thirds of a dream, which often illustrates the issue you are dealing with and how you feel about it.

If a symbol comes in the form of a resolution, outcome, insight, solution or conclusion in the climax, usually at the end of the dream, then it may indicate a consequence, result or your dream advice to you.

Symbol	Meaning or Symbolism *Look for feelings, desires, needs, beliefs or situations, explore literal meanings, apply any puns and idioms*	Ask Yourself *You can rephrase these questions, if necessary, using other words with similar meanings to expand their personal relevance*
Aborigine	Feeling dispossessed; being transient; suffering prejudice or injustice; moving on; feeling unsettled; being deprived; Dreamtime.	Where are you feeling unaccepted? Are you moving from one thing to another?
Actor	See Acting in Chapter 10.	
Alchemist	Release and liberation; initiating change; having influence; alchemy; spiritual growth.	Where are you taking an alternative approach? What are you transforming?
Alien	Strange and unfamiliar; uncharacteristic behaviour; different approach; novel and innovative.	Are you feeling like you don't belong? Where are you alienating yourself or others?
Amateur	Lay person; feeling incompetent; being unprofessional; in training; striving for perfection; admiring others; amateurish.	What has no financial gain? Where do you need to improve your skills?
Analyst	Self-perception; self-analysis; inner realisations; looking within; cause and effect; getting to the bottom of things; needing to look deeper; final analysis.	What do you need to look into? Where are you feeling insecure?
Apron	Housekeeping; feeling tied; responsibilities; giving of yourself; feeling used; apron strings.	Where do you feel dominated? Where are you protecting yourself?
Armour	Being unyielding or stubborn; delivering a blow; confronting others; being hard-hearted; lack of trust; defending yourself or your values.	Are you being defensive? Where are you on the offensive?
Artist	Feeling complete; being in tune; being creative, imaginative or	Where are you showing skill and talent?

Symbol	Meaning or Symbolism	Ask Yourself
	original; unrealistic expectations; feeling inadequate; taking risks.	What are you devoted or committed to?
Attacker	Taking the initiative; intruding influences; being undermined; turning your energies to a task; being caught by surprise; being decisive.	Where are you feeling threatened or intimidated? Are you on the offensive?
Attendant	Guiding others; intruding; offering your service; making an appearance; attendance.	What are you representing? Where are you supporting others?
Audience	Onlookers; lack of involvement; being received or listened to; recognition and reward; being entertained; absorbing new ideas.	Where are you being applauded for your efforts? Are you being sensitive to the opinions of others?
Aunt	Supportive; confidant; having a bond; kind influence; familiarity; 'Auntie': Australian Broadcasting Corporation.	What's familiar and well known? Where are you being a role model?
Author	Pushing boundaries; power of the imagination; communication; keeping or making a record; founder; teaching others; occupation.	What are you creating or initiating? Where are you considering new possibilities?
Baby	New concept, idea or project; feeling vulnerable or dependent; having potential; innocent.	Are you pampering or indulging yourself? Where do you need to grow up?
Bachelor	Stage of life; unencumbered; on your own; needing release; seeking intimacy; loneliness; lack of loyalty; bachelor: holding a degree; expertise.	Are you looking for independence? Where are you able to please yourself?
Backer	Feeling confident; profiteering; dealing with uncertainty; enthusiasm; financial matters; seeing potential.	Are you taking or weighing up risks? Where are you providing support?
Baker	Fermenting feelings; foundations; rising tensions; expansion;	Are you being the breadwinner or bringing home the dough?

Symbol	Meaning or Symbolism	Ask Yourself
	needing; changing gradually; transformation.	Are you supporting others?
Barbarian	Uncontrolled feelings and actions; uncivilised behaviour; violent outbursts; undermining others; barbaric; showing bad taste.	Where are you being brutally honest? Are you being destructive?
Bartender	Attending to others' needs; feeling ordered about; socialising; supporting dependency.	Are you listening to problems? Where do you need to be cooperative or accommodating?
Bathers	Self-exposure; showing off; competitive attitude; needing to cool off; spiritual pursuits; relaxed approach.	Do you need to reveal yourself? Where are you being informal?
Beggar	Impoverishment; lack of success; loss of status; falling behind; low self-esteem; pitiful situation; feeling inadequate; needing support; lucky beggar; beggary; beggarly.	Where are you being dependent? What are you turning your back on?
Belt	Productive areas of your life; economising; rushing; punishment; providing support; belting; belting along; wheat belt.	Do you need to economise or tighten your belt? Where do you need to be more reticent or belt up?
Besieged	Many demands; giving in; holding out; coerced or manipulated; harassed or pestered; being hemmed in or restricted.	Are you feeling overwhelmed or pressured? Where do you need inner strength or self-reliance?
Bogey man	Mischievous actions or motives; fears; source of annoyance.	Are you feeling vulnerable or threatened? What's haunting you?
Bookkeeper	See Accountant's office in Chapter 4.	
Boss	Opportunities; being decisive; leadership qualities; taking responsibility; conscience; spiritual wisdom; taking control; looking at the bigger picture.	Are you being bossy or domineering? Where are you seeking or lacking independence?

Symbol	Meaning or Symbolism	Ask Yourself
Boy	Energetic; active; childhood memories; childish; insecure; inexperience; immaturity; group solidarity: the boys; emerging power and determination.	Where are you starting to take the initiative? Are you developing courage?
Boyfriend	Lover; passion; exploration; emotional attachments; associating with others; joining forces; feeling accepted; being loved.	What are you attracted to? Where are you feeling a strong connection?
Bra	Receiving support; presenting yourself; standing out; making an impression; projected feelings and attitudes; getting prepared.	Where are you feeling encouraged or uplifted? What are you keeping close to your chest? (Also see Panties and Underwear in this chapter.)
Broach	Seeking attention; presenting or promoting yourself.	Where do you need to broach a subject? What are you presenting in the best light?
Brother	Showing kindness and loyalty; childhood memories; competing needs; being challenged; brotherly; brotherhood.	Where do you have a sense of belonging? Where are you being competitive?
Bus driver	Taking a predetermined course; regular routine; monotonous circumstances; traversing obstacles; running on time; missing the bus.	Where are you making predictable choices? Have you missed an opportunity?
Butcher	Being brutally honest; heartless; inhuman; mortality; being aggressive; lacking compassion; making a killing.	What part of yourself have you killed off? Are you making a mess or botching things up?
Captain	Drive; decisiveness; conscience; commanding position; higher self; gaining mastery; leadership; feeling responsible; having responsibilities; brief account: caption.	Where are you taking control? Do you feel dominated?

Symbol	Meaning or Symbolism	Ask Yourself
Carpenter	Hard feelings or attitudes; traditional values; reinventing yourself; shaping yourself; being practical.	Are you making things work? Where are you constructing new plans or projects?
Cheerleader	Supporting or standing by others; showing allegiance; encouragement; approving of yourself or others.	Are you leading or inspiring others? Where are you being optimistic or good-humoured?
Children	Being trusting; innocent; having potential; immature and naive; annoyance; undisciplined; inexperienced; dependence.	Where do you need instruction or training? Are you being natural and spontaneous?
Children's clothes	Not thinking for yourself; childish reactions; naive attitudes; fresh or youthful outlook; not understanding the consequences.	Are you developing your thinking? Where do you need a more mature approach?
Choir	Inner peace; expressing yourself; cooperation; compatibility; feeling in tune with yourself; celebrating the spirit; working with others.	Where are you achieving harmony? Are you sharing common goals?
Christ	Christianity; oath; Christ consciousness; making spiritual progress; higher power; divine intervention; Jesus.	Do you need to show love and forgiveness? Where are you seeking guidance?
Cloak	Disguised or veiled feelings; cover up; self-protection; defensive reactions; cloak of secrecy; an earlier time.	What are you trying to hide? What's obscure or difficult to understand?
Clothing	See Common Dream Theme at the end of this chapter.	
Clown	Seeking attention; disguising insecurity; needing a sense of humour; ability to make people laugh; not taking things too seriously; needing to laugh at yourself.	What's amusing you? Where are you clowning around?

Symbol	Meaning or Symbolism	Ask Yourself
Comedian	Seeing the absurd; new perspective; being good-humoured; standing back from things; indulging yourself; humouring others; needing to laugh at yourself.	Can you see the funny side of things? Are you being witty and clever?
Cook	Being creative; preparing; making palatable; what's cooking; presenting to others; offering support; cook up; cook the books.	What are you dishing out to others? What are you inventing or fabricating?
Costume	Not being true to yourself; pretence; putting on an appearance; ability to perform; adopting others' values; entertaining yourself and others.	Are you playing a role? Where are you kidding yourself?
Crowd	Public demands or opinion; mass or unconscious reactions; lack of individuality; crowded out.	Are you part of the in-crowd? Where aren't you being noticed?
Dark-skinned person	Shadow (or unknown) side of yourself; negative thoughts or gloomy feelings; bias or prejudice.	What have you suppressed? What part of you seeks acknowledgment and recognition?
Dealer	Commercial interests; wealth; profiteering; managing others; handling responsibilities; getting involved.	Are you wheeling and dealing? What are you dealing with?
Debt collector	Having a conscience; pursuing others; paying for past mistakes; unable or unwilling to pay the price; calling in favours.	Where are you feeling obligated? Are you feeling accountable or responsible?
Dentist	Consider a dental check-up; self-image; fears; valuing appearances; needing to watch what you say.	What do you need to check-up on? Where are you dealing with painful situations?

Symbol	Meaning or Symbolism	Ask Yourself
Detective	Being discerning; finding a new perspective; seeing the true nature of something; looking deeper; looking inwards; subconscious mind; suspending your judgments; discovering your inner self.	What have you exposed? Where do you need to consider all the facts?
Devil	Villain; abusing your power; fear of future consequences; feeling unworthy; devil is in the detail.	Are you tempting others? Where don't you trust yourself?
Diplomat	Delicate or sensitive issues; compromising; being polite; respecting differences; saving face; pleasing others; immunity from prosecution.	Where are you showing tact and diplomacy? Do you need to be a skilful negotiator?
Disabled person	See Wheelchair in Chapter 18.	
Doctor	Know-how and training; taking advice; healing; self-healing; remedial action; doctoring or tampering.	Where are you offering or needing support? Do you need to help yourself?
Dreamer	Out of touch with reality; being naive; dare to dream; unrealistic; dream; daydream; go like a dream.	What seems unreal or unbelievable? Where have you got hopes and aspirations?
Dress	Self image or public image; covering or concealing; wanting to be seen; roles you play; your moods; dress circle.	What are you dressing up or putting a good slant on? Where do you need to express your feminine side?
Drunkard	Numbing your feelings; drowning your sorrows; inability to cope; lack of self-control; alcoholism; dependency; addictions.	What are you blocking out? What can't you face?
Dwarf	See Dwarf in Chapter 12.	
Editor	Compiling information; correcting others; evaluating values and opinions; being right;	What are you censoring? What needs amending or adapting?

Symbol	Meaning or Symbolism	Ask Yourself
	having authority; exercising control.	
Elected official	Power; authority; prioritising; representing others; making choices; official office; politics; being accountable.	Are you choosing your values? Where are you having your say?
Embryo	Pregnancy; inner awareness; immaturity; undeveloped; needs time; feeling defenceless; potential.	What's in the early stages of development? Where are you feeling protected or supported?
Enemy	Opposing and competing with others; hostilities; competing needs; not liking or accepting yourself: enemy within; shadow self.	Where don't you trust yourself? What are you confronting?
Evacuee	Running away from issues; avoidance; releasing feelings or responsibilities; losing patience; lacking courage; retreating; cutting your losses.	What are you withdrawing from? Where are you concerned with your safety?
Faceless person	Feeling anonymous or overlooked; unidentified issues or feelings; fears; unknown part of yourself; doing an about-face.	What can't you see? What do you need to face up to?
Famous people	See Common Dream Theme in Chapter 13.	
Farmer	See Farmhouse in Chapter 4.	
Father	Authority; power; respect; leadership; responsibility; discipline; guidance; dominating; control; religious teacher: father; father figure.	Are you creating or founding something new? Where are you being protective and kind?
Fellow pupil	Intellectual or studious part of yourself; common interests; growing with others; rivalries.	Where are you sharing common beliefs? What are you learning with others?

Symbol	Meaning or Symbolism	Ask Yourself
Female	Intuition; communication; feelings; compassion; openness; receptivity.	Do you need to express your feminine side? Where are you listening or wanting to be heard?
Fireman	Role model; charging in; protective; burning ambitions; intense feelings; getting your fingers burnt; helping others; dampening passions; taking responsibility; confronting adversity; devotion to duty; courage and daring; fiery temper.	Are you inflaming a situation? What do you need to rescue?
Foreigner	Rich and rewarding experiences; different perspective; unpalatable; dissimilar; irrelevant views or options.	Where are you being open to different views or ways of thinking? What feels strange or unfamiliar?
Friend	Offering encouragement; self-acceptance; understanding yourself; guidance; deep inner-most secrets; confidante; befriending an unknown part of yourself.	Do you need to be kind to yourself? Where do you feel supported and understood?
Fugitive	Trouble; feeling threatened or guilty; feeling like you don't belong; unaccepted; deserting others; abandoned.	What are you running away from? What can't you face?
Gangster	Destructive tendencies or forces; criminal inclinations; uncontrolled forces; using violence; overly assertive; railroading others.	Are you being ruthless? Where are you exerting pressure or influence?
Girl	Developing female energies; innocence; intuition; communication; feelings; cute; immature; childhood memories; potential.	Are you starting to express your emotions? Where do you feel undervalued; inexperienced or vulnerable?
Girlfriend	See Friend in this chapter.	

Symbol	Meaning or Symbolism	Ask Yourself
Gloves	Protecting yourself; taking a situation in hand; leaving no trace; glove box.	What do you need to handle carefully with kid gloves? What are you coming to grips with?
Grandfather	Ancestors; family roots or connection; patriarch; influence; ageing; having time; supporting others; personal history; giving of yourself; old man.	What have you originated or been the forefather of? Where have you got traditional values?
Grandmother	Ancestors; family roots or connection; matriarch; influence; ageing; having time; traditional values; personal history; Great Mother; giving of yourself.	Where are you showing wisdom or patience? Who or what are you supporting?
Group of people	Collection of thoughts and feelings; public opinion; representing others; needing approval; group consciousness.	Where are you trying to reach an audience or market? Are you trying to influence others?
Guard	Being prepared; lack of trust; defending or preserving your values; security; realistic expecta-tions; pessimism; not sharing; emotional defences; feeling secure.	What are protecting? Where are you being on your guard?
Guru	See Sage in Chapter 20.	
Gypsy	Itinerant; wanderer; bad reputation; romany; suspicion; lack of trust; transition; intuition; psychic abilities; moving on.	Are you finding it hard to settle? Where do you feel like you don't fit in or belong?
Hacker	Illegal access; intruding; lacking authority; unauthorised behaviour; uncontrolled; forcing boundaries; unethical behaviour.	Where are you breaking conventions? Are you refusing to be confined or restricted?
Hairdresser	Hairy or difficult situation; new self-image; having an impact; hair-raising; hairline; hairsplitting; hair's breadth.	Are you walking a narrow line? Where are you changing your thinking?

Symbol	Meaning or Symbolism	Ask Yourself
Handshake	Acknowledgment; making deals; giving your word; patching up differences; being true to yourself.	What are you agreeing to? What are you being introduced to?
Harry Potter	Being victorious; solving problems; acquiring useful skills; fantasy; making a valuable contribution; unbelievable; out of touch with reality.	Are you showing special talent? Where are you overcoming enormous challenges?
Headband	Having self-control; identifying with others; making a statement; being defiant; being narrow-minded.	Are you restricting your thinking? Have you got alternative attitudes?
Hermit	Time for reflection and evaluation; keeping to yourself; questioning; turning inwards; self-analysis; independence; alchemy; hermetic.	Do you want to run away or break free? What are you trying to avoid or can't face?
Hero	See Hero in Chapter 20.	
Husband	Partnership; love; protection; self sacrifice; domineering; intimacy; proper management; husbandry.	Who do you feel an alliance with? Where are you involved in a mutually supporting relationship?
Intruder	See Attacker in this chapter.	
Jeans	Being a free spirit; casual attitude; making a statement; practical; hard-wearing attitudes.	Are you being informal? Where are you being strong and enduring?
Judge	Evaluating or assessing situations; wisdom; authority; independence; higher self; conscience.	Are you judging yourself or others? What are you presiding over?
Kin	Allegiance; bonding; competing needs; similar interests; common goals; family roots; shared history.	Where are you relating to others? Do you feel a sense of belonging? (Also see Relatives in this chapter.)

Symbol	Meaning or Symbolism	Ask Yourself
King	Dominating others; important role; respect; sense of destiny; giving approval; feeling privileged; king-size; king hit; kingdom.	Are you feeling superior to others? Where do you have power and influence?
Knight	Being principled and determined; heroic tendencies; courage and daring; being trusted; showing loyalty; night; knighthood; loyalty.	Where are you being honourable and reputable? Are you waiting for someone to rush you off your feet?
Lawyer	Playing by the rules; justifying yourself; having influence; needing to conform; conscience; rule of law; arguing the point; authority; establishment; justice.	Are you evaluating your position? Where are you standing up for what you believe in?
Linen	Natural approach or way of thinking; authentic; luxury; linen press; dirty linen.	Are you feeling crushed? Where do you need to iron out difficulties?
Lobbyist	Having your our own agenda; applying pressure; self-interest; being biased or narrow-minded.	Are you pushing a particular line? Who are you trying to influence?
Lover	Sexual passions; intimacy; mistrust; being an enthusiast; jealously; bonding; feeling whole; complementing or balancing qualities; pairing up with common purpose.	What have you great affection for? Are you tempted to act improperly?
Magician	Trickery; unbelievable; concealed; extraordinary events; unable to see; magnetism; subtle effect; cover up; being manipulated.	What are you conjuring up? Where have events taken a miraculous turn?
Maid	Needing to nurture yourself; virgin; pure motives; unblemished record; feeling unwanted; lack of choice; old maid: unmarried.	Where are you serving others? Are you feeling used or unappreciated?

Symbol	Meaning or Symbolism	Ask Yourself
Mailman	See Post office in Chapter 4.	
Male	Drive; energy; action; aggression; courage; resourceful.	Do you need to develop your masculine side? Where are you being logical and methodical?
Man	See Male in this chapter.	
Manager	Higher self; conscience; leadership qualities; vision; bigger picture; managing yourself or others; taking responsibility.	What are you managing? Where do you need self-control?
Matador	Basic impulses; uncontrolled desires; seeking grandeur; sexual anxieties; confronting yourself or others.	What are you pursuing? What do you need to eliminate?
Mate	See Friend in this chapter.	
Maternity clothes	Expanding your potential; developing project; having expec-tations; big or happy outcomes; supporting; nurturing; promoting.	What are you enlarging or extending? Where are you evolving?
Mechanic	Physical body or ailment; self-maintenance; repairing problems; needing to get going; being technical.	Are you reacting automatically or unconsciously? Where are you solving problems?
Medium	Channels of communication; guidance; looking beyond; being open; other worldly matters; hidden influences; being sensitive; medium: moderate.	Where are you channelling your energies? Are you acting as a go-between?
Merchant	Selling yourself; exchanging ideas; entrepreneur; taking opportunities; seeking to profit.	Who or what are you exploiting? Do you need to adopt a business-like approach?
Midget	See Dwarf in Chapter 12.	
Mime artist	Unable to express yourself; poor communication; can't relate to others; imitating others; being direct or unclear.	Do you need to speak up? Are you putting your feelings into action?

Symbol	Meaning or Symbolism	Ask Yourself
Minister	See Monastery and Temple in Chapter 4.	
Mob	Disorderly behaviour; basic instincts; appealing to the masses; needing to regain your power; feeling threatened; needing to protect yourself.	Are things getting out of control? Where are you feeling besieged or harassed?
Monk	See Monastery and Temple in Chapter 4.	
Mother	See Mother in Chapter 20.	
Musician	Harmonious relationships; inspiration; establishing a rhythm; having talent; being in harmony with yourself; facing the music or consequences.	What are you creating? Where are you performing?
Negligee	Need for transparency; passion and intimacy; feeling tempted; desirable; appealing situations.	Where are you revealing yourself? Are you being seductive?
Neighbour	Having to get on; help and assistance; connecting issues; working together; offering support.	Who are you feeling close to? What do you have to deal with?
Nun	See Monastery and Temple in Chapter 4.	
Officer	See Police in this chapter.	
Older person	Out-of-date beliefs or values; ageing; maturity; role model; tradition; inflexibility; dependency.	Where have you got experience and wisdom? What's outlived its usefulness? (Also see Grandfather and Grandmother in this chapter.)
Oriental person	Inner reflection; philosophical; East; Asia; orient yourself.	What's feeling unfamiliar? Do you need to adapt or change?
Orphan	Needing to nurture yourself; neglected values; self-neglect;	Where are you feeling deprived?

Symbol	Meaning or Symbolism	Ask Yourself
	forced independence; needing to be loved.	Are you feeling alone or unsupported?
Overalls	Being practical; being strong; down to earth; self-protection; the whole picture: overall.	Where are you working hard? Do you need a hands–on approach?
Overweight person	Obesity; lack of moderation; exaggerating; overindulgence; weighty issues; out of balance or proportion; important person: big man; low self-esteem.	Are you suffering from an inflated sense of self-importance? What are you enjoying the best of?
Panties	Privacy; hidden feelings; intimacy; seductive; looking deeper; foundations; working under someone; touch bottom; bottom up; bottomless.	What are you considering from a female perspective? What are you uncovering? (Also see Bra and Underwear in this chapter.)
Pants/Trousers	Management skills; power; drive; leadership qualities; dominant force; pant: gasping or choking.	Who's wearing the trousers or is in control? Are you asserting your authority?
Parents	Balance of male and female energies; nurturing yourself or others; having rapport; noticing resemblances; protecting; self-sacrifice; training; needing unconditional love.	What are you creating or manifesting? Who or what are you feeling responsible for?
Passenger	Lack of control; not taking responsibility; relying on others; going places; being supported; common direction.	Where do you need to make a contribution? Have you been taken for a ride?
Patient	Needing to nurture yourself; seeking advice; enduring situations; out of balance; taking remedial action; tolerance: patience.	Do you need healing? Where are you trying to regain control?
People	Self-image; public opinion; acceptance or lack of it; appearances; mass or unconscious behaviour	Where are you relating to others? Are you looking at trends?

Symbol	Meaning or Symbolism	Ask Yourself
	(Also see Introduction in this chapter.)	
Performance	Being acknowledged or recognised; applauding yourself; showing off; receiving rewards; high self-esteem.	Are you putting on an act? Where have you got a sense of achievement or satisfaction?
Philanderer	Lover; provoking yourself or others; indiscriminate behaviour; promiscuous; manipulating others; lack of trust.	Are you flirting with new ideas? Where are you leading others on?
Pilgrim	Spiritual values; inner search; feeling inspired; trying to find yourself; being dedicated and committed.	Where are you on a journey? Do you need to look within?
Pilot	Going places; plans taking off; exploring new ideas; professionalism; leading or guiding others; testing; pilot study or program.	Where are you in control? Are you charting your course?
Pioneer	New paths, frontiers or ways of thinking; being driven; highly motivated; setting trends; taking the initiative; showing courage; perseverance.	Are you preparing the way? Where are you showing leadership?
Pirate	Transgressing; rebellious side of yourself; being out of control; attacking others; feeling outcast; not accepting authority; taking but not giving.	What are you violating? Are you committing piracy or infringing copyright?
Poet	Feeling inspired; inner wisdom; expressing yourself; being articulate; having magnetism and charm.	Are you being imaginative or creative? Do you need a philosophy of life?
Police	Higher self; conscience; sense of justice; confronting others; following procedure; protecting yourself and others; rebellious side of yourself.	Are defending your values? Where are you maintaining control?

Symbol	Meaning or Symbolism	Ask Yourself
Politician	Tact and diplomacy; bigger picture; public good; self-interest; authority; watching your back; short-term thinking.	Are you dealing with a lack of trust? Have you made a promise you can't keep?
Pope	Moral conduct; beliefs; conscience; religious aspirations; Catholicism; God; influence; fear of retribution.	Where are you adhering to a way of thinking? Are you delegating authority?
Postman	See Post Office in Chapter 4.	
Potter	Forming new ideas; taking it easy; earthiness; expressing your creativity; wasting time; pottering around; potter away.	What are you moulding into shape? Where are you being shaped by circumstances?
Priest/Monk	See Monastery and Temple in Chapter 4.	
Prince or Princess	See Prince/Princess in Chapter 12.	
Promoter	Elevating yourself; receiving a promotion; having your own agenda; higher status; being forward; seeking attention; needing to take notice; self-promotion.	What are you supporting? Are you advertising or marketing yourself?
Prostitute	See Prostituting in Chapter 10.	
Prowler	See Prowling in Chapter 10.	
Pyjamas	Needing to reflect; relaxation; sleep; taking time out; hopes and dreams; needing to slow down; can't get started.	Are you feeling unprepared? What can't you face?
Queen	Fulfilling others' expectations; respect and reputation; arrogance; being reserved; over-bearing; observing formalities; self-control; privilege and responsibility; authority; Queen's Counsel; queen bee; ice queen.	Do you have a sense of destiny and purpose? Where are you in control?

Symbol	Meaning or Symbolism	Ask Yourself
Real estate agent	Security; professional advice; lifestyle; property; wealth; personal investment; buying and selling; exchanging ideas; your rights; moving on; transition.	Are you weighing up your personal values or assets? What do you need to dispose of?
Relatives	Related issues or events; family concerns or formalities; blood ties; having common origins; in-laws; obligations.	What do you have to deal with? Where are you relating to others? (Also see Kin in this chapter.)
Role	See Introduction in this chapter.	
Rich person	Abundance; wealth; enjoying respect; desirable; successful endeavours; feeling generous; ability to give.	Are you feeling talented or valued? Where are you being productive or resourceful?
Robber	See Attacker in this chapter.	
Sailor	Embarking on an endeavour; adventurous or unsettled spirit; taking it easy; flowing with life; set sail.	Are you setting your course? What are you sailing through and finding easygoing?
Saint	Living your spiritual principles; doing the impossible; being noble; put on a pedestal; sainthood.	Where are you being virtuous or unselfish? Are you enjoying respect and admiration from others?
Salesman	Entrepreneurial skills; meeting needs; being business-like; profiteering; selling yourself; salesmanship.	Where are you being influential or persuasive? Are you maximising opportunities?
Sarong	Casual approach or lifestyle; easygoing; freedom; feeling comfortable; Sri Lanka; Malaysia.	Where are you being open to other points of view? Do you need to loosen up?
Scarf	Warmth; comfort; protection; expecting the worst; making predictions; being prepared.	Are you bracing yourself? Where have you got expectations?
Scientist	Self-knowledge and examination; seeking	Are you being logical and systematic?

Symbol	*Meaning or Symbolism*	*Ask Yourself*
	understanding; self-analysis; being observant; objective; dealing with causes; Scientology.	What are you investigating or looking into?
Scotsman	Scotland; conserving energy; preserving or economising; stockpiling resources.	Where are you being frugal? Are you being too extravagant?
Secretary	Relying on others; nurturing yourself; love affairs; being competent; feeling dependent; used; taking the pressure off; secretary-general; secretary of state.	Where should you be delegating? Are you supporting others?
Seducer	Sexual passions; lack of self-control; fanciful imaginings; bribery; emotional desires.	Are you feeling manipulated or persuaded? What are you finding tempting or irresistible?
Servant	See Maid in this chapter.	
Shadow	See Shadow in Chapter 14.	
Shepherd	Mentoring; teaching; security; protecting yourself or others; protective feelings; shepherding.	Who are you watching over or feeling responsible for? Where are you leading the way?
Shopkeeper	See Merchant in this chapter.	
Sister	Family issues; competing needs; religious affiliations; nursing yourself; assisting others; expressing kindness; sisterhood; sister-in-law; sisterly.	Are you competing for affection? Where are you sharing a bond?
Skirt	Bordering on; considering change; borderline situation; womanising; taken to the edge; hanging on to a situation; skirt an issue; bit of skirt.	What are you avoiding? Who or what are you attracted to?
Socks	Warmth and comfort; needing to be quiet; being forceful; put a sock in it; sock it to.	Do you need to pull your socks up? Where are you protecting your beliefs?

Symbol	Meaning or Symbolism	Ask Yourself
Soldier	Defending yourself or others; disciplined; confronting others; forcing the issue; standing up for what you believe in; mercenary: soldier of fortune.	Where are you soldiering on? What are you opposing or resisting?
Soul mate	Love and understanding; past connection; future links; passing the test of time.	Where are you feeling an enduring bond? Are you feeling content and fulfilled?
Sports jacket	Recreation; leisure; good-humoured; keeping fit; informality; being appropriate; sportsmanship; sporting of you.	Are you being competitive? Where have you got a sense of fair play?
Stranger	Unfamiliar; unawareness; feeling like you don't belong; uncomfortable; different approach; strange; strange manner.	What don't you recognise or haven't seen before? What seems extraordinary or hard to explain?
Suit	Formal approach; flattering; fitting in; being business-like; combining resources; putting things together; matching skills; follow suit; suits you; suitor; lawsuit.	Where are you feeling suitable? Are you suiting yourself without considering others?
Surgeon	Having something taken from you; detachment; last resort; remedial action; healing potential or talent; needing healing; skill; respect; reputation.	What do you need to eliminate? Have you lost part of yourself? (Also see Operating in Chapter 10.)
Sweater	Keeping things in; being warm-hearted; covering up; self-protection; being informal; sweat; sweated over; sweatshop.	Are you feeling overworked and undervalued? Where are you being defensive?
Tailor	Feeling stylish; up to date; looking the part; repairing your image; satisfying requirements; being adaptable; tailor-made.	Do you need to alter your attitude? What's fitting into your life perfectly?
Thief	See Thief in Chapter 20.	

Symbol	Meaning or Symbolism	Ask Yourself
Three people	Trio; triplets; trilogy; body, emotions and mind; Trinity: father, son and Holy Spirit.	Where do you need balance between mind, body and spirit? What are you dealing with that has three aspects to it?
Tie	Family or karmic ties; formalities; duties and obligations; unfinished business; tied up; tie in; tie-breaker.	Are you feeling tied down? Where have you got connections?
Tourist	Being non-committal; considering your options; taking a journey; new ways of thinking.	Are you gaining a new perspective? Where do you feel like you don't belong?
Trickster	See Trickster in Chapter 20.	
Twins	Partnership; two sides of an issue; duality; being paired together; zodiac sign of Gemini; couple; two.	What seems identical or very similar? Where are you being balanced or even-handed?
Umpire	Irrevocable; having the last say; presiding over situations; authority; evaluating your performance or others.	Are you making hasty decisions? Where are you being decisive?
Underwear	Privacy; intimacy; secret; keeping feelings or information to yourself; foundations; essential principles.	Are you hiding your feelings? Where are you needing or giving support? (Also see Bra and Panties in this chapter.)
Uniform	Conforming with others; unchanging conditions; feeling in harmony with others; monotonous; employment opportunities; uniformity.	Have you lost your individuality? Are you enjoying a sense of belonging?
Unknown people	Subconscious thoughts or feelings; obscure fears and issues; unawareness; shadow (unknown/negative) side of you.	What are you suppressing? What part of you is seeking recognition?
Veil	Showing or needing discretion; cover up; keeping to yourself;	Do you need greater transparency?

Symbol	Meaning or Symbolism	Ask Yourself
	respecting others; private thoughts or feelings; mystery; religious symbol; can't see; needing clarity.	What are you trying to hide?
Vest	Heart-warming feelings; feeling close; coordinating yourself and your tasks; self-protection; emotional defences.	Where are you using the power vested in you or your inner strength? What are you keeping close to your chest?
Victim	Victimising others; not taking responsibility; being a martyr; looking for sympathy; sense of fate; blaming others.	Where do you need to be careful? Are you feeling helpless or lacking control?
Virgin	Feeling inexperienced; being chaste or modest; untested project; unexplained opportunity; pure intentions or motives.	Are you finding new qualities within you? What are you exploring that's new or doing for the first time?
Waitress	See Bartender in this chapter.	
Wedding dress	Making a commitment; love and loyalty; marriage; forming allegiances.	Where are you taking vows or making a promise to yourself? What are you dedicating yourself to?
Wiseman	See Sage in Chapter 20.	
Woman	See Female this chapter.	
Wool	Self-protection; emotional defences; warm-hearted; being comforted; feeling comfortable; hiding your feelings; wild and woolly.	Where do you need to keep your wool on or hold your temper? Are you pulling the wool over someone's eyes or deluding yourself?
Youth	Prime of life; feeling invulner-able; going back in time; memories; prime time; reached its peak; needing to mature; showing vigour, strength or enthusiasm.	Do you need to grow up? What's showing potential?

Common Dream Theme: Trying on clothes

Trying on clothes can symbolise exploring issues from different points of view or your need or desire to reinvent yourself or take on a different role.

If you're trying on clothes that are too tight, the new ideas or changes don't meet your requirements or won't work for you. If they are old fashioned or worn out they could be referring to outmoded ways of thinking that would be better discarded. If, on the other hand, they are new fashionable clothes, you may have found a style of thinking or a role that suits you.

Chapter 18
Vehicles

*Your automatic guidance system cannot
guide you when you're standing still.*
Maxwell Maltz

Vehicles can symbolise your body, state of health or current lifestyle. They can also represent your progress or lack of it, taking control, inability to get started, backing out of a situation, driving yourself too hard, your self-image or social status. Consider these possible meanings with any others specifically listed.

How to get the best value from this chapter

- See if you relate to any of the key words or questions and explore your own meanings which may override those given here.
- Look at all possibilities and apply the most appropriate for your situation.
- Rephrase the Life Issue questions to broaden their personal relevance to you, if necessary, by using other words with similar meanings.
- You can also turn any question around (including those you formulate) to see if you relate to them better, by asking them in a slightly different way. For example, rephrase it as a need rather than a desire or belief or vice versa.
- The Symbol in Action examples show how to apply context or link meaning with action.

Desires and needs as opposed to outcomes and results

If a symbol represents an issue you are currently facing, then it may be indicative of your feelings, desires, beliefs or needs. This would usually occur in the first two-thirds of a dream, which often illustrates the issue you are dealing with and how you feel about it.

If a symbol comes in the form of a resolution, outcome, insight, solution or conclusion in the climax, usually at the end of the dream, then it may indicate a consequence, result or your dream advice to you.

Symbol	Symbol In Action *Look for feelings, desires, needs, beliefs or situations, explore literal meanings, apply any puns and idioms*	Possible Life Issues *Look for where, what and who this reminds you of, apply key words to thoughts, feelings or situations, explore literal meanings, apply word plays and figures of speech*
Ambulance	See Emergency Vehicle in this chapter.	
Antique car	**Valuable vintage car:** Past views or values; treasured possession **Being a passenger in a vintage car:** Revisiting the past from someone else's perspective **Restoring a vintage car:** Old values that are still relevant.	Older lifestyle; old times; feeling sentimental; old fashioned; treasured values or possessions Are you ageing or feeling worn out? Where is your thinking out of date?
Armoured car	**Delivering money to a bank:** Delivering the goods; feeling trusted and valued; abundance **Armoured car with a flat tyre:** Feeling vulnerable; being a target **Holding up an armoured car:** Questioning your defences; taking what's not yours; feeling desperate; rebelling against authority.	Keeping things to yourself; self-defences or protection; needing to be more open; authority; separating yourself from others Are you being heavy-handed, forceful or aggressive? Where have you got a lack of trust or are playing it safe?
Balloon	**Travelling in a hot-air balloon:** Taking a new journey; gaining a new perspective; having a sense of adventure; letting go **Child letting a balloon go:** Releasing your cares; being irresponsible **Balloon bursting:** Reaching saturation point; change; anxiety; overdoing things.	Being idealistic; soaring interest; personal journey; higher point of view; rising up; rising above; new frontiers Have you got an inflated sense of self-importance? Are you full of hot air or are your words lacking substance?
Barge	**Barge docking:** Achieving your goals; giving back; receiving support **Overloaded barge:** Taking on	Hard work; dignified (stately); imposing presence; heavy-handed approach: barging into

Symbol	Symbol In Action	Possible Life Issues
	too much; expectations that are too high; achieving great things **Barge sinking:** Plans falling through; feeling inadequate; loss of support.	Where are you delivering the goods? What won't you touch with a barge pole or have a loathing for?
Bicycle	See Cycling in Chapter 10.	
Big car	**Driving a big car:** Feeling in control; powerful; higher social standing; big responsibilities **Repairing a big car:** Needing to regain your position or status; big health issue or concern **Oversized big car:** Inflated ego; bigger issue than you expect; out of place.	Selling yourself; showing off; boasting; pride; enjoyment Are you exaggerating your sense of self-importance? Where do you feel influential or important?
Boat	**Sailing a boat:** Enjoying the journey; feeling in tune **Launching a boat:** Presenting a new product; making a new start; new hopes and aspirations **Boat capsizing:** Feeling inadequate; being out of your depth.	Journey or transition; moving on; taking risks with others; being in the same boat What are you launching? Are you sailing through life or cruising along?
Bulldozer	**Driving a bulldozer:** Feeling in control; making things happen; carrying on regardless **Repairing a bulldozer:** Compromising your power; needing to restore your status or influence **Protestors lying in front of a bulldozer:** Intimidating others; holding a firm position; acting on principle; seeking attention.	Making a new start; major reforms; transformation; power and influence; weighty issues; significant undertakings Are you intimidating others or feeling coerced? Where are you forging your way or overcoming obstacles?
Bus	See Bus driver in Chapter 17.	
Campervan	**Loading a campervan:** Preparing for change; accumulating emotional baggage **Repairing a campervan:** Needing to change	Leaving no trace; breaking with the past; phase or temporary situation; change; refreshment; time out; broader perspective Are you in a state of transition?

Symbol	Symbol In Action	Possible Life Issues
	Old decaying campervan: Being unable to move on; feeling stuck or trapped.	Where are you changing your outlook?
Canoe	**Building a canoe:** Seeking balance; being prepared; making plans **Sinking canoe:** Feeling out of balance; being unable to flow with life; going under; can't cope; plunging hopes **Several canoes:** Group agreement or harmony.	Simple approach; linking with nature; recreation; natural alternative; serenity; peace; fitness Where are you setting your own pace? Are you feeling in harmony with yourself or others?
Car	See Common Dream Theme at the end of this chapter.	
Caravan	See Campervan in this chapter.	
Carriage	**Loading a carriage:** Making preparations; accumulating emotional baggage **Travelling by horse and carriage:** Taking your time; special occasion; memories; having style **Broken carriage:** Unable to progress; can't take what you need.	Old-fashioned views or thinking; enjoying the journey; holding on; having access; carriageway Are you dealing with the past? Where are you making slow progress?
Catapult	**Building a catapult:** Fast-tracking your career or plans **Loading a catapult:** Preparing or releasing a project **Broken catapult:** Unrealised expectations; weakened influence.	Old-fashioned views or thinking; impulsiveness; having momentum What are you launching? Have you been propelled into a new role?
Chariot	**Riding a chariot:** Being proactive or daring; past issues that demand attention **Oversized chariot:** Past issues that are now a big problem; exaggerating the importance of the past	Past; ancient ties; old-fashioned thinking; belongs to another era Are you being aggressive? What's becoming irrelevant or redundant?

Symbol	Symbol In Action	Possible Life Issues
	Chariot with one wheel broken: Past impediment; old values that are holding you back; feeling old and worn out.	
Convertible	**Driving a convertible:** High self-esteem; being open-minded; wanting to impress; in an enviable position; freedom **Being a passenger in a convertible:** Wanting to adapt; being with the in-crowd; wanting to improve your self-image **Stolen convertible:** Lost flexibility; loss of status or position.	Openness; enjoyment; self-esteem; image; flexibility; convert Where are you being adaptable? Are you folding under pressure?
Crane	**Driving a crane:** Feeling in control; being a driving force; shifting or fulfilling your responsibilities; gaining a higher perspective **Several cranes:** Group responsibilities; group of people you look up to or feel intimidated by **Broken-down crane:** Being ineffective; lacking the means to achieve; faulty mechanism; lack of vision.	Weighty issues; being effective; relocating your energies; bird What do you need to see more clearly? Are you bearing heavy burdens; or responsibilities?
Cruise ship	**Taking a cruise:** Change; needing to reflect; taking things more slowly; romance **Cruise ship held hostage:** Self-sabotage; having another agenda **Sinking cruise ship:** Losing hope; sinking finances; failure of a new project.	New ideas; personal journey; prosperity Are you in a state of transition? Where are you cruising along and enjoying life?
Digging equipment	**Using digging equipment:** Having determination and endurance; getting to the bottom of things; using your resources	Defending yourself; strength and power; being capable; uncovering deeper aspects of yourself; mining for information

Symbol	Symbol In Action	Possible Life Issues
	Digging equipment lying idle: Wasted opportunity; untapped potential; economising **Rusty digging equipment:** Outdated means; feeling unprepared; inattention.	Are you digging in and standing your ground? Where are you undermining yourself or others?
Dump truck	**Buying a dump truck:** Acquiring strength or the tools to achieve **Driving a dump truck:** Feeling in control; being a driving force; shifting responsibilities **Empty dump truck:** Releasing feelings; avoiding responsibilities.	Overturned decision; being capable; power; responsibility; strength; endurance; disposing of responsibilities; transferring energies What are you needing to unload or are unloading onto others? Are you carrying a heavy burden or feeling weighed down?
Dune buggy	**Going for a joy ride:** Not thinking of the consequences; having fun **Maintaining a dune buggy:** Supporting irresponsible attitudes **Overturned dune buggy:** Changing your ways.	Being irresponsible; thoughtless; damaging thoughts or actions; haste or speed; enjoyment Where are you travelling light? Are you being flexible or adaptable?
Emergency vehicle	**Driving an emergency vehicle:** Offering support; ability to move quickly; having priority **Being a passenger in an emergency vehicle:** Life-and-death situation; receiving support; evaluating procedures **Repairing an emergency vehicle:** Sorting out your priorities; rectifying serious problems.	Unforseen event; things breaking down around you; martial law; state of emergency Where do you need support? What needs immediate attention?
Family car	See Station wagon in this chapter.	
Ferry	**Catching a ferry:** Making a change; going places; exploring and sharing new ideas; adventurous spirit **Missing a ferry:** Missed opportunities; bad timing; wrong priorities; being unprepared	Communication; sense of accomplishment; transition; delivery of ideas; bringing about change Who or what are you supporting? Where do you need to move on?

Symbol	Symbol In Action	Possible Life Issues
	Sinking ferry: Warning; plunging hopes; unable to deliver; bad move.	
Fire engine	See Fireman in Chapter 17.	
Freight train	**Driving a freight train:** Feeling in control; being a driving force; expecting others to give way **Jumping off railway tracks ahead of freight train coming:** Taking a risk; giving into power; coming to your senses; facing the inevitable **Derailed freight train:** Business or economic obstacles; going off the rails; losing control.	Commercial values or concerns; sequence of events; unstoppable; predictable thinking What are you going along with? Are you bearing a heavy load? (Also see Railway Station in Chapter 4.)
Harvester	See Harvesting in Chapter 10.	
Hearse	See Coffin in Chapter 16.	
Helicopter	**Flying a helicopter:** Manoeuvring into position; gaining access; taking risks **Helicopter gun ship:** Danger; feeling vulnerable; threatening others **Helicopter on a rescue mission:** Warning; providing support.	Upward mobility; rise in status; important visitor; vulnerable; short-term transition; versatile Where are you hovering about or lingering? Do you need to lift your game?
Jeep	**Buying a jeep:** Acquiring skills; coping with difficult situations; changing your lifestyle **Damaged jeep:** Unable to move forward; setback to your lifestyle **Jeep with oversized wheels:** Nothing to hold you back; unstoppable; no limits; proceed with confidence.	Traversing the landscape; need for fun; vigorous and strong; surprise: jeepers Where are you finding the going tough and rugged? Are you surmounting hardship and obstacles?
Juggernaut	**Trying to hold back a juggernaut:** Avoiding difficulties	Disaster; forcing your way; being superstitious

Symbol	Symbol In Action	Possible Life Issues
	Running toward a juggernaut: Confronting demands; facing pressures head-on **Warning others of an oncoming juggernaut:** Forewarning of struggles ahead; predicting trouble.	Are you making a big sacrifice? Where are you dealing with strong pressures?
Limousine	**Driving a limousine:** Serving important objectives; feeling used **Being a passenger in a limousine:** Seeking power and prestige; feeling superior to others; taking opportunities; receiving acknowledgment or acclaim **Repairing a limousine:** Reinstating your position or reputation.	Wealth; abundance; success; image; appearance; separation; pride; self-importance; luxury Are you making a statement? Where are you seeking attention or personal glory?
Model car	**Building a model car:** Being original; making plans; selecting ideals **Displaying a model car:** Showing what can be done; pushing boundaries; exploring possibilities **Damaged model car:** Flawed idea; blemished reputation.	Small scale; ideals; being creative; building and constructing; role model Are others imitating you? What are you showing others?
Motorbike	**Riding fast on a motorbike:** Seeking freedom; being reckless; creating an impact **Motorbike with a sidecar:** Manipulating others; taking others with you **Overturned motorbike:** Emotional setbacks; facing consequences.	Compromise; emotional stability; power and strength; vulnerability; freedom; image; independence Where do you need balance? Are you being rebellious?
Moving van	**Loading a moving van:** Taking emotional baggage; needing to move on **Oversized moving van:** Big opportunity; being thoroughly prepared; emphasising the past	Making progress; going places; getting a move on; being on the move What's changing? Are you in a state of transition?

Symbol	Symbol In Action	Possible Life Issues
	Empty moving van arriving at its new destination: Being unprepared; making a clean break or fresh start.	
Paddleboat	**Paddleboat with oversized peddles:** Progressing well through your own efforts; effective teamwork **Sinking paddleboat:** Unsuccessful efforts; futile struggle **River overcrowded with paddleboats:** Competition; popular goals and ambitions; taking a slower pace; recreation.	Working together; recreation; propelling yourself forward Where are you being self-sufficient or making your own way? What are you putting your energy into?
Plane	See Airport in Chapter 4.	
Police car	See Police in Chapter 17.	
Pram	**Pushing a baby in a pram:** Promoting a new idea or project; motherhood; getting fit **Oversized pram:** Hard-going; making a real effort **Broken pram:** Avoiding your responsibilities; lack of support; faulty mechanism.	Support; childhood; responsibility Where are you being pushed or are you pushing others? Are you feeling dependent?
Racing car	**Driving a racing car:** Handling pressure; being a driving force; precarious position; admiration **Oversized racing car:** Inflated sense of self-importance; overemphasising the need for speed; needing to act quickly **Having an accident in a racing car:** Warning; not thinking ahead.	Speed; haste; rivalries; seeking glory; ancestry; common attitudes; race; racing around Are you being impulsive? Where are you being competitive?
Raft	**Lying on a raft:** Drifting through life; being supported **Raft sinking:** Plunging hopes;	Emotional ups and downs; feeling buoyant; helpless; lack of control; abundance; large amount

Symbol	Symbol In Action	Possible Life Issues
	lack of support; feeling overwhelmed **Several rafts:** Family support; group of volunteers.	Where are you being supported? Are you drifting or taking life as it comes?
Rickshaw	**Riding in a rickshaw:** Being guided; new experiences **Pulling a rickshaw:** Feeling used; hard work; desperation; lack of options **Selling a rickshaw:** Regaining your independence; freedom.	Adventurous spirit; leading others; needing direction; unfamiliar; unknown; feeling insecure Are you being guided? Where have you delegated responsibility?
Road-construction vehicle	**Driving a road-construction vehicle:** Pushing hard; handling pressure; steering big plans **Loading road-construction vehicles onto a truck:** Carrying a heavy load; shifting your responsibilities; being a big support; delivering the goods **Organising several road-construction vehicles:** Managing a powerful team; being firm with others.	Blazing new trails; forging a new role or direction; endurance and determination Are you being heavy-handed? Where are you getting things done?
Rocket	**Launching a rocket:** Plans taking off **Rocket landing on the moon:** New possibilities; results that exceed expectations **Exploding rocket:** Unsuccessful ventures.	Self-sufficient; new ideas; rising feelings or tensions; sudden progress; moving boundaries; clever: rocket science Are you exploring new frontiers? Where are you propelling yourself forward?
Rubbish truck	See Rubbish in Chapter 16.	
Sailboat	See Sailor in Chapter 17.	
School bus	**Driving a school bus:** Feeling responsible or trusted; helping others grow; providing opportunities **Repairing a school bus:** Needing to reinstate your position; lack of growth; undeveloped potential	Collective growth; group information; learning experience; humanity; common goals and aspirations Where are you learning from others? Are you being accepted by your peers?

Symbol	Symbol In Action	Possible Life Issues
	School bus being held hostage: Limiting your and others' growth.	
Sleigh	**Enjoying a sleigh ride:** Enjoying life; taking time out; nostalgia **Building a sleigh:** Making things run smoothly; causing friction; making tracks **Repairing a sleigh:** Being at the cutting edge.	Gliding or coasting along; being pulled along; pleasure; romance; love What are you letting slip? Where are you sliding back into old habits? (Also see Snow in Chapter 14.)
Small car	**Trying to squeeze into a small car:** Restricting yourself; wanting to fit in **Washing a small car:** Attending to detail **Repairing a puncture on a small car:** Amending details; empowering yourself.	Low self-esteem; suffering limitations; humility; minor details; modest lifestyle Where are you feeling insignificant, inadequate or inferior? Are you lacking power and strength?
Sports car	**Buying a sports car:** Adopting speed; being manoeuvrable; raising social status **Driving a sports car:** Being competitive; driving yourself hard; wanting to be noticed **Dented gold sports car:** Loss of reputation; financial loss.	Recreation; enjoyment; having style; prestige; fit and healthy; success; wealth; casual approach Are you being competitive? Where are you being a good sport or needing to show sportsmanship?
Station wagon	**Driving a loaded station wagon:** Feeling weighed down; family responsibilities; supporting others; ignoring your own needs **Oversized station wagon:** Big family problem; exaggerating your responsibilities; strong family loyalties **Wrecked station wagon:** Family dislocation or divisions.	Family values; responsibilities; endurance; hard work; wear and tear; loyalties Where are you feeling burdened or loaded up? Are you supporting others?

Symbol	*Symbol In Action*	*Possible Life Issues*
Stolen car	**Stealing a car:** Living others' expectations; allowing yourself to be influenced or manipulated; giving into your temptations **Car chase using a stolen car:** Things getting out of control; circumstances taking a turn for the worst; being rebellious; running from your conscience **Setting fire to a stolen car:** Fear of consequences; unwilling to take the blame.	Taking from others; acting against your conscience; taking all the praise What haven't you acknowledged? Where aren't you being true to yourself?
Taxi	**Hailing a taxi:** Putting yourself in others' hands; trusting; giving directions; having expectations **Driving a taxi:** Feeling used; always on the move; exploring new ideas **Taxi involved in an accident:** Disappointment; being let down.	Hiring and firing; being guided; easy options; other ways of thinking; transition Are you moving on? Where are you delegating authority?
Tractor	**Driving a tractor:** Feeling in control; making things happen **Oversized tractor:** Exaggerating your power to achieve; being very capable; large or intimidating responsibilities **Overturned tractor:** Unable to progress; feeling inadequate.	Heavy responsibilities; forging a new path; assistance; hard work; having means Where are you forging ahead? Are you overcoming obstacles?
Trailer	See Wagon in this chapter.	
Train	See Railway station in Chapter 4.	
Tram	**Catching a tram:** Sharing common goals with others; old-fashioned values; towing the line **Driving a tram:** Revisiting your past; being in control; following a set course; sequence of events **Jumping off a tram:** Breaking with your past; questioning your goals.	Expecting others to give way; keeping on track; rigid views; past; personal track record Where is your thinking behind the times? Are you being predictable?

Symbol	Symbol In Action	Possible Life Issues
UFO	See Alien in Chapter 17.	
Vehicles	See Introduction in this chapter.	
Wagon	**Packing a wagon:** Making preparations; hanging onto feelings or situations; taking things with you; building responsibilities **Oversized wagon:** Heavy workload; big responsibilities; emotional baggage **Broken axle:** Liabilities; unable to progress; leaving the past behind.	Feeling tied down; relying on yourself; being restricted; station wagon Where do you feel loaded up or overburdened? Who are you pulling along or what baggage are you taking with you? (Also see Station wagon in this chapter.)
Wheel	**Wheel turning:** Karma: what goes around comes around; change; repetition **Wheels bogged:** Unable to make progress; feeling stuck or trapped **Wheels falling off:** Going nowhere; feeling ineffective.	High roller; cycles; mortality; feeling pushed; unavoidable; wheeling and dealing; wheel of fortune; wheel of life What's gathering momentum? Where do you feel like you are going around in circles?
Wheelbarrow	**Pushing a full wheelbarrow:** Shifting your responsibilities; clearing your clutter **Miniature wheelbarrow:** Inadequate support; lack of influence; feeling ineffective **Rusty wheelbarrow:** Unreliable support.	Small responsibilities; manageable affairs; force and influence What are you pushing? What needs cleaning up or clearing away?
Wheelchair	**Being in a wheelchair:** Feeling self-conscious; being dependent; feeling impeded or ineffective; low self-esteem **Old-fashioned wheelchair:** Irrelevant limitations; past impediments **Broken wheelchair:** Lack of support.	Working against the odds; feeling self-conscious; making slow progress Where do you feel deprived? Are you dealing with limitations or crippling circumstances?
Wrecked vehicle	**Being in a wrecked vehicle:** Warning; making an unwise	Dealing with remains or leftovers; shattered lifestyle; ruined plans

Symbol	Symbol In Action	Possible Life Issues
	decision; not looking after yourself; lacking energy or self-worth **Towing away a wrecked vehicle:** Dealing with an unsatisfactory outcome; facing consequences; clearing a situation **Wrecked vehicle being demolished:** Ending of health, relationship, habit, status, plans or lifestyle; recycled experiences.	Where are you feeling like a write-off? Are you undermining your health?
Yacht	See Boat in this chapter.	

Common Dream Theme: Driving a car and the brakes won't work
*Finding yourself unable to brake the car can symbolise going
too fast, a hectic lifestyle, driving yourself too hard, feeling out of
control or being impulsive or reckless. A car crashing, on the
other hand, can symbolise danger, being on a collision course,
negative impact, a bad decision or consequence or an unavoidable
situation. Is it you who is driving and in control or are you
a passenger who's powerless and going along for the ride?*

Part Three

Getting the Most From Your Dreams

Chapter 19
Dream Feelings

The fastest way to freedom is to feel your feelings.
Gita Bellin

Dreams can often be associated with one prevailing feeling which holds the clue to your current life issues and offers the first key to understanding your dreams. Listed in this chapter are some dream feelings you might wake up with and questions you could ask yourself to help you reveal the dream topic. Look for the answer in the 24 to 48 hours preceding the dream. Refer to the introduction—Putting it all together—for more information.

How to get the best value from this chapter

- Identify the dream feeling you woke up with and see if you relate to any of the associated questions.
- Rephrase the questions to broaden their personal relevance to you, if necessary, by using other words with similar meanings.
- You can also turn any question around (including those you formulate) to see if you relate to them better, by asking them in a slightly different way. For example, rephrase it as a need rather than a desire or belief or vice versa.

Predominant Dream Feeling	How the Feeling Could be Symbolised in Your Dream	Possible Life Issues *Questions to ask yourself about your life the day you had the dream or the previous day*
Abandoned	Baby left by itself Being lost.	Where are you feeling alone or left in the lurch? Are you withdrawing into yourself?
Accepted	Being applauded on stage Coronation.	Where are you being included or acknowledged by others? Are you enjoying approval?
Agitated	Being cross with a child Being in a hurry and trying to get out of a locked door.	Where are you feeling annoyed or unsettled? Are you stirring up trouble?
Aimless	Wandering around Window shopping.	Where are you drifting or lacking direction? Are you being passive and compliant?
Aloof	Hermit Standing out from a crowd.	Where are you feeling disconnected or detached? Are you being unsympathetic?
Amorous	Making advances to a lover Courting another with flowers.	Who or what are you feeling affection for? Where are you being playful and passionate?
Anger	Smacking a child Expressing road rage.	Are you feeling annoyed? Where are you feeling resentful?
Anticipation	Opening a present Sitting down to a meal.	What are you hoping for? Where is the outcome unknown?
Anxiety	Seeing a ghost Being followed.	What are you fearful of? Do you have lingering feelings?
Apathy	Not eating a meal Sitting in a corner.	Where are you feeling detached? What are you indifferent about?
Assertive	Auctioneer slamming down a hammer Teacher reprimanding a class.	Where are you feeling self-assured or decisive? Are you being outspoken or dogmatic?

Predominant Dream Feeling	How the Feeling Could be Symbolised in Your Dream	Possible Life Issues
Awe	Looking at a beautiful landscape Seeing an angel.	Where have you been amazed or have great respect? What are you dreading?
Awkward	Falling over Dropping a vase.	Where are you feeling uncomfortable? Are you being clumsy or inept?
Betrayed	Friend informing the police on you Mother abandoning a baby.	Where are you dealing with disloyalty or injustice? Are you feeling deceived or misled?
Bold	Bungee jumping Winning a medal.	Where are you taking risks? Are you feeling confident or courageous?
Boredom	Naughty child misbehaving at school Person sitting with nothing to do.	What doesn't interest you? What's proving monotonous or tedious?
Carefree	Walking along the beach Taking off your business suit.	Are you ignoring your responsibilities? Where do you feel happy or content?
Cheated	Bank foreclosing on your house Losing at poker.	Where have you been deprived or deceived? Are you dealing with dishonesty or injustice?
Confined	Being tied up Locked in a room.	Are you feeling trapped or held back? What's limiting or restricting you?
Confused	Being caught in fog Traffic lights not working.	What's disorganised? Where do you need clarity or direction?
Connected	Plug in a power point Talking on the telephone.	Where are you enjoying good communication? Are you relating well to others?
Contempt	Pointing your finger at someone Holding an object underwater in a bath.	What are you disapproving of? What have you put down?

Predominant Dream Feeling	How the Feeling Could be Symbolised in Your Dream	Possible Life Issues
Convinced	Customer standing firm wanting a refund Premier delivering a victory speech.	Are you being arrogant or assertive? Where are you persuading yourself?
Corrupt	Policeman taking a bribe Printing counterfeit money.	Are you being dishonest or disloyal? Where are you questioning your motives?
Curious	Looking into a box Cat.	What are you eager to learn? Are you being nosy?
Cynical	Gossiping to another Shutting the door in a salesperson's face.	Where are you being sceptical or distrusting? Are you seeing the worst in people or putting others down?
Degraded	Working as a prostitute Slipping down an eroded slope.	Are you lacking self-worth or have you fallen from grace? Where are you feeling humiliated or dishonoured?
Depressed	Sitting alone in a dark room Being held under a heavy weight.	Where have things slumped? Are you being pessimistic?
Deserving	Winning a court case Bowing to an audience.	Where are you feeling justified? Are you receiving approval or recognition?
Despair	Dangling from the end of a rope Holding a heart in your hands.	What seems hopeless? Do you want to give up?
Determined	Running a marathon Training in the gym.	Are you being focused or single-minded? Where are you being decisive and deliberate?
Discord	Seeing an angry face Hearing a musical instrument that's not tuned.	Are you feeling conflicting emotions? Where is there friction?

Predominant Dream Feeling	How the Feeling Could be Symbolised in Your Dream	Possible Life Issues
Disgusted	Getting sunburnt Walking away from an argument.	What's offended or appalled you? What can't you tolerate?
Dispossessed	An Australian aborigine or native American Having your wallet stolen.	Have you been displaced or robbed of an opportunity? Where do you feel like you don't belong?
Dissatisfied	Person with a sad face Being turned away from a department store.	Are you disappointed? Where have you got unfulfilled expectations?
Drained	River flowing into the sea Tap left running.	Where are you being deprived? What's sapped your energy or enthusiasm?
Dynamic	Winning a swimming marathon Jumping out of a plane with a parachute.	Where are you feeling enthusiastic and energetic? Are you being ambitious or achieving your goals?
Eager	Beaver collecting twigs Camping out in order to get good tickets for a show.	What are you enthusiastic about? Where are you feeling impatient?
Elated	Going up in an elevator Jumping for joy.	What's turning out well for you? Where are you feeling happy or relieved?
Embarrassed	Having a red face Hiding.	Where are you feeling humiliated or self-conscious? Are you trying to save face?
Empty/ Unfulfilled	Empty glass Swimming pool with no water.	Are you lacking purpose or direction? Where are you feeling drained?
Enriched	Discovering a gold mine Nuclear power plant.	Where are you feeling fulfilled? What are you improving?
Exhilarated	Jumping up and down for joy Happy face.	Where are you feeling elated? What's exciting you?
Exposed	Being naked in public Taking a lie-detector test.	Where do you feel embarrassed or vulnerable? What have you revealed?

Predominant Dream Feeling	How the Feeling Could be Symbolised in Your Dream	Possible Life Issues
Fascinated	Seeing Christ Reading a good book.	What's aroused your interest? Where are you looking deeper?
Fearful	Seeing a ghost Going to the dentist.	What are you afraid of? What do you need to face?
Fraud	Committing a robbery Cooking the books.	Are you living a lie? Where are you dealing with irregularities or deception?
Freedom	Skydiving Being released from prison.	What's eased or opened up for you? What are you releasing?
Frustrated	Having a boulder in your way Empty glass.	What's blocking your progress? Where are you feeling unfulfilled?
Fulfilled	Full glass of water Eating a meal.	Where have you lived up to expectations? Have you got a sense of achievement?
Futile	Bucketing water out of the ocean Climbing a slope only to keep falling down.	Where have your efforts been thwarted or fruitless? Are you feeling that things are pointless?
Greedy	Pig in a trough Overweight person.	Where can't you get enough? Are you ignoring limits?
Grief	Person sobbing Standing near a grave.	What have you lost? What's causing you sorrow?
Guilt	Can't see your reflection in the mirror Holding your head in your hands.	What are you regretting? Where are you blaming yourself?
Heartbroken	Surgeon taking out your heart Heart-shaped jigsaw puzzle with piece missing.	What have you lost? Are you feeling rejected?
Helpful	Holding a child's hand Helping an elderly person to cross the street.	What can you give to others? Are you supporting others?

Predominant Dream Feeling	How the Feeling Could be Symbolised in Your Dream	Possible Life Issues
Hopeful	Opening a gift Holding your hands in prayer and looking up expectantly.	Where have you got expectations? What are you feeling optimistic about?
Humiliated	Face with unattractive make-up Being naked in public.	Do you need to save face? Where have you been embarrassed or put down?
Impatient	Pushing a child forward Starting a race before the starter's gun goes off.	What can't you tolerate? Where are you feeling frustrated?
Inadequate	Looking small in size Being incapacitated.	What do you feel you could do better? Where are you lacking self-worth?
Indifferent	Not barracking at a sporting event Handing back a menu without choosing your meal.	What's not holding your interest? Where don't you have a preference?
Indignant	Disagreeing with a judge's decision Being angry at missing out on a promotion.	What's hurt your pride? Where are you dealing with unfairness or injustice?
Indiscreet	Passing on a secret Wearing inappropriate clothing.	Have you been undiplomatic? Where should you have been more careful?
Insignificant	Being in a crowd Homeless and living on the streets.	Are you feeling inadequate or overshadowed? What's not important?
Inspired	Seeing an angel Meeting a famous person.	Where are you feeling stimulated? Are you feeling creative?
Intimidated	Seeing a much bigger, larger person Being sentenced.	Where are you feeling restrained or discouraged? What's frightening or threatening you?

Predominant Dream Feeling	How the Feeling Could be Symbolised in Your Dream	Possible Life Issues
Irritated	Being angry with another Scratching profusely.	Where are you feeling frustrated? What's annoying you?
Joy	Having a big smile on your face Laughing on a sideshow ride.	Where are you feeling satisfied and content? Are you letting yourself go?
Lazy	Lying on the lounge Ignoring dirty dishes in the sink.	Where have you lost interest or motivation? What needs your attention?
Left wanting	Being left at a bus stop Jilted lover.	Are you feeling inadequate? What's not meeting your requirements or expectations?
Lonely	Person eating by themselves in a restaurant Hanging from a cliff.	Where are you feeling isolated or abandoned? Are you feeling deprived?
Lost	Trying to find your group Looking at street signs all pointing in different directions.	What are you looking for? Are you off-track or disorientated?
Love	Passionately embracing others Two intertwined wedding rings.	What are you attached to? Where are you making a commitment?
Lucid	Waking up and looking around Transparent tropical beach.	What seems crystal clear or obvious? Where are you switched on?
Naive	A child playing Blind puppies suckling their mother.	Where have you got innocent motives? Are you being too trusting?
Numb	Mountaineer with hypothermia Pricking your thumb with a needle and feeling no pain.	What are you suppressing? Where are you protecting yourself?
Overlooked	Jogger running past without saying hello Overstepping a twig.	Where are you feeling disregarded? What have you failed to notice or take into account?

Predominant Dream Feeling	How the Feeling Could be Symbolised in Your Dream	Possible Life Issues
Paralysed	Person in a comatose state Being in a wheelchair.	Where have you lost control? What's come to a halt?
Pity	Embracing another Looking at someone with tears in your eyes.	Where are you being compassionate? What are you regretting?
Pride	Pride of lions together Person in a business suit.	Are you feeling important? Where have you done well?
Protected	Having a blanket around you Being in a cocoon.	Where do you feel secure? Are you being guided?
Rebellious	Youths driving fast in a car Skinheads.	Do you want to be free? Where are you disregarding limits?
Receptive	Accepting an invitation Hugging another person.	Are you being open or responsive? What are you embracing?
Reckless	Running across a busy road Choking on your food.	Where are you disregarding consequences or being irresponsible? Are you acting without thinking?
Relief	Threatening lion who turns and walks away Starting to drown and being pulled out of the water.	Where are things easing up for you? Are you receiving help and support?
Resentful	Being punished Person being pushed forward onto a stage.	What are you begrudging or disliking? Are you feeling jealous or envious?
Resigned	Resigning from your job Being a passenger in a plane that is about to crash.	What are you relinquishing? What have you come to terms with?
Satisfied	Eating a delicious meal Receiving high marks in a test.	Are you feeling fulfilled and content? Where have you got a sense of achievement?

Predominant Dream Feeling	How the Feeling Could be Symbolised in Your Dream	Possible Life Issues
Seductive	Attractive woman in lingerie Model of the opposite sex calling you over.	Where are you enticing others? What do you find attractive or fascinating?
Serene	Looking at a reflection in a lake Person sitting in meditation.	Where have you got peace of mind or inner peace? What are you accepting?
Sleazy	Walking through a red-light district Propositioning a prostitute.	Where can't you trust yourself or others? What are you exploiting?
Sneaky	Peeking from behind a curtain Looking smug.	Are you being underhanded or secretive? Where have you got your own agenda?
Sorrow	Looking at a grave site Wiping away tears.	What have you lost? What are you regretting or grieving over?
Stale	Leftover bread Old newspaper.	Do you need to embrace change? Where do you need a fresh approach?
Strength	Lifting heavy weights Muscular body.	Are you going from strength to strength? Where do you have power and influence?
Stressed	Receiving a high blood pressure reading Fast-pumping heart.	Where are you feeling pressured or overburdened? What are you overemphasising?
Stretched	Tightening elastic Stretching your muscles.	What's been exaggerated? Where are you spreading yourself too thin?
Susceptible	Child being led away Doctor giving a patient an injection.	Are you being easily influenced? What's affecting you emotionally?
Suspicious	Not opening the door to someone Being unwilling to participate in a telephone survey.	What are you questioning? Where have you got misgivings?

Predominant Dream Feeling	How the Feeling Could be Symbolised in Your Dream	Possible Life Issues
Sympathetic	Sending someone a card Holding an embrace.	Where are you feeling affinity or are reaching out to others? What are you supporting or giving your loyalties to?
Trust	Baby looking into its mother's eyes Getting married.	Where have you got faith or conviction? What have you got confidence in?
Uninhibited	Stripping in public Dancing wildly around the room.	Where are you being spontaneous or free and easy? Are you being frank or unreserved?
Urgency	Running to catch a train Mother feeding a crying baby.	What can't wait? What needs priority?
Vain	Looking in a mirror Beauty quest contestants.	Where are you self-absorbed or self-obsessed? Are you feeling proud or being conceited?
Vengeful	Plotting against a person Vigilante group.	Are you seeking revenge? Where are you inflicting harm or damage?
Violated	Being raped Being robbed.	Where have you breached boundaries or been disrespectful? What have you infringed or abused?
Weak	Being sick in bed Trying to pick up weights.	What are you struggling with? Where do you need inner strength?
Weighed down	Holding heavy bags Wearing a diver's weight belt.	Are you being overly responsible? Where are you feeling burdened or overwhelmed?

Did you know?
The feelings embodied in the dream images, themes and unfolding storyline holds a vital key to its meaning.

Chapter 20

Human Archetypes or Universal Life Patterns

One may not reach the dawn save by the path of the night.
Kahlil Gibran

Your dreams show the roles you play and the unconscious beliefs that support your behaviour. We all act out various universal stereotypes or life patterns as these drives and urges play out over a long period in our lives. Your dreams bring these to light so that you can consciously work with or change them.

This chapter lists some common archetypes that you might recognise or see as recurring symbols or themes in your dreams. Awareness of these will help you see where you act out the line of least resistance. You can then see the potentials and limitations that need to be managed or enhanced in order to receive the empowerment that these learning pathways offer.

How to get the best value from this chapter

- Identify the archetypal theme or symbol in your dream and see if you relate to any of the key words or questions associated with its positive or negative qualities.
- Look at all possibilities and apply the most appropriate for your situation.
- Rephrase the questions to broaden their personal relevance to you, if necessary, by using other words with similar meanings.
- You can also turn any question around (including those you formulate) to see if you relate to them better, by asking them in a slightly different way. For example, rephrase it as a need rather than a desire or belief or vice versa.

The Aim

To gain the empowerment that each archetype offers by blending the positives and transforming the negatives in the manner indicated. This will harmonise the energies, bringing stability and balance.

Archetype Universal symbol	Positive and Negative Aspects Look for feelings, desires, needs, beliefs or situations, explore literal meanings, apply any puns and idioms	Aim Focus on blending qualities in this way
Addict	**Positive:** Passionate; committed Where are you working with external influences? **Negative:** Manipulated; weak willpower Where are you lacking self-control?	Learn to commit without being consumed.
Artist	**Positive:** Intuition; dedication; talent Where do you desire to create? **Negative:** Procrastination; unconventional Where is the fear of imperfection or failure holding you back?	Sense the beyond and express it with courage.
Athlete	**Positive:** Strength; endurance; values Where are you exceeding expectations? **Negative:** Competitive; lacking integrity Where are you misusing your power?	Balance achievement with honour and grace.
Beggar	**Positive:** Ability to ask for help; open to others Where do you know your limitations? **Negative:** Seeking attention; dependency Where have you got insufficiency?	Build generosity of spirit.
Bully	**Positive:** Meeting challenges; confronting yourself Where have you got a sense of justice? **Negative:** Timid; short-sighted; self-interest Where are you lacking courage or principles?	Overcome your fears and liberate your inner conviction.

Archetype	Positive and Negative Aspects	Aim
Child	**Positive:** Confidence; hopeful; positive Where do you believe in others? **Negative:** Hanging on; naive Where are you relying on others?	Try to remain open and safe.
Companion	**Positive:** Devotion; understanding; trust Where are you being supportive? **Negative:** Treachery; unfaithfulness; misgivings Where have you exposed others?	Give and receive support.
Creator	**Positive:** Innovation; new choices; leadership Where are you moving boundaries? **Negative:** Drained; workaholic; preoccupied Where are you overdoing things?	Redefine yourself with new realities and balance.
Destroyer	**Positive:** Reform; letting go; liberation Where are you campaigning for change? **Negative:** Undermining yourself and others; addictions Where are you being destructive?	Make room for the new by releasing the old.
Detective	**Positive:** Makes no assumptions; open-minded Where are you looking deeper or within yourself? **Negative:** Suspicious; sceptical; fastidious Where are you being hard to please?	Blend knowledge and intuition to find satisfying solutions.
Father	**Positive:** Vigilant; self-sacrifice; guidance Where are you showing leadership? **Negative:** Autocratic; domineering Where are you being authoritarian?	Initiate and supervise with love and understanding.

Archetype	Positive and Negative Aspects	Aim
Fool	**Positive:** Natural; inquiring; playful Where are you enjoying yourself? **Negative:** Self-gratification; laziness; insatiable Where are you being self-centred?	Achieve balance between enjoyment and responsibility.
Gambler	**Positive:** Intuition; courage; vision Where are you managing risk? **Negative:** Obsession; addiction; irresponsibility Where do you need to win at all costs?	Accept change at its own pace.
Healer	**Positive:** Love; compassion; assistance Where are you giving to others? **Negative:** Burn out; attachment Where are you absorbing others' problems?	Nurture yourself and others.
Hermit	**Positive:** Contemplation; independence Where are you looking within? **Negative:** Antisocial; lack of contribution Where are you seeking escape?	Blend inner withdrawal with outer service.
Hero	**Positive:** Bold; determined; talented Where are you being fearless? **Negative:** Callous; critical; fear of imperfection Where are you being relentless?	Strive to achieve and keep detached.
Judge	**Positive:** High ideals; taking a stand Where are you being principled? **Negative:** Critical; cynical Where are you being arrogant?	Balance justice and wisdom with mercy.
Liberator	**Positive:** Freedom from tradition; justice Where are you opposing exploitation?	Release the old without imposing the new.

Archetype	Positive and Negative Aspects	Aim
	Negative: Abuse of power; self-advancement Where are you seeking power?	
Lover	**Positive:** Enthusiastic; dedicated; passionate Where are you getting the most out of life? **Negative:** Controlling; intense; jealous Where are you being possessive?	Learn to love without attachment.
Martyr	**Positive:** Courage; devotion; principles Where are you making sacrifices? **Negative:** Persecution; obsessive; extremist Where are you victimising yourself?	Aspire to high ideals without condemning others.
Mediator	**Positive:** Working things out; harmonising Where are you bringing people together? **Negative:** Indecisive; procrastination Where are you unable or unwilling to move forward?	Allow your open mind to lead to inclusiveness.
Mentor	**Positive:** Assistance; faith; admiration Where are you guiding others? **Negative:** Authoritarian; arrogant; self-importance Where are you controlling others?	Serve through empowering others.
Miser	**Positive:** Reserving energy; self-protection Where are you valuing your resources? **Negative:** Holding on; exploiting others Where are you unwilling to give?	Value what you have and use for the greater good.

Archetype	Positive and Negative Aspects	Aim
Mother	**Positive:** Abundance; fertility; encouragement Where are you nurturing yourself or others? **Negative:** Possessive; jealous Where are you being overbearing?	Learn to love and forgive unconditionally.
Networker	**Positive:** Adaptability; empathising with others Where are you expanding your influence? **Negative:** Scandal; gossip; putting others down Where are you using others?	Find your power through helping others.
Nurturer	**Positive:** Benevolent; tenderness; duty Where are you being dutiful and reliable? **Negative:** Consuming; engulfing Where are you acting the victim?	Learn to give and receive.
Observer	**Positive:** Discerning; objective; intellectual Where are you being perceptive? **Negative:** Indecisive; non-achiever Where are you lacking involvement?	Maintain an interested detachment.
Orphan	**Positive:** Self-reliant; down to earth Where are you being independent? **Negative:** Anxiety; oppressor Where are you persecuting others?	Learn to become interdependent.
Perfectionist	**Positive:** Idealistic; energetic; honourable causes Where are you striving for perfection?	Blend striving for excellence with patience.

Archetype	Positive and Negative Aspects	Aim
	Negative: Intolerant of failure; hesitates; superiority Where are you dissatisfied with your best?	
Performer	**Positive:** Accomplishments; presenting yourself Where are you leading the way? **Negative:** Uninvolved; aloof; unrealistic Where are you out of touch with reality?	Speak the truth and enlighten others.
Pioneer	**Positive:** Initiating; founding; reform Where are you setting trends? **Negative:** Rejecting the past; scorning tradition Where are you leaving everything behind?	Discover your self through emerging stages.
Pirate	**Positive:** Independence; freedom; challenge Where are you acting on your own convictions? **Negative:** Using others; profiteering Where are you exploiting others?	Find your own value and worth.
Prostitute	**Positive:** Displaying your talents; self-promotion Where are you selling yourself? **Negative:** Control; entrapment Where are you selling yourself short?	Find and honour your inner worth.
Queen	**Positive:** Guidance; admiration; respect Where are you providing leadership? **Negative:** Power; manipulation; repression Where are you expecting others to seek your approval?	Balance power and responsibility.

Archetype	Positive and Negative Aspects	Aim
Rebel	**Positive:** Courage; defiance; vision Where are you challenging limited thinking? **Negative:** Discontent; uncontrolled emotions Where are you opposing authority?	Expand your personal boundaries.
Ruler	See Queen in this chapter.	
Sage	**Positive:** Wisdom; guiding others Where are you seeking the truth? **Negative:** Uninvolved; aloof; unrealistic Where are you out of touch with reality?	Seek truth to serve others.
Seeker	**Positive:** Direction; motivation; vision Where are you searching for meaning? **Negative:** Unrealistic; dissatisfied; overly critical Where have your expectations not been met?	Allow higher meaning to bring greater achievement and fulfilment.
Shaman	**Positive:** Altered awareness; higher consciousness Where are you transforming energies? **Negative:** Abusing your abilities; dominance Where are you manipulating others?	Use self-mastery for the highest good.
Slave	**Positive:** Endurance; personal change Where are you finding yourself? **Negative:** Limiting yourself and others; suppression Where do you feel disempowered?	Find freedom by blending your personal will with divine purpose.

Archetype	Positive and Negative Aspects	Aim
Storyteller	**Positive:** Sharing information; learning Where are you teaching others? **Negative:** Embellishing facts; changing principles Where are you bending the truth?	Express your wisdom in a meaningful way.
Student	**Positive:** Receptive; open-minded Where are exploring the new? **Negative:** Unapplied or misapplied knowledge Where are you learning but not giving?	Use new knowledge for betterment of yourself and others.
Thief	**Positive:** Seizing the moment; opportunistic Where are you valuing what others have? **Negative:** Not taking responsibility; deceiving yourself Where are you not being true to yourself?	Love yourself and find your own inner strength.
Trickster	**Positive:** Sense of humour; reorganisation Where are you questioning accepted norms? **Negative:** Unsettling others; malicious Where are you being irresponsible?	Reveal your truth and expose pretence.
Victim	**Positive:** Compliant; submissive; humble Where are you being accommodating? **Negative:** Martyrdom; not accepting responsibility Where are you exploiting others?	Value yourself while giving to others.

Did you know?
It is wise to transform and incorporate negative energies into your personality.
Repressed, they play out rebelliously in the unconscious and absorb energy
that you could otherwise use for constructive living.

Chapter 21
Dream Messages

A loving outcome acknowledges reality,
respects everyone involved and speaks the truth.
Stephanie Dowrick

When you unravel your dream messages using the steps outlined in the introduction you will see that each dream message comes to help you. They offer constructive insight, comment, communication, creative ideas or solutions about your present life circumstances and issues you are facing. Each dream provides extra insight or another piece of the puzzle, and dreams often repeat important themes in different ways until another more pressing issue takes precedence.

Your dream and its message will be unique to you and will therefore have more power than the dream examples listed in this chapter. Your dreams seek to guide, encourage and empower you.

What to do next

When you've analysed your dream, reduce your dream message to its essence as illustrated in this chapter and then formulate your corresponding affirmation. Work with this as often as you can during the day. This will give you the tools you need to implement your dream solutions.

Dream Theme	Possible Dream Message	Manifesting Affirmation
Achieving	Set worthy goals. They will demand the best of you. They'll bring with them the greatest rewards.	'I commit to the highest within me. I grow into what I can become.'
Balancing	Slow down. Take it easier. This will give you head room. It will give you time to tune into yourself.	'My life is filled with beauty and purpose. I live with balance and wisdom.'
Centring	Stay connected to your source. Your empowerment lies there.	'I am true to myself. My power lies within. All things are possible.'
Clearing	You're moving forward in your career. On the journey you'll clear blockages of your own.	'I know myself as I really am. I like what I see. I am open with others.'
Defending	Beware danger! There's something you haven't seen. Attend to it. Protect yourself.	'I am aware of all eventualities. I am watchful and cautious. I carefully prepare my way.'
Developing	Grow into the next experience that awaits you. Let it evolve. Move through it with ease and grace.	'I welcome all that lies ahead of me. It brings out the best in me.'
Easing up	Be more relaxed in your relations with others. There's nothing to lose!	'I am at ease with others. I am calm and quietly assertive.'
Embracing	Accept the opportunity offered to you. This is a fateful moment. The unexpected can lead to other openings.	'I gratefully accept each and every opportunity. It guides me to where I need to be.'
Ending	Let go and allow new beginnings to take their course. Move on.	'I embrace change. I let go of the past. I trust what lies ahead.'

Dream Theme	Possible Dream Message	Manifesting Affirmation
Evaluating	Look at the cause of this conflict. Find solutions. Blame will deplete you.	'Solutions present themselves to me. I am open to all possibilities.'
Fearing	Your fears are imagined and exaggerated.	'I can do the task ahead of me. Look what I've done and what I've become.'
Grasping	Pride plays a part in wanting to hold on.	'I contribute to the whole. I enjoy adopting my part and being one with others.'
Guiding	You'll find yourself in helping others.	'I look within and find my purpose. With strength I give to others.'
Helping	Assistance will come to your aid. However, you will have to do something first.	'I gratefully receive whatever help is available to me. I willingly play my part.'
Hesitating	An opportunity will present itself. You will be reluctant to take it. It will benefit your cause.	'I take every opportunity offered to me. I go where I've never been before.'
Honouring	You will experience a drop in financial status. Your decision, however, is morally and spiritually sound.	'I am true to myself. I follow my inner convictions. I enjoy doing what's right.'
Hurting	You're hurting yourself. Heal your wounds rather than avoid them. Strength will come.	'I am gentle with myself. I work with the healing process. I allow others to do the same.'
Intuitive	Strengthen the interaction between your sleeping and waking consciousness. Build your awareness.	'I tune into my higher awareness. It guides me. I am open to where it leads.'
Learning	Not all information has been disclosed. There is more to this issue.	'I watch and learn. I reserve my judgment. I act when I have all the facts.'
Liberating	Release your pain. Let healing begin.	'I express my pain. I let it go. My new awareness begins to grow.'

Dream Theme	Possible Dream Message	Manifesting Affirmation
Losing	Home life and relationship with others holds the key to losing self.	'I have found myself. I am one with myself and others.'
Openings	You will have privileged and unfettered access to the top. You're in a desirable position.	'Everything has its time and place. I am in the right place at the right time.'
Organising	You'll need time. Delegate.	'I am working on my highest priorities. I am achieving my inner purpose.'
Playing	Be playful and joyous. You'll discover a new side of yourself. Let it out!	'I am fun-loving and free. I enjoy being spontaneous.'
Programming	Program your thinking so that thoughts come to mind quickly. You'll need to be able to think on your feet.	'I am skilful at what I do. I enjoy improving my skills every day.'
Resisting	Let go. You don't need to win or lose. Simply be.	'I open my heart. My difficulties become easier with love.'
Resolving	Peace will come by looking deeply and choosing the essentials.	'I am at peace with my choices. I see the essence. I embrace the new.'
Restricting	Take control. Reign in your impulses. Don't be reckless.	'I proceed carefully and slowly. I prepare the way and consider all factors.'
Retreating	Love that which you've neglected. Then look for a change within you.	'I focus on that which needs attention. I enjoy balance and harmony.'
Seeking help	Put back-up in place. You will need back-up.	'I welcome the opportunities offered to me. I am supported and ready to move forward. I am inspired.'

Dream Theme	Possible Dream Message	Manifesting Affirmation
Simplifying	Don't try too hard. Speak from the heart. Keep it simple and heartfelt.	'I act as a channel. I let my words speak their own truth.'
Suffering	Suffering is functional. It is a cleansing progress and can be worthwhile.	'I look behind my pain. I see the lesson. I gain the wisdom.'
Timing	Deal with others kindly and helpfully. Allow events to progress at their own pace. It will serve the good of all concerned.	'I am patient and tolerant. I serve the highest good.'
Trusting	Wait and see what presents itself. You're not in a strong position. Something will come and conclude the matter.	'I am patient and expectant. I am open and flexible to what comes. It will serve my highest good.'
Viewing	Look at how far you've come. But there is still more to be done.	'I see the bigger picture. Each day paints more of the scene.'
Vulnerability	Don't accept limitations. Free yourself from doubt. Leap into your future.	'I look at my accomplishments. I move forward with courage and vision.'

Did you know?

Dream messages are alway constructive. In nightmares the imagery becomes frightening to wake you up to an important issue. Quite often it's been building in earlier dreams that have been ignored. Even in nightmares the dream message (or the emotional adjustment presented in trauma nightmares) is offered for your benefit. If followed, it will lead to further growth.

Chapter 22
Triggering a Dream

For not to mention the wonders of dreams in which we invent,
without effort, but also without will, things which we should have to
think a long time to discover when awake.
Gottfried Leibniz

You can trigger a dream to receive honest and constructive guidance, inspiration, healing, creative ideas and solutions on a subject of your choice.

Dwell on the desired issue before going to bed from various perspectives. Ask yourself, or write out why you need help and what you would do with the insights you receive. Think about the options you have and what it would take, or what you would be prepared to give up, to get this information.

Form a concise, direct and specific phrase to invoke help from within. You can use the ones listed in this chapter or create your own. Write it down, put it under your pillow, let the issue go and then sleep on it. Be prepared, if necessary, to repeat the process and allow up to three days for a response. Then watch your dreams invent an idea or create a solution.

Don't forget to say thank you after your question or request. It acknowledges your source and gratitude and opens you to receive. For example, after asking the question, 'How can I love myself and feel worthy of the love of others?' make sure to say 'Thank you'.

Area of Life	*Dream-invoking Questions/Requests*

Beliefs:
- How can I love myself and feel worthy of the love of others?
- Show me how to express my anger and frustration in appropriate ways.
- How can I stop blaming myself?
- Why do I take ownership of what others project onto me?
- Are my expectations of myself and others too high and unrealistic? If so, what can I do about it?
- Am I selling myself short?
- Why am I submissive and afraid to assert myself?
- How can I be accepted and loved by others?
- Why do I need to control others?
- How can I gain control of my feelings?
- What's stopping me from loving others?
- Why am I afraid of getting hurt?
- What's the underlying cause of my jealousy?
- Why am I judgmental?
- How can I feel wanted and desirable?
- Why is being right so important to me?
- Help me let go of the past so that I can focus on the present.
- Why am I still holding onto pain?
- Show me how to feel less tense and anxious.
- What's the positive side of this situation?
- Show me how to accept and love myself.
- What's holding me back from becoming who I want to be?
- Show me how to connect and communicate more clearly with others.
- Help me achieve inner peace.
- I am willing to learn. Teach me what I need to know.

Business:
- Provide me with a name for my new business.
- How can I make my business grow?
- Show me how our efficiency can be improved.
- What new products or services can we offer?
- Would it be better to restructure the company? If so, how?
- Have we got unproductive management practices? If so, where?
- What will be the outcome of my forthcoming business meeting?
- Is anyone undermining or about to ambush me?
- Provide me a solution to my problem.
- Will we win our litigation?
- Who will lease our warehouse?
- What's the source of my colleague's, or employee's, lack of motivation?

- Will the economy pick up? When?
- What are the strengths and weaknesses of my associates?
- Improve on this idea if it can be done.
- Shall I relocate my business? Will it be a wise move?
- Provide me with a new incentive program for my employees.
- Design a simpler and less complicated contract.
- Where does my business go from here?
- Why am I encountering so many obstacles? Is there a better way?

Career:
- Provide me with inspiration for my next book.
- What's the next step forward in my career? Where do I go from here?
- Where will I find meaning and purpose in my life?
- What's holding me back from achieving my goals?
- Where does my future lie?
- Show me how to be the architect of my own life.
- Give me a progress report on my career.
- What can I give to the world?
- How can I increase my income and fulfilment?
- What's my true and deeper purpose in life?
- How can I be happy in my job?
- Why do I keep changing jobs?
- How can I reduce my stress?
- What's the cause of the conflict between myself and my colleagues?
- What's stopping me from taking risks?
- How can I obtain a more harmonious or satisfying job?
- Show me how to overcome my fear of failure.
- How can I deal with my frustration at work?
- What's the perfect job for me?
- How can I be more appreciated in what I do?
- Why am I stuck in my career?
- Where am I being undermined or manipulated?
- How can I increase my sense of achievement?
- Show me how to balance work and home commitments.
- How can I build my confidence and self-esteem?
- What's my best career path or option?

Family:
- Is my new lover the person for me?
- How do I cope with my child's tensions?
- Is there a soul waiting to be born?
- Where do I proceed from here?
- How can I best guide my child?
- What is the deeper purpose in the relationship between myself and my child?

- How can I best deal with my child's problems at school?
- Show me how to gain control of my life.

Health:
- I seek healing. Please do what can be done.
- What's the cause of my present health problems?
- Am I contributing to my illness?
- What can I do to improve my health?
- Why do I keep getting sick?
- What will be the outcome of this present course of treatment?
- Show me how to be at peace with myself through this healing journey.
- What can having this disease teach me?
- Show me how to accept what I'm going through.
- Can I influence the course of this disease? How?
- What will happen to me now?
- Why am I supporting my addictions?
- Am I abusing my body? How?
- Where do I go from here?
- What am I suppressing?
- Show me what my future holds.
- Why am I feeling resentful?
- Am I still in denial?
- Why don't I feel comfortable with my body?
- What can I do to support those around me?
- Will I have another heart attack?
- How can I make this a positive experience?
- What should my attitude be now in this time of ill-health? Show me. Make it clear so I can understand.
- Why am I feeling so depleted?
- Why am I abusing my body?
- Is it possible to cure my disease?
- Why is my healing such a slow process?
- How can I cope better with my allergies?

Money:
- What's holding me back from living abundantly?
- Show me how to give as well as receive.
- Why am I not earning what I believe I am worth?
- What other sources of income are open to me?
- How can I achieve financial security?
- What is my life's work?
- How do I best support myself and my family?
- Why do I feel guilty earning good money?
- How do I avoid bankruptcy?
- Why do I feel guilty spending money?
- Show me how to manage money?
- What will be the outcome of the contested will?

- Why do I link my personal value with money?
- Show me how to use money for good.

Relationships:
- Will I be loved and respected in this relationship?
- Is this marriage made in heaven?
- Will I find love? Is there someone for me?
- What's holding me back from letting go and moving on?
- Why are my relationships unsuccessful and unfulfilling?
- What's the cause of my present unhappiness?
- Show me how to choose rewarding relationships?
- Why don't I feel safe and secure?
- What attracts me to negative and abusive relationships?
- Why do I have difficulty with trust and intimacy?
- Show me how to be liked.
- Why do I feel dependent on others for their approval, love or affection?
- What can I give to this relationship?
- Why can't I ask for help when I need it?
- What can this relationship give to me?
- Why don't others accept me?
- What is the next step I need to take towards independence?
- Why am I afraid of being disappointed?
- Show me how to give and receive love.
- How can I express my feelings freely?
- Why am I feeling trapped in my present relationship?
- Show me the nature of our relationship.
- Why do I fear rejection and criticism?
- How can this relationship better serve my needs?
- Is my new lover the person for me?
- Why don't others value me?
- Is this relationship going to last?
- How can I get out of this unhappy relationship?
- Why am I worried that people won't like or understand me?
- Will this guilt end?
- Am I making the same mistakes again?
- Why do I look after others and forget myself?
- How can I ease the grieving process?
- Why does intimacy scare me?
- Do I sabotage myself and my relationships? If so, how?
- Why don't I like socialising?
- Will I ever be able to like myself?
- Why do I feel guilty about my failed relationships?
- How can I achieve the support I need?

Security:
- Will I ever be able to buy my own house?
- What will happen when I die?

- How can I make my growing dependence on others a positive experience?
- Will I be able to provide for my retirement?
- How long will I have my independence?
- Will I be able to support myself if I live alone?
- Show me where to go from here. What's my best option?
- Is my job secure?
- Where does my future lie?
- Will I be able to manage without help? If so, how?

Sex:
- Why do I feel uncomfortable with my sexuality?
- Show me how to gain self-control.
- Why do I want to dominate and control my lover?
- Show me how to express my sexuality appropriately.
- Why don't I enjoy making love?
- Show me my true sexual preference.
- Why am I scared of intimacy?
- Show me how to work through my fear of being inadequate.
- Why am I confused about my sexuality?
- Why don't I feel passionate and desirable?

Did you know?
If your dream initially overrides your incubation request then it must be an important issue and one that your dreaming mind believes takes precedence. Keep trying and your patience will be rewarded.

Part Four

Working With Your Dreams

Dream Diary Pages

Go confidently in the direction of your dreams!
Live the life you've imagined.
Henry David Thoreau

The Dream Diary Pages have been designed for you to photocopy and bind (or put in a folder) for your Dream Journal.

Compiling your Dream Journal

I recommend photocopying the following pages in order for your Dream Journal:

- Insert the Title page
- Insert two copies of the Contents page
- Photocopy 50 sheets of each of the four pages below (enough for 50 dreams) which relate to recording and analysing your dreams . . .
  1. Dream Incubation Question page
  2. Date and Dream Type page
  3. Dream Insights—Feeling page
  4. Dream Insights—Dream Message page
- Insert four Recurring Dream Symbol pages
- Insert four Recurring Dream pages
- Finish with four Dream Review pages.

You now have a functional Dream Journal with prompts to guide you through the process. Just answer the questions and watch your dream messages unravel. Refer to the Introduction for more information regarding each step.

DREAM JOURNAL

Date: _____

Ph: _____

Contents

Dream Title	Page

Dream Incubation Question

(You can trigger a dream on a subject of your choice. Create a simple and specific statement)

_____
_____
_____
_____

My Dream

_____
(Title)

Day Notes

(To remind you of the day's emotional highlights)

_____
_____
_____
_____
_____
_____
_____
_____
_____

Date___ / ___ / ___   **Dream Type _____**

(Prophetic, instructional, communication,
spiritual progress report, recollections of real experience,
retrospective or creative problem solving dream)

Title _____

(Give the dream a title that embodies the main image or feeling in the dream)

Dream Insights

Feeling _____
(Name the predominant feeling associated with the dream, if there was one)

Background _____
(Health, relationships or work)

Major Dream Themes
(Rephrased broadly in general terms using your own words)

_____

_____

_____

_____

_____

Linking Questions
(Select a major dream theme and ask how or where in your life at the moment do you feel …)

_____

_____

_____

_____

Dream Issue
(This is the issue that your dream has identified. It would relate to you current
life circumstances)

_____

_____

_____

_____

Symbols & Associations

_____ _____

_____ _____

_____ _____

_____ _____

_____ _____

Dream Insights

Dream Message
(Look for the climax of the dream – a resolution, solution, conclusion or outcome)

_____

_____

_____

_____

_____

_____

Dream Gem (or Words of Wisdom)
(Create a short phrase or sentence that embodies the essence of the dream message)

_____

_____

_____

Affirmation
(Create a positive statement of belief to anchor the recommended feeling or attitude
into waking life)

_____

_____

_____

Action
(What action will you take based on the insights you have been given?)

_____

_____

_____

Gratitude
(Don't forget to honour your dreams and close the circle)

_____

_____

_____

_____

Recurring Dream Symbols

Dream Symbols	Associations
_____	_____
	_____
	_____
_____	_____
	_____
	_____
_____	_____
	_____
_____	_____
	_____
_____	_____
	_____
	_____
_____	_____
	_____
	_____
_____	_____
	_____
	_____

Recurring Dreams

Summarised Dream

Title

_____
_____
_____
_____
_____
_____
_____
_____

Dream Message

_____
_____
_____
_____
_____
_____
_____
_____

Affirmation

_____
_____

Title

_____
_____
_____
_____
_____
_____
_____

Dream Message

_____
_____
_____
_____
_____
_____
_____

Affirmation

_____
_____

Dream Review

Dream Gems
(or Words of Wisdom)

Personal Comments

Personal Dream Notes

There is only one journey.
Going inside yourself.
Rainer Maria Rilke

Suggestions to help you on your journey:

- If you're short of time, set aside one hour each week to analyse your dreams and build up your skills. Your dreams will repeat themes on issues they think have special importance.
- Find a dream partner to discuss your dreams with and explore ideas together. This will help you both gain deeper insights and keep you motivated while you are learning.
- Have fun. Be explorative and creative. There are no right and wrong answers— only insights to be gained. Follow the leads that speak to your heart and see where they take you.
- Regular practice will reap rewards.

The journey of a thousand miles
begins with the first step.
Lao Tzu

Personal Dream Notes

_____
_____
_____
_____
_____
_____
_____
_____
_____
_____
_____
_____
_____
_____
_____
_____
_____
_____
_____
_____
_____
_____
_____
_____
_____
_____
_____
_____
_____
_____
_____
_____
_____
_____

Personal Dream Notes

Bibliography

All About Symbols — Andrew T Cummings. (Astrology Publishing House 2002)

Aura Soma — Irene Dalichow & Mike Booth. (Hay House, 1997)

Australian and New Zealand Fishing — Paul Hamblyn. (Spectrum Books, 1973)

Australian Fishing Guide — Gregory's. (Gregory's Publishing Company, 2001)

Awakening the Heroes Within — Carol S Pearson. (HarperCollins, 1991)

Classical Mythology — Mark PO Morford & Robert J Lenardon. (Longman, 1991)

Colours & Numbers — Louise L Hay. (Hay House, 1999)

Concise Dictionary of First Names — Patrick Hanks & Flavia Hodges. (Oxford University Press, 2001)

Dictionary of Dream Symbols — Eric Ackroyd. (Cassell Illus, 1993)

Dictionary of Symbols — J E Circlot. (Routlege & Keegan Paul, 1962)

Dictionary of Symbols — Carl G Liungman. (Norton, 1995)

Dream Book — Patricia Garfield. (McLelland & S Dump, 2002)

Dream Cards — Strephon Kaplan-William. (Simon & Schuster, 1991)

Dream Deck — David Fontana. (Chronicle Books, 2002)

Dream Dictionary — Jo Boushala. (G P Putnam's Sons, 1992)

Dream Dictionary — Tony Crisp. (Bantam Doubleday, 2002)

Dream Encyclopedia — James R Lewis. (Gale, 1995)

Dreamer's Dictionary — Barbara Condron. (SOM Publishing, 1997)

Dreamlife — David Fontana. (Element, 1990)

Enneagram — Helen Palmer. (HarperCollins, 1991)

Enneagram Made Easy — Renee Baron & Elizabeth Wagele. (Harper San Francisco, 1994)

Favourite Names for Boys and Girls — Patrick Cook. (Unwin Paperbacks, 1983)

First Steps to Dream Power — Diane Bellchambers. (Axiom, 2001)

Flower Remedies Feel Better Naturally — Mark Wells. (Thomas C Lothian, 2002)

Foods that Heal — Bernard Jensen. (Avery Publishing Group, 1993)

Freshwater Fishes of Australia — Stephen Booth & Bill Classon. (Australian Fishing Network, 2002)

Grower's Guide to Trees — Margaret Hanks. (Murdoch Books, 1998)

Healing Colour — Theo Gimbel. (Gaia Books, 2001)

Healing Power of Gemstones — Harish Johari. (Destiny Books, 1996)

Hero Within — Carol S Pearson. (HarperSan Francisco, 1998)

Interpreting Dreams A–Z — Leon Nacson. (Hay House, 2001)

Love is in the Earth	Melody. (Earth-Love Publishing House, 1995)
Love Yourself, Heal Your Life Workbook	Louise L Hay. (Hay House, 2002)
Macdonald Encyclopedia of Amphibians and Reptiles	Massimo Capula. (Macdonald Orbis, 1990)
Medicine Cards	Jamie Sands & David Carson. (Saint Martin's Press, 1988)
Mystical Magical Marvelous World of Dreams	Wilda B Tanner. (Sparrow Hawk Press, 1988)
Numerology of Names	Laureli Blyth. (Brumby Books, 2001)
Penguin Dictionary of Symbols	Jean Chevalier & Alain Gheerbrant. (Penguin, 1996)
Pocketful of Dreams	Denise Linn. (Piatkus Books, 1993)
Sacred Contracts	Caroline Myss. (Bantam Australia, 2002)
Secrets of Dreams	Caro Ness. (DK, 2001)
Secrets of Numerology	Dawne Kovan. (DK, 2001)
Symbols and their Meanings	Jack Tresidder. (Duncan Baird Publishers, 2000)
Symbols in Art & Religion	Karel Werner. (Routledge Curzon Press, 1990)
Talismans & Amulets	Felicitas H Nelson. (Sterling Publishing, 2000)

Index